Date Du

COMPETITION AND REGULATION IN FINANCIAL MARKETS

Financial markets recently have been characterised by fundamental and rapid changes. Among the most important are the breakdown of product market segmentation and despecialisation of the intermediaries, the internationalisation of banking activities and the innovations in financial technology, especially the electronic funds transfer system. In addition, financial markets have been troubled in the seventies by an enduring economic crisis and a highly inflationary environment, affecting strongly the level and structure of interest rates.

These developments have raised a considerable new interest in the structure and performance of financial markets and in financial regulations. In this book several competitive and regulatory issues are treated, especially from the point of view of their effects on the working of the financial system and also on monetary policy. Contributions are included not only on the USA, where these aspects have been analysed the most extensively, but also on Belgium, France, Greece, Italy, the Netherlands and the United Kingdom.

While for some countries the topics studied are the relation between financial markets structure, the behaviour of the intermediaries and the effectiveness of monetary policy, the largest part of the book is devoted to problems of financial regulation. It is shown how financial regulation may become obsolete and ineffective with respect to the goals pursued and how it may enhance a lot of inefficiencies.

Dr Albert Verheirstraeten, the editor, is Associate Professor of Economics at the Katholieke Universiteit Leuven. He is the author of *Geld, Krediet en intrest in de Belgische Financiële Sector* and co-author of *De Geld — en Kapitaalmarkt,* I *and* II.

Also by Albert Verheirstraeten

De Geld – en Kapitaalmarkt (*two volumes, co-author*)

Geld, Krediet en Intrest in de Belgische Financiële Sector

COMPETITION AND REGULATION IN FINANCIAL MARKETS

Edited by
Albert Verheirstraeten

First published 1981 by
THE MACMILLAN PRESS LTD
London and Basingstoke
Companies and representatives
throughout the world

ISBN 0 333 29388 6

Printed in Hong Kong

To
Lieve, Jeroen and Michiel

Contents

List of Tables
and Figures

TABLES

FIGURES

Preface

In the economy, the financial sector takes a special position. Indeed, its functioning affects all other sectors, as it is determining for the overall liquidity, for the working of the money exchange mechanism and for the transfer of funds from surplus units to various deficit spenders. As a consequence, there is a continuous interest in the performance and regulation of the financial sector.

In many countries, financial structures show a high market concentration, in the USA as well as in Europe. This constitutes a source of concern for the degree of competition, for the behaviour and market power of the intermediaries and for the optimality of financial market results, from the point of view of allocative efficiency as well as operational efficiency. Therefore, a study of the structure–behaviour–performance relationship and its change over a time – frequently examined in the USA, but rarely in Europe – seems to be a necessary condition to evaluate the need either for a more appropriate regulation of the financial sector, or for its deregulation.

Besides, the economic situation in the industrialised countries in the 1970s has been characterised by high inflation rates and an enduring economic crisis. Macroeconomic policy measures have turned out to be unsuccessful to cope with these problems. From this derives the importance of a more disaggregated approach, giving more attention to the microeconomic aspects of the economic system and to the efficiency of its working and regulation. This applies the more so for the financial sector because of its strategic position in the economy.

On the grounds of these considerations, on 13 and 14 September 1979, a conference was organised at the Catholic University of Leuven on the issue of financial structures, performance and regulation. Papers were presented on different European countries and on the USA, of which the main are included in this volume. These contributions contain to a varying degree theoretical arguments, institutional analysis and empirical evidence. (Note that in the data given a billion stands for a thousand millions.)

The first two chapters in the book treat the general debate on regulation versus deregulation in the financial sector. In this debate, on the one hand critical remarks are made with respect to the considerable government intervention in the financial sector, aiming at its safety and soundness, but also at changing credit allocation and influencing income distribution through interest rate restrictions. Attention is drawn to different negative side-effects of those regulations. On the other hand, proposals for deregulation are often treated as if they would enhance the risk of more failures and of bank runs, enhancing large detriments for the savers and a threat for financial intermediation and for the use of the checking account payments system.

Maybe somewhat surprisingly, here it is strongly argued however that regulation on the one hand and increased competition and efficiency on the other have to be considered not in opposition, but rather as complements. The arguments derive from the increased economic instability, from the effects of inflation especially on interest rates, from the internationalisation of the financial sector, from the growing despecialisation of the different kinds of intermediaries and finally from the impact of new financial technologies, especially the electronic funds transfer system.

Those developments cause serious concern about the stability of the financial sector and about the controlling power of the monetary authorities. At the same time, however, it is also stressed that several kinds of government intervention not only are ineffective with respect to the goals pursued, but in addition involve a lot of inefficiencies. This is especially to be expected in the case of regulations such as market entry and activity restrictions, several allocative interventions and finally interest-rate setting. With respect to the latter, in Chapter 3 an extensive study is included on the effects of the interest ceilings in the USA.

Inefficiencies may also derive from the financial markets' structure – being partly determined by the applied system of regulations – as it may induce, for example, oligopolistic behaviour and give eventually an opportunity to the intermediaries to realise excess profits. This is examined in two chapters on Belgium. Chapter 4 highlights one important aspect of financial market structure: its degree of concentration. Also in Belgium this concentration is very high, raising serious questions about the degree of competition, especially in mainly domestic markets. An explanation is then sought in the existence of economies of scale. Turning to the results of the intermediaries, in Chapter 5 the yields are analysed of the shares of some important Belgian financial institutions, after having them made easier to interpret by means of a risk-adjustment.

The following five chapters treat different forms of government intervention in the financial sector and their implications in Italy, France, the Netherlands, the United Kingdom and Greece.

In Chapter 6 it is shown how subsidies and risk reducing interventions of the government in the Italian financial sector have led to allocative inefficiencies and to an overexpansion and overliquidity of the Italian banking system, enhancing an inflationary threat. Numerous channels of intervention in the credit allocation for France are described in Chapter 7. In Chapter 8 it is demonstrated how a specific regulation of the discount window as in the Netherlands may impair, in an oligopolistic banking system, the effectiveness of some instruments of monetary policy.

Financial intermediaries are, however, not indifferent with respect to the regulations imposed on them. In Chapter 9 it is shown for the UK how non-market-based control systems lead to portfolio shifts, market distortions and interest-rate instability. In the same sense, Chapter 10 clarifies the complex system of financial controls and inducements in Greece and explains why regulation may become ineffective as a consequence of unforeseen reactions of the intermediaries and their customers.

The closing Chapter 11 gives an impressive account of the main lessons that can be learnt from the research included. Regulation in all countries considered is confronted with financial markets that are rapidly and fundamentally changing, due among others to a decrease in market segmentation, internationalisation and innovations in financial technology. The applied regulatory arrangements in several cases seem to fail or even to create additional problems. This leads to a rather pessimistic view on the future possibilities to control the money stock and its velocity, as well as to maintain the stability of the financial system. To respond to those challenges, an appeal is made for a dynamic and integrated analysis, encompassing both the macroeconomics and the microeconomics of financial markets.

ALBERT VERHEIRSTRAETEN

Acknowledgements

This book has grown out of a conference held at Leuven in September 1979. It was made possible through financial support by the Research Council of the Katholieke Universiteit Leuven, by the Faculty of Economics and Applied Economics at the same university, and finally by the National Fund for Scientific Research in Brussels through the intermediation of the Seminar for Industrial Organisation and Policy (SIOP). Co-organisers of the congress were R. De Bondt and L. Vanthienen (Leuven), A. Jacquemin (Louvain-la-Neuve) and especially my collaborator J. Pacolet. The last not only contributed much to the conception of the colloquium, but was also very helpful in preparing the final text of this volume; in addition, he compiled the index. Finally, the practical execution of the project was entrusted to the administrative staff of the Centre for Economic Studies at the Katholieke Universiteit Leuven. To all of them many thanks.

A. V.

List of the Contributors

FLORIN AFTALION, ESSEC, Ecole Supérieure de Sciences Economiques et Sociales, Cergy.

ROY A. BATCHELOR, Centre for Banking and International Finance, City University, London.

FRANK BOLL, Katholieke Universiteit Leuven.

ANTHONY S. COURAKIS, Brasenose College, Oxford.

PAUL DE GRAUWE, Katholieke Universiteit Leuven.

MICHEL DE SMET, Economic Department, Belgian Bankers' Association.

FRANKLIN R. EDWARDS, Columbia University, New York.

LIEVEN GHEYSENS, Katholieke Universiteit Leuven.

BRIAN GRIFFITHS, Centre for Banking and International Finance, City University, London.

DIRK HEREMANS, Katholieke Universiteit Leuven.

HERWIG LANGOHR, INSEAD, European Institute of Business Administration, Fontainebleau.

MARCEL MAES, Banking Commission, Brussels.

GEORGES MARTIN, Economic Department, Belgian Bankers' Association.

MARIO MONTI, Università Bocconi, Milano.

JOZEF PACOLET, Katholieke Universiteit Leuven.

ALMARIN PHILLIPS, University of Pennsylvania, Philadelphia.

ANGELO PORTA, Università Bocconi, Milano.

JACK R. S. REVELL, Institute of European Finance, University College of North Wales, Bangor.

ALAIN SIAENS, Université Catholique de Louvain, Louvain-la-Neuve.

ROBERT A. TAGGART, Northwestern University, Evanston, Ill.

ALBERT VERHEIRSTRAETEN, Katholieke Universiteit Leuven.

ALFONS VERPLAETSE, National Bank of Belgium, Brussels.

GÉRARD VILLA, Université Catholique de Louvain, Louvain-la-Neuve.

JOZEF VUCHELEN, Vrije Universiteit, Brussels.

ROBERTO E. WESSELS, Economic Institute, Leyden University.

1. Financial Institutions and Regulation in the 21st Century: After the Crash?[1]

FRANKLIN R. EDWARDS

1. INTRODUCTION

The 1970s mark the beginning of a new area in financial regulation. Structural changes are now taking place which promise to make obsolete our present system of regulation. Many of our existing regulations are addressed to problems that no longer exist, and many are now, or will soon be, hopelessly ineffective because of changes that either have or soon will take place. The development of new markets, and of new ways of doing business in old markets, has brought new problems that are going unrecognised and unattended. New views and fresh perspectives must be forged so that regulation can be reforged into a system more compatible with current and future needs. If we are to achieve this end, it is important that we understand the social goals that underlie financial regulation and that we recognise how current changes are threatening the achievement of these goals. Such an understanding must be the compass for our efforts to modernise regulation. Otherwise these efforts will be sabotaged by political pressure groups that seek only to sustain or enhance their positions of special privilege.

2. GOALS OF FINANCIAL REGULATION

While financial regulation has many purposes, some of which change with market conditions and political ideologies, it has one goal which is of overriding importance: to maintain stability in financial markets and to guarantee that vicissitudes in economic activity do not undermine the economic health of nations and of the world economy. Other goals, such as those of maintaining low interest rates, allocating credit to favoured groups, protecting the financially unsophisticated, and curbing monopoly power are of lesser importance. A regulatory system that achieved these while failing to maintain financial and economic stability would be a clear failure.

The theme of this chapter is that current changes in financial institutions and markets threaten the stability of financial systems and the health of our economies, for which the remedy is not more but different regulation. What is needed is a regulatory system that is both more compatible with today's realities and more responsive to changes in market conditions. In most cases this calls for less regulation, although in a few situations additional regulation may be desirable.

There are two regulatory objectives that must remain firm if we are to have financial and economic stability. First, central banks must have the power to control 'money', or to control relevant monetary aggregates; and, second, the solvency of financial institutions in general, and especially that of banks, must be assured by appropriate regulatory safeguards. Economic stability is not compatible with widespread bank failures and 'bank panics', nor with untempered cyclical swings in the money supply. In the United States, the key regulatory pillars are the Federal Reserve, with its control over commercial banks' reserves and the money supply, and deposit insurance, which is in turn supported by solvency regulations aimed at specific aspects of financial soundness.[2]

I believe that changes now under way strike at the foundations of these regulatory pillars: some tend to dilute monetary control, while others allow risk-taking by banks to go undetected and unchecked by regulatory surveillance.

3. A CONCEPTUAL FRAMEWORK FOR THE CURRENT EVOLUTION OF FINANCIAL INSTITUTIONS AND MARKETS

With so many changes taking place in financial markets, it is inevitable that the important will often be obscured by the trivial, and the long-lasting by the ephemeral. To ferret out the major regulatory implications of what is happening, it is essential that we focus on what is fundamental, and not on 'cyclical' problems that come and go with changes in economic activity and interest rates. To achieve this, we need to conceptualise and to generalise about what is occurring, so that fundamental aspects of this evolution are identified and responded to.

I believe a central element in this evolution is the decline of market segmentation that is taking place. The erosion of both product and spatial market segmentation is responsible for many of the regulatory pressures now besetting us.

3.1 Product markets

Product segmentation is eroding rapidly. Non-bank financial institutions are perilously close to being banks, or to doing a banking business. Non-bank savings institutions already provide their customers with deposit accounts that can be accessed by cheque or by electronic funds transfer devices: savings and loan associations and mutual savings banks provide 'NOW Accounts', and credit unions 'Share Draft Accounts'. Both are interest-bearing transaction accounts that threaten to make obsolete the traditional non-interest-bearing commercial bank demand deposit account. An even more dramatic intrusion into the banking business is the provision by brokerage firms of transaction account facilities in conjunction with money market mutual funds. These facilities permit customers to make deposits and write cheques on their money market funds in amounts as little as two hundred dollars. Indeed, in what may prove to be the harbinger of future developments, Merril Lynch's 'Cash Management Account' presently allows customers to access their invested funds for transaction purposes through use of either a charge card or bank drafts written on a zero-balance demand deposit held in an associated bank. The essential aspect of all of these plans, of course, is that they permit customers to keep transaction balances fully invested at all times – they eliminate the need for conventional transaction accounts. These innovations, however, are only the beginning: we are moving swiftly towards a system in which all financial assets will be accessible for transaction purposes, even bonds and stocks, and, with the maturing of electronic funds transfer systems, this trend should accelerate.

Commercial banks, as well, are diversifying into non-traditional financial activities. Both directly and through bank-holding company affiliates, they have entered financial markets that have been the exclusive preserve of non-banks since the 1930s. They now engage in extensive leasing activities (airplanes, automobiles and other business equipment), provide sophisticated management consulting and data-processing services, sell and, in some instances, underwrite insurance, and are rapidly expanding the scope of their investment advisory and money management activities.

In the United States, attempts by banks to enter the securities business and to push back the frontiers of the Glass–Steagall Act have probably attracted the most attention.[3] Banks' attempts to compete directly with investment bankers and brokerage firms have stirred up a hailstorm of legal, regulatory and political fury. Proposals to offer comingled investment funds and to provide more extensive underwriting facilities have resulted in litigation and Congressional hearings that have at their heart the definition or redefinition of banking. The old question, 'What should commercial banking be?' has again moved to the forefront.

These development – banks expanding into areas that have traditionally been the preserves of non banking institutions, and non-banks engaging in conventional banking activities – have blurred the distinction between commercial banks and other institutions. The historically based legal definition of a commercial bank as an entity that both accepts demand deposits and makes commercial loans is no longer reflective of economic realities, and a system of regulation that is premised on such a legal foundation is tilting at windmills. As non-bank financial institutions become more like commercial banks, it seems clear that new regulations will have to be imposed on them; and, as banks expand into non-traditional financial activities, bank regulation will similarly have to be revised to meet new problems.

3.2 Spatial markets

Another central feature of financial markets in the past has been the competitive insulation afforded to banks and other financial institutions by the existence of geographically separate markets. Often this insulation has seemed to be the very aim of regulation itself. The most obvious case is the restrictive branching laws that have been adopted by many states in the United States. More generally, there exist wide disparities in state and country regulations, which have the effect of fracturing markets.

Both the economic and the technological changes now occurring in financial markets, however, seem destined to greatly diminish regulatory and economic barriers to spatial competition.

In the United States, utilisation of bank-holding companies has permitted banks to operate widely in states that prohibit branching, and has enabled them to cross state lines through the device of non-bank affiliates, something they have never been able to do directly. Large bank-holding companies, such as Citicorp and Bank of America, presently operate financial affiliates in nearly every state that provide all major banking services except for the acceptance of consumer deposits.

Future developments in the technology of electronic funds transfer systems will further remove impediments to spatial integration. Customers will soon be able to access their accounts through various alternative transfer systems, resulting in *de facto* nationwide branching. In addition, the logic of current bank-holding company regulation suggests that, eventually, savings and loan institutions will become permissible affiliates of bank-holding companies. When this occurs, we will have nationwide branching savings institutions now provide both savings deposits and cheque account facilities. While the Federal Reserve Board has been understandably reluctant to take this final step, deferring to the Congress on the basis that such a step would be tantamount to a sweeping change in the financial structure, the apparent logic to that step will, I believe, ultimately dominate. (Indeed, this step may ultimately come to be viewed as a solution to a problem, rather than as a problem that needs a solution. I refer, of course, to the growing vulnerability of savings institutions to cyclical swings in interest rates.)

In the international sphere, the breakdown of geographical barriers is even more apparent. Money and credit are commodities that travel easily, and international banks have formed worldwide financial networks to smooth their journeys. In all major countries, national and foreign banks compete aggressively for the business of major international corporations. Increasingly, this competition is being extended to purely domestic businesses and to retail banking. In the United States, foreign banks, because of differential regulatory treatment, can and do operate branches in more than one state, and both foreign and US banks utilise 'Edge Act' subsidiaries to branch interstate for 'limited' purposes, where 'limited' is neither 'strictly limited' nor 'time inelastic'.

The development of the Eurodollar market is the pinnacle of international integration: it surmounts all regulatory barriers and is the inevitable result of economic forces to internationalise pushing against national regulations designed for unintegrated economies. The Eurodollar market has resulted in two types of banking systems, but with one kind of regulation. There is domestic banking, which is regulated unevenly by disparate national banking laws, and there is international banking, which is regulated only partially by the same domestic banking laws. The extent to which international banking has escaped national banking regulation is readily apparent from the recent US proposal to establish a 'Free-Banking Zone' in New York City for international banks. Such proposals are obvious attempts by national regulators to respond to international competitive realities.

In summary, the decline of both product and geographical market segmentation has resulted in a number of regulatory problems, some more important than others. In the next section an attempt is made to identify the major problems and to determine their regulatory implications.

4. REGULATORY IMPLICATIONS

The erosion of market segmentation strikes at the heart of our ability both to maintain monetary control and to preserve bank solvency. Diminishing institutional insularity has resulted in two central economic trends: it has reduced and may soon eliminate the distinction between commercial banks and other financial institutions; and it has increased competition in US and world financial markets to levels that exceed most historical experience. The current competitive environment in major financial markets, and especially in international markets, may surpass the competitive frenzy that financial markets reached in the late 1920s. It is the narrowing distinction between commercial banks and other financial institutions, however, that holds the major implication for monetary control, while the chief impact of the increased competition we are experiencing falls on bank solvency.

The integration of financial markets throughout the world, and the development of international financial markets, such as the Eurodollar market, have also reduced the ability of regulation and of regulators to control events. Competition among alternative and quite different national regulatory systems, each designed to cope with quite different financial systems, is driving regulation to its lowest common denominator, despite efforts towards greater international regulatory co-operation and towards the establishment of more harmony among national regulatory systems.

4.1 Monetary control

As banks and other financial institutions grow more alike, the problem of monetary control grows more complex. In the United States, the primary lever of monetary policy is the Federal Reserve's control over the supply of commercial banks' reserves. Through control of these reserves, coupled with regulations that require banks to maintain minimum reserve requirements with the Federal Reserve, the Federal Reserve controls the volume of 'money' and the supply of related monetary aggregates. Traditionally, only commercial banks provided transaction balances, or demand deposits, so that direct control of only these transaction balances gave the Federal Reserve a reasonable degree of control over all related monetary aggregates (such as M2 or M3). With non-bank financial institutions also providing transaction balances, however, the power of the Federal Reserve to control either the volume of transaction balances or the supply of other monetary aggregates has clearly been diminished.

This loss of control stems from the fact that non-bank financial institutions, such as savings institutions and credit unions, are not required to hold legal reserves in the same way that banks are (as 'idle balances'). Thus, as more and more transaction balances are shifted to non-banks, less total reserves are required to be held, with the result that the money supply multiplier becomes larger and larger. It is, however, widely recognised that at some point an equilibrium will occur, and at a finite multiplier, since depository institutions all wish to hold some small amounts of cash as liquidity cushions against deposit withdrawals. Indeed, it is precisely this phenomenon that has induced some economists to argue that there is no need to regulate bank reserves, or to impose reserve requirements on banks. As a narrowly construed theoretical proposition, this argument is probably correct; as an operational proposition, however, it is certainly questionable. The complete elimination of minimum reserve requirements, and the lack of regulatory control over 'money-creating' financial institutions, may substantially increase the difficulty of controlling the money supply in at least two ways: it will increase the Federal Reserve's uncertainty about variations in the money supply multiplier, and will reduce the amount of information the Federal Reserve has about monetary aggregates.

This problem is made even worse by the existence of money market funds which provide cheque-writing privileges, and by innovations in electronic funds transfer systems. Non-depository financial institutions which provide transaction account facilities (such as brokerage firms) need not maintain cash balances as a liquidity reserve against withdrawals. Withdrawals from these funds are made totally on a market value basis, with the customer taking the risk of any fluctuation in the market value of his asset holdings. While there is some question about the extent to which customers see these transaction facilities as substitutes for traditional depository transaction accounts, there can be no doubt that they are substitutable to an important degree.

Declining market segmentation impinges on monetary control in still another way: the increased competition that has resulted has provoked banks to quit the Federal Reserve system, compounding and accelerating its loss of control. Also, the growing activity in the United States of foreign banks, which are not members of the Federal Reserve system, has further complicated the issue.

Finally, the development and growth of the Eurodollar market raises a fundamentally similar issue. Eurodollars (or at least those which represent liabilities to non-banks, which constitute a pool of about 120 billion dollars) can be viewed as close substitutes for the United States money supply, and Eurobanks are not required to hold legal reserves against these liabilities (just as savings banks do not have to hold reserves against their transaction–deposit liabilities). Thus, the extent to which United States' monetary authorities can or should control these transaction balances is uncertain.

In summary, the changes in financial markets now under way are moving us to a radically new financial system – one without legal reserve requirements and without a Federal Reserve system as we have always known it. At this juncture it is still unclear whether this system will be as viable as the old, or whether it will permit as much monetary control as the system we are leaving behind. What is clear is that important changes in our monetary system are taking place, and these changes should be carefully considered before they are embraced.

4.2 Bank solvency and financial soundness

More competitive financial markets also make the financial system more vulnerable to insolvency and panic. Financial soundness has two dimensions: the vulnerability of individual banks to insolvency, and the vulnerability of the entire financial system to 'bank runs' and crises of confidence. Governments have sought to diminish these risks both through direct solvency regulation and through the establishment of central banks as 'lenders of last resort'. In addition, in the United States these have been supplemented by a governmentally backed deposit insurance scheme.

In general, direct regulation to maintain the solvency of individual banks seeks both to restrain competition among banks and to keep them from engaging in activities that result in risk exposures that are unacceptably high. Examples of the first kind of regulation are entry restraints, either on *de novo* entry or entry via branching, and 'pricing' restrictions, such as the prohibition against paying interest on demand deposits and the setting of maximum rate ceilings on savings and time deposits. Examples of regulations which restrict high-risk activities, or constrain protfolio choices, are prohibitions against banks holding common stocks for their own account, prohibitions against engaging in investment banking activities, and the impositions of minimum capital and liquidity requirements.

In the context of portfolio theory, these kinds of solvency regulations can be viewed as attempts to alter the parameters of the earnings distributions of individual banks and of the entire banking system. By limiting competition, banks' expected earnings should increase, and their entire earnings distribution should shift to the right. By restricting the ability of banks to engage in risky activities, the spread (or variance) of banks' earnings distributions should be reduced. Thus, for a given level of bank capital, the probability of insolvency for a given bank should be reduced.

Government intervention to guard against 'bank panics' is of a different nature. Here, the major concern is interdependence among banks: the fear that even a handful of bank insolvencies could trigger a crisis of confidence in all banks, however intrinsically sound they may be. The primary governmental defence against this happening is the timely and forceful intervention of central banks. Central banks must know what is happening, have detailed knowledge about the principal parties involved, and be prepared and willing to intervene on a massive scale, if necessary. Timeliness is the key. Central banks must act without hesitation and with confidence in their decisions. To do this, they must be kept fully informed and, themselves, be integral participants in the operations of financial markets and institutions.

The changes presently occurring in financial markets weaken both of these regulatory supports to financial soundness, at least in the absence of an appropriate prudential response. Increased competition among financial institutions is reducing their earnings cushions, making them more susceptible to bankruptcy (everything else remaining the same). It is also resulting in increased pressure to maintain earnings, causing bankers to search for new activities as sources of additional income. High-risk activities, which carry higher earnings, are becoming increasingly attractive – evidence exists which clearly suggests that competition drives banks to increase their risks.[4] In recent years, regulators have also become more permissive in allowing banks to pursue riskier activities.

These tendencies are further exacerbated by the internationalisation of financial markets, and by competition among nations to acquire a larger share of international banking. Motivated by the desire to permit their own banks to compete successfully internationally, US regulatory authorities and those of other countries have relaxed restrictions on their banks' activities abroad. US banks, for example, may engage in a wide range of investment banking activities abroad, but not at home. Also, in order to attract foreign banks, some nations have exempted them from regulations that apply to domestic banks. In other instances, as in the United States, foreign banks have been able to circumvent important domestic banking restrictions through loopholes in the law (such as their ability to avoid important Glass–Steagall Act prohibitions).[5] These developments are diluting traditional bank solvency regulation just at the time that enhanced competition is driving banks towards a greater reliance on high-risk activities. Bankers are demanding more freedom from regulatory restrictions to meet increased market pressures, and regulators are supplying less regulation in response to increased international political and economic pressures. The obvious question is: where will it stop? Will there be a new 'equilibrium' at a reduced level of solvency regulation, and will this degree of regulation be sufficient to maintain financial soundness?

Still another way that recent international developments threaten soundness is by diminishing the ability of central banks to cope with 'bank panics'. International banks are closely linked to each other through international financial markets: in the Eurodollar and Eurocurrency markets, they are connected by elaborate networks of deposits and credits, and in foreign exchange markets, they are linked by enormous spot and forward exchange positions. This interdependence makes the many vulnerable to the calamities of the few. To guard against such a crisis requires a higher degree of international co-operation than we have ever had before. Successful international crisis management requires the continual exchange of information among central bankers and a clear understanding of their international and domestic responsibilities. While some progress has been made in this direction during the past five years, we have not yet developed the institutions and the degree of international understanding that can assure successful international crisis management.

In summary, the major goals of financial regulation are to protect the soundness of financial systems and to provide a framework for effective monetary control. Recent developments and innovations in financial markets threaten the attainment of both goals. I have argued in this chapter that monetary authorities are less able to control monetary aggregates now than in the past, and that banks and entire banking systems are presently more vulnerable to bankruptcy and to crises of confidence than in the past.

As a general proposition, more integration of markets and greater competition are desirable ends, since both enhance economic efficiency. Financial markets, however, provide some exceptions to this general proposition. Any meaningful definition of economic efficiency for financial markets must clearly incorporate financial soundness and effective monetary control as essential dimensions, and competition in financial markets must be compatible with the attainment of these social goals.

The key problem at present is that changes in financial markets are occurring in a haphazard, unmanaged way. The problem is not so much that competition is increasing, but that the new market environment which is developing is being superimposed on a regulatory structure that is outdated and slow to change.

5. REGULATORY REFORM: SOME GENERAL PROPOSALS

The thrust of my discussion so far has been to warn of potential dangers rather than of an imminent crisis. The dangers that exist, however, are likely to grow over time if appropriate measures are not taken. Thus, careful consideration should be given to beginning the process of regulatory reform.

Any changes adopted should obviously attempt to preserve wherever possible the benefits of the increased market integration and the heightened competition we are now experiencing. If anything, financial markets in the past have been less competitive than is desirable. Greater integration of markets and increased competition have been, in that sense, a welcome development. The result has undoubtedly been better customer service and a better allocation of financial resources. Our objective, therefore, should be to preserve these benefits while containing the potential dangers.

I believe we can accomplish this by working towards three long-run regulatory goals. These goals, by necessity, are transnational in scope, and I envisage them as ultimately being applied to all of the major financial institutions throughout the world. As a consequence, the political and economic steps necessary to reach these objectives will be arduous. It is important, nevertheless, that we have a firm idea of where we want to go, even though the path we must follow to get there is difficult. These goals are the following:

(i) Either uniform legal reserve requirements should be imposed on all financial institutions offering 'transaction balances', or monetary authorities should adopt a consistent system of paying interest on bank balances that are in effect bank reserves.

(ii) Capital, liquidity and portfolio constraints designed to assure institutional soundness should be adjusted to reflect the enhanced competitive environment in which financial institutions now operate and, where feasible, these regulations should be uniform across competing institutions.

(iii) A supranational lender of last resort facility should be established, supported by at minimum the Group Ten Central Banks.

The first of these proposals will preserve the ability of monetary authorities to control the volume of money and liquidity, and hopefully to conduct effective stabilisation and anti-inflation policies. The second and third will assure the continued soundness of the financial system: the second by keeping the risk of institutional insolvency to acceptable levels, and the third by preventing short-lived crises of confidence in financial markets from precipitating 'bank runs' that bring about a chain reaction of banking collapse.

These proposals will not diminish competition nor erect obstacles to further market integration. They will encourage both developments by assuring competitive equality and fairness of regulatory treatment. They will also have a minimal distorting effect on the allocation of resources. Indeed, if these proposals were adopted, much of existing financial regulation could be eliminated, so that many of the present regulatory-induced distortions could be corrected. These proposals represent the minimum government interference consistent with the attainment of the overriding social goals of maintaining monetary control and assuring financial soundness.

NOTES

1. This project was funded in part through the General Motors Corporation Faculty Research Fellowship, 1978–9.
2. For a fuller discussion of the rationale and structure of bank regulation, see F. R. Edwards and J. H. Scott (1979).
3. F. R. Edwards (1979).
4. F. R. Edwards and A. A. Heggestad (1973).
5. F. R. Edwards (1979).

REFERENCES

Edwards, F. R. (1979) 'Banks and Securities Activities: Legal and Economic Perspectives on the Glass–Steagall Act', in L. Goldberg and L. White, *The Deregulation of the Banking and Securities Industries* (Lexington, Mass.: Heath) pp. 273–94.

Edwards, F. R. and A. A. Heggestad (1973) 'Uncertainty, Market Structure and Performance: the Galbraith–Caves Hypothesis and Managerial Motives in Banking', *Quarterly Journal of Economics* (August) pp. 455–73.

Edwards, F. R. and J. H. Scott (1979) 'Regulating the Solvency of Depository Institutions: a Perspective for Deregulation', in F. R. Edwards (ed.), *Issues in Financial Regulation* (New York: McGraw Hill) pp. 65–105.

Comment on Edwards

ALFONS VERPLAETSE

I agree with Professor Edwards's description and analysis of financial developments in the recent past and with the changes he foresees for the future. It is clear that changes require appropriate adjustments in the financial regulations. This does not mean a complete deregulation. On the contrary, the efficient functioning of a modern economy implies some 'good' regulation. In principle, financial regulation should be as 'market-oriented' as possible and should not intervene in the competitive position of individual institutions. Even such measures as credit ceilings which are by nature not 'market-oriented' can be improved – for example, by the trading of unused amounts.

One feature in the analysis of Professor Edwards struck me particularly: until now I thought that the United States were in every field a decade ahead of Europe, and of Belgium in particular. However, with regard to the decrease in market segmentation, I think that my country (Belgium) is a leading one. Indeed, the erosion of financial product segmentation started in the early 1960s and is, by now, probably more advanced than in most other countries. The despecialisation of the credit institutions and the large possibilities of substitution between a very wide range of financial assets have definitely influenced the conduct of monetary policy. All measures taken in that regard always apply to all main credit institutions (banks, savings institutions, public credit institutions). Monetary authorities are paying no attention to M1, M2 or . . . M27.5 but to the whole spectrum of financial assets and more specially to the factors bringing about changes in these assets (overall credit to the private sector, financial deficit of the public administrations, external factors). Supervision of the financial institutions has evolved in the same direction, but on a more pragmatic basis and with some delay.

As to regulation goals for the long run, I agree that the same monetary requirements should apply to all the operations of the same nature, without regard to the kind of involved credit institution. It is, however, not my opinion that this should be a uniform reserve requirement. The need for compulsory reserves, in fact an imposed participation by the credit institutions in the financing of the assets of the central bank, depends on the financial structure and on the economic circumstances. In a lot of cases, compulsory reserves only bring about a useless or even harmful increase in the cost of credit or an equally useless decrease in the interest rates fixed on financial assets or, in rare occasions, an erosion of the profit margin of credit institutions. Moreover, I fear that compulsory reserves which would be uniform across countries would prevent adjustments required by the economic situation of individual countries and would thus mean the end of using them as a tool for active monetary policy.

Uniform reserve requirements and uniform regulations assuring institutional soundness of the financial system will not prevent international capital movements as these are brought about by a number of factors.

Finally, I consider that the suggested supranational lending facility of last resort should not be granted directly by the central banks themselves but should be supported by a supranational guaranty fund, fed by a pool of financial institutions, a recourse to the central bank being provided only in the very last resort. A permanent and too direct concern of central banks for difficulties of individual banks would divert central banks from their first task: to control monetary developments in order to help to achieve the final objectives of the real economy. In the proposal, conflicting situations between macroeconomic and microeconomic responsibilities might even occur. The concentration of both responsibilities in one hand might lead to a paralysing of both activities and might be detrimental to the monetary control as such.

2. The Complementary Nature of Competition and Regulation in the Financial Sector

JACK R. S. REVELL

1. THE DEBATE ON DEREGULATION

The main theme of this chapter is that competition and regulation are not alternatives to each other in the financial sector, but that a competitive financial system requires close regulation and supervision by the authorities. I decided on this theme largely because in Europe the debate is often carried on in terms of 'competition versus regulation'. This seems to echo the current debate in the United States on the deregulation of depository institutions and, indeed, the chapters of F. R. Edwards and R. A. Taggart in this volume (chapters 1 and 3) are concerned with that debate. I think there are great dangers in transposing the debate into a European context without being aware of what it is about and what it does not call into question.

The word 'regulation' covers two rather different forms of control. The first is what I shall call *structural* regulation. It is concerned with the kinds of activity permitted to different classes of institution, the conditions for establishment of new institutions and the branches of existing ones, and various controls on interest rates and charges for services (Regulation Q and state usury laws in the American context). The second form is *prudential* regulation and is concerned with balance-sheet controls to ensure liquidity and solvency. It is true that many of the structural regulations originally had a prudential aspect, but I doubt whether many of them are really necessary to the soundness of the financial system. It is the structural regulation, far more than the prudential regulation, that inhibits competition.

What makes the American debate largely irrelevant to European conditions is the fact that most of the structural regulations have either been abandoned or drastically reduced in Europe over recent years. The French abandoned their compulsory split between *banques de dépôts* and *banques d'affaires* in 1966, and even the structural restraints implied in several countries by the restriction of commercial banks to short-term deposits and short-term loans have been partly lifted.

There is little doubt that the American financial system has for some time been over-burdened with structural regulations, and there is a strong case for them to be dismantled. It would be a great pity, however, if the general theme of the American debate were to be used in an attempt to call into question the need for the sort of prudential regulation exercised by central banks and banking commissions in Europe. There is room for debate about the nature and form of this regulation, and I shall return to this point later. However, the abolition of this prudential regulation is not on the agenda, either in the United States or in Europe. The participants do not see competition and prudential regulation as effective alternatives.

2. COMPETITION

The discussion of competition in the financial sector is nearly always confined to retail banking services, but this is only one of many markets in which banks compete. Since the war the breakdown of specialisation among credit institutions has led to commercial banks facing competition from a range of non-bank institutions such as savings banks, agricultural credit associations and credit unions, which offer much the same range of services either individually or through central organisations, which have sometimes become major international banks. The scope of the ancillary services offered by these institutions has also been extended greatly since the war, from the traditional trust and foreign exchange business into credit cards, leasing, factoring, travel services, insurance broking and computing facilities. Each market has its own margin of profitability, its own degree of competition, and its own split between retail and wholesale elements. It is thus unrealistic to single out one of the markets as the touchstone of competition, especially as the opportunities for cross-subsidisation between all the markets and within many of them are very great.

The reason for concentrating the discussion on the retail banking services is clearly because that is the only part of banking business for which information can be obtained with any facility. In retail business, prices are posted and the services are standardised. In the nationwide branch banking networks that are the norm in Europe both the prices and the types of service offered by different institutions tend to be very similar if not identical, and this fact is sometimes used to point to the lack of competition. This is surely a very naive view, because identical prices can be found both in perfectly competitive and in monopolistic markets; in between these two extremes, identical prices may indicate either collusion or competition between a small number of large sellers. The product offered by each bank is likely to be very similar to that of its competitors because there is no means of patenting financial innovations. Naive though it is, this view sometimes puts pressure on banks to create differences between each other just to appear competitive.

Discussing the reality of bank competition in terms only of the retail services has never been justified, and it is even less justified today with the development of wholesale banking, both domestic and international. Competition between banks for large customers has always been particularly intense, with negotiated terms for services that are designed to suit the particular needs of the customer; identical prices for standard packages of services do not apply in this sphere.

The special significance of large customers was recognised before the war by L. V. Chandler, who spoke of them as having two great advantages in bargaining over terms with banks.[1] The first was that they tended to use the services of more than one bank, a fact that is true for very large customers in the nationwide banking systems of Europe, but presumably even more so for the geographically restricted banking system of the United States. The second advantage is that they have the further alternative of raising funds in their own names on either the money market or the capital market. Quite apart from these structural advantages, the largest of the customers are often larger than the banks themselves. They are in a specially good position to play off one bank against another and to obtain the keenest terms for the banking services that they use.

Banks react to the strength of their largest customers by arriving at conventions or explicit agreements about the greatest concessions that they are collectively prepared to grant to the most favoured customers. Agreements on maximum rates of interest payable on current accounts (demand deposits) in some European countries probably have this significance. Agreements on loan rates usually specify only one rate, that charged on loans to prime customers, and price leadership secures the same result in banking systems in which cartel practices have been abandoned. In other words, the answer of the banks to their powerful customers is a suspension of interbank competition and the presenting of a united front. Somewhat paradoxically, they usually leave a loophole by diverting some powerful customers to branches outside the country that are not subject to the agreements; the branches of Scottish banks in London used to fulfil this function.

Whatever may be the position in the retail market, there can be no doubt that wholesale and international banking are highly competitive. There are virtually no agreements or conventions to inhibit interbank competition, the customers have a wide choice of banks in both domestic and international business, and they can raise money in their own names. At the present moment, the doubt is whether competition has not reduced margins to the point of zero profitability in international banking, the so-called Eurocredits.

One of the most important features of competition between banks, and increasingly among non-bank institutions and between them and banks, is the extent to which they attempt to secure the continued loyalty of their customers by making it worth their while to take a whole range of services from the same institution. This is the basis of the 'customer relationship' to which D. R. Hodgman drew attention.[2] Hodgman was talking of the position of the large customers, the prime customers of the previous discussion. The main relationship that he described was the granting of loans to large depositor customers at a preferential rate of interest, with the prime rate as an irreducible minimum. The banks were able to do this because the other services that they provided for these customers were profitable.

The customer relationship is not limited to large customers, and for the present purposes the way in which it applies in the retail market is of even greater importance. As in the case of the large customer, the key service is that associated with the operation of the customer's current account. In most European countries, some interest is paid on current accounts, but it is only at the low rate of $\frac{1}{2}$ per cent, or 1 per cent on personal accounts; in countries where no interest is paid, such as the United Kingdom and Ireland, there is no law against payment. Fees and commission are charged for current account services, but there is almost no information on the extent to which these charges cover the cost of operating the payments service. Generally speaking, it is probably true to say that in Europe the case of the personal current account depositor is the opposite of that considered by Hodgman: the loan margin has to be increased to make good a shortfall between costs and charges on payments services.

What makes the current account so potent a weapon for tying the customer to one bank or savings bank is that the personal account holder sees access to credit when he needs it as one of the implicit benefits of holding deposits with the institution. The same is true, but to a lesser extent, of savings deposits. Unlike the large corporate customer, whose creditworthiness is established and who can obtain credit from a variety of sources, the personal customer has to build up his creditworthiness by the prudent operation of his account, and he is loath to begin this process all over again when he switches his account from one bank to another.

The competitive process, even in the most competitive of banking systems, thus has the fatal weakness of 'bundling' services and using profits on one service to compensate for losses on another. Only rarely is the pricing of services related directly to the costs of providing them. It is arguable that the greatest increase in competition within the financial sector and the greatest increase in allocative efficiency would come about if the institutions were forced to pay market rates for all funds they attracted and to recover the full cost of each service. Over the next decade or so the introduction of electronic funds transfer systems in all developed countries will force governments to make critical decisions that will affect the extent and nature of competition in the financial sector, and we should give further consideration to the question of competition in an EFTS context.

3. ELECTRONIC FUNDS TRANSFER

After many official and unofficial reports and several tentative experiments, the technical features of an EFT system are reasonably clear. There will be three kinds of terminal through which access to the system is possible. Point-of-sale terminals will enable shoppers to pay for their purchases without the use of either currency or a cheque in most cases; the seller will be able to verify before completing the sale that the customer has sufficient funds in his account. The other two types of terminal, automatic teller machines in public places and push-button telephones in homes, will both give access to a customer's accounts in a number of different institutions; the former will also dispense currency.

One of the factors that will determine the shape of an EFT system is the existence of considerable economies of scale. These are at their greatest with point-of-sale terminals, and it is almost certain that most countries will end up with one, or at the most two, networks linking these terminals to institutions. For the purposes of the present discussion, it does not matter whether the network is publicly or privately owned. The economies of scale are not nearly so great for automatic teller machines, and they do not really exist at all for home telephone terminals.

Since only the major banks could begin to think of establishing EFTS, the key question is the ease of access to the full facilities of the system by other depository institutions. This question has been debated in the context of the US banking system by M. J. Flannery and D. M. Jaffee and in that of the United Kingdom by D. Hopton.[3] The consensus seems to be that the authorities will insist that access be free to all in the interests of greater competition. We can hope that this will be so, but not all the competitive consequences of EFTS depend on equal access to the system for all kinds of financial institution.

The first, and in many ways the most important, consequence arises as soon as any sort of automatic access to the computer of an individual institution is provided by a terminal in a public place or in the customer's home. The consequence is that location ceases to have any competitive advantage for routine transactions. In Europe, branching on a national or regional scale has been one of the most important competitive weapons, but much of the advantage of a branch network will be lost when access through computer terminals becomes widespread. The degree of competition would obviously be greater if the terminals in public places were provided cooperatively by all institutions, but many institutions at present without branches would find it much cheaper to provide their own terminals individually than to establish and man a normal branch. In very few European countries would they have to seek permission to do this. The cost of entry into full-scale deposit business would be drastically reduced.

The second consequence is that of instantaneous transfer of a balance from an interest-bearing account to a current account. As recent experience in the United States shows, this so erodes the differences between a demand deposit and a savings deposit that the two become one for all practical purposes. This would largely circumvent the legal prohibition of the payment of interest on demand deposits in the United States, even if the law were not abolished, and it would remove the inhibitions of banks in most European countries against paying a market rate of interest on current accounts.

The third consequence is that the cost of transferring money would be so much reduced that it would be easy to move over to a position of charging the customer with the full cost even when he had become accustomed to 'free' or subsidised money transfer facilities. The marginal cost of each transaction would be little above zero, and the average cost with full recovery of overheads would be much lower than with our present paper-based system.

The fourth consequence that seems to be envisaged by most writers on the subject is that the customer would have access to credit lines previously authorised: in European terminology, overdrafts would once again be the norm for consumer lending. Some writers take this question even further and suggest that the consumer could automatically mobilise such assets as the surrender values of his life assurance policies. One of the main points, however, is that the personal customer will no longer be so dependent on the bank manager's knowledge of his reliability through monitoring the operation of his current account; his creditworthiness will depend far more on credit-scoring devices that give marks for such factors as his income and its assured continuance, his ownership of a house, and his possession of a telephone. The link between a current account and access to credit will be severed, and the consumer will be able to maintain his interest-bearing transactions-cum-savings account with one institution and borrow from one or more others.

No doubt, the authorities in each country could prevent most of these consequences of an EFT system or they could permit the dominant banking institutions to deny equal access to all deposit institutions. Even if they sought to do this, the possibility of each customer having automatic access at all hours to his account with an individual institution, which the authorities probably could not deny him, would open the door quite wide to a more competitive system. What is certain is that the authorities must shortly make up their minds what sort of deposit and credit system they want to see developing. There must undoubtedly be a long transition period, but the decisions on the ultimate shape of the system must be taken fairly soon, and they must be taken with all the technical possibilities in mind. These possibilities add up to a system in which each deposit is rewarded at a market rate of interest and each loan and service is charged at full cost and one in which the customer has the possibility of selecting a different institution for each service.

4. CYCLES, CRISES AND AGREEMENTS

So far the discussion has been entirely about competition, but now the time has come to introduce the second theme of regulation. The line of argument will be that aggressive competition in the financial sector tends to lead to financial crises, and that the motivation behind the agreements into which banks and other deposit institutions enter is as much the avoidance of risky business as the securing of abnormal profits. The link between agreements and regulation is that the suspension of interbank competition implied by the agreements was a primitive form of self-regulation, designed to preserve the safety of the financial system and the continued existence of established institutions. In the course of the discussion we shall have to survey briefly the significance of the recent literature on the subject of financial crises associated with the names of Minsky and Kindleberger.

Over the past few years the subject of financial crises has begun to arouse interest in academic circles, following three severe crises or near-crises in 1966, 1969–70 and 1973–5. H. P. Minsky has long been arguing that the financial system of the United States shows a condition of 'systematic fragility', and the evidence that he adduces could be paralleled in most industrialised countries.[4]

Minsky's interest is largely in the postwar period, but other writers have been driven to explore the lessons to be gained from history by going back over the important financial crises of the past, starting in the seventeenth century. C. P. Kindleberger is undoubtedly the most eminent of these, and he concludes his study with an analysis of the lessons to be drawn from history.[5] For our immediate purposes, an especially interesting study is that made by C. R. Barclay, in which he compared nineteenth century financial crises in Britain with our fringe banking crisis of 1973 and 1974.[6] In the course of this comparison he developed a model of the way in which pockets of excess profitability attracted new entrants to an industry, reducing the level of profits down to a more normal level and often below the level that was necessary for the continuance of the enlarged number of firms in the industry. It is, if you like, a cobweb theorem model. It applies particularly to banking because it is an industry that can be entered most easily unless government regulation inhibits it, a state of affairs that did not apply in the nineteenth century.

This model of the banking industry can be developed to show that the increase in competition led in almost all instances to the growth of bad banking practices. What makes such practices very likely is that retribution for bad banking does not follow immediately; it is delayed until the next financial crisis, which may be sparked off by some almost fortuitous event, although it is unlikely to occur until the banking system is in a state of what Minsky would describe as fragility. The losses and failures resulting from bad banking are not spread evenly over time but are bunched. Before this crisis arrives, the profit advantage will lie with the aggressive banks that indulge in unsound and speculative practices and the established banks will be drawn into bad banking in order to rescue their profitability. This results in a kind of Gresham's law of banking, in which bad banking drives out good banking.

At a more analytical level we can identify the particular features of a boom period that will draw banks into unsound practices. The general price level is rising and the prices of equities and properties rise with it, so that capital gain looms much larger in financial calculations. Not only do banks themselves indulge in speculation on rising price levels but they also issue loans that can be serviced only if the price of the borrower's output rises continually. During a boom period the yield curve is usually tilted, so that the financing of long-term assets with short-term deposits offers the prospect of high profits. The importance of these features is magnified when, as in the postwar period, a rising trend of inflation is superimposed on the business cycle.

The implication of the bunching of banking losses at times of financial crisis is that risk is not some immutable factor associated with a particular type of banking asset. Risk varies over time, and in general we can say that the probability of loss increases with every year that has passed since the last crisis.

This analysis, bald though it has to be for reasons of space, provides justification for associating a high degree of competition with a high degree of risk in banking. The next step in the argument is one that cannot be documented to any great extent. It consists of the hypothesis that one of the reactions of established banks, which had by definition survived one or two financial crises, was to resist the continuance of this cyclical process, in which increased risk and increased competition went hand in hand, by banding together to restrain interbank competition. The history of the interbank agreements that we have come to call 'cartels' has not been investigated in any country that I know of, although I hope to find some material in due course. In the meantime, I can only indicate why I think it likely that one of the main motives behind these cartels was self-regulation to make the banking industry safer. For this to be true it is not necessary to pretend that bankers are angels who never use their cartels to their own profitable advantage; all that need be done is to demonstrate that the self-advantage sought through cartels was partly the increased safety of the banking system. I must admit that the indications are rather flimsy, but fortunately this hypothesis, interesting and useful though it is, is not essential to the general theme of this chapter.

5. RECENT EVENTS

The changes in the regulatory environment that took place in Europe some ten or twelve years ago form an important link in the argument. They were designed to increase competition between banks and between different sorts of credit institution, but the significant fact is that they were followed within a very few years by the most dangerous financial crisis since the war. Competition was certainly not an adequate substitute for regulation in this instance.

These measures were nearly all structural. They abolished restrictions on branching and legally-enforced specialisation of types of institution, such as that between deposit banking and investment banking in France. In the case of the United Kingdom, the 'Competition and Credit Control' reform of 1971 changed the method of applying monetary policy regulations on banks, moving from credit ceilings to controls over a reserve assets base. In many ways the most important feature was that the new controls applied to all recognised banks instead of only to clearing banks, thus seeking to bring under official control the largely separate group of wholesale banks that had grown up during the previous decade. In some countries, including the United Kingdom, the cartels were abandoned as a result of pressure from the authorities, and the banks were set free to compete as vigorously as possible. By contrast, no changes were made in the forms and content of prudential regulation.

What followed in late 1973 and throughout 1974 has been well documented, but there are some points that need clarifying. The first is the nature of the bad banking that led to banks in all countries failing or having to be rescued from failure by the authorities. Although much publicity has been given to losses in foreign exchange dealings, they were rarely the fundamental cause of failure. The foreign exchange market after the Smithsonian agreement was certainly a dangerous place for operators who had consistently produced good profits for their banks in the days of fixed exchange rates, when the official reserves absorbed all losses and when the only question was not whether one could make a profit but how much. As recognised profit centres, the foreign exchange departments of banks were expected to produce equally good results under the regime of floating exchange rates. It is no wonder that some were led to plunge even more heavily after initial losses and that some did so for their own profit rather than for that of the bank. Even when the failure of a bank appeared to be caused by foreign exchange losses, however, closer inspection reveals that the bank was led into greater speculation on the exchanges in an attempt to recoup losses made on domestic banking. This was certainly true of both Herstatt and Franklin National.

The pattern of bad banking can be seen most clearly in the fringe banking crisis of 1973 and 1974 in Britain because many banks got into difficulties at the same time or soon after one another and because the pattern of unsound practices was consistent. On the liabilities side the banks relied on short-term deposits, drawn either from the interbank market or from retail operations, and they invested the funds in either longer term loans or in speculative ventures that yielded no immediate income so that the interest due had constantly to be added to the principal ('Ponzi finance'). Much of the lending was to property companies, many of which were linked to the bank in common ownership. In addition to these general examples of unsound and speculative banking there were, of course, many cases of straight-forward fraud and embezzlement.

This particular episode in the history of banking had many features that were peculiar to Britain. Banks were free to establish themselves with a minimum of interference and to continue in their business with a bare minimum of supervision by the authorities; the Bank of England concentrated its supervisory function on those established banks to which it had given various recognitions, and it had no responsibility for the 'fringe'. These features may explain why all these fringe banks got into trouble at much the same time and also why no major bank was in trouble, but they cannot explain why much the same sort of bad banking was to be found in nearly every country at the same time.

In looking at the descriptions of the types of domestic business that was conducted by the banks that failed in European countries and the United States in 1974 and 1975, I am struck by the similarities to the business of the fringe banks in Britain. In nearly every case there was, for example, some connection with the property market, whether it was the involvement of American banks with real estate investment trusts or the links between small German banks and property companies. The fact is that this phenomenon of bad banking was worldwide and it existed in countries where the prudential regulation of banks was exceedingly tight, as much as it did in the permissive regulatory climate of the United Kingdom. There must be some common reasons, and the elucidation of these is essential to the argument.

The two main reasons have already been mentioned, and they are linked together. The first reason, to my mind, was the move towards the relaxation of structural controls over banks with a view to making the banking system more competitive. I would not claim that this, by itself, could explain everything. It was rather the association of these relaxations of control with the acceleration of inflation and general euphoria that accompanied it. Had the moves towards greater competition taken place at a time of general stability in the financial system, there would probably have been no ill effects, but the combination of greater competition with inflation and euphoria was lethal. Since any prudent man at the present time must reckon with the continuance of inflation, we must take heed of this lesson in deciding how much more competition the financial sector can stand in the immediate future.

To my own satisfaction at least, I have demonstrated the close connection between competition and risk, but there remains one weak link in my argument. The regulatory changes of the period from 1966 to 1971 did not extend to a formal relaxation of the prudential aspects of control. My thesis requires me to show that increased competition in the financial system should be accompanied by increased prudential regulation, and yet during the early part of this decade even the tightest systems of prudential control in some countries were unable to prevent the unsound and unsafe banking practices that were associated with the fringe in all countries, a fringe that grew as much by the changes in the management teams of established institutions – Herstatt was established in 1720 – as by the influx of new banks.

Competition may not be able to ensure a sound banking system, but it is no use relying on increased prudential regulation if that too is impotent.

6. FORMS OF PRUDENTIAL REGULATION

A useful point at which to begin is the consideration of the purposes that a system of regulation of the financial sector ought to serve from the point of view of society. The supreme purpose is the safety of the financial system. The working of the system depends so completely on public confidence in the ability and willingness of institutions to carry out the contracts into which they have entered that the authorities must always seek to prevent failures and to contain the effects of those failures that are inevitable. As this formulation implies, it is impossible (and probably undesirable) to ensure complete safety, and the problem reduces itself to a series of trade-offs between safety and a number of other factors, the safety of the system remaining the paramount concern.

A number of other considerations, such as consumer interests in privacy, the prevention of conflicts of interest and so on, enter the picture, but there are three main factors that must be balanced against safety:

(i) the cost of intermediation;
(ii) the allocative efficiency of the financial system;
(iii) the ability of the system to sustain strong measures of monetary policy.

A greater degree of competition is likely to lower the cost of intermediation and to improve the allocative efficiency of the system, but it may well be at the cost of safety if institutions are not prevented from indulging in speculative and unsound banking practices. On the other hand, safety works in the same direction as the ability of institutions to sustain strong measures by the authorities in the interests of macroeconomic policy: the sounder the balance-sheet structures of banks and other credit institutions the greater is the power of the authorities to impose and sustain such measures until they begin to bite, and conversely the weaker the balance sheets the sooner such measures will have to be reversed. This point has been made forcefully by E. P. M. Gardener.[7]

In the conditions of the early 1970s the British system failed to prevent the fringe banking crisis, but the more formal regulatory systems of the United States and Europe also failed to prevent bank insolvencies. The failure of the British system lay in the fact that most of the dubious operators escaped supervision of any kind, but the parallel failure of the other systems must have lain in the nature of the supervision. If we are to rely on regulation to permit a greater degree of competition in the financial sector, it is important to analyse the weaknesses and to suggest a more effective system.

With the sole exceptions of the British and some American systems, the supervisory and regulatory systems of all countries rely on a number of rules of thumb. As we have seen, these may be simple ratios, applied across the board to all institutions, or they may be based on elaborate breakdowns of the asset and liability structure of each institution. However elaborate they may be, the numbers applied to the ratios or to the capital coefficients are arbitrary, and they are usually drawn from the practice of institutions at the time when the regulations were formulated, often many years in the past. One of the main lessons to be drawn from the experience of accelerating inflation in recent years is that the rules of thumb that have served the managements of financial institutions, in place of a more theoretical approach, have begun to break down, in many cases completely. Regulatory systems based on such rules of thumb are also liable to break down.

Linked with this point is the fact that all present supervisory systems are much more concerned with what has happened in the immediate past than with what is likely to happen in the months or years ahead. The figures that are inspected are drawn from a balance sheet that is already several months out of date. The only forward-looking elements occur in those systems, like many in the United States, in which loans in the current portfolio that carry the seeds of trouble are identified and assessed for risk. Earlier, I made the point that risk is not an immutable attribute of a particular asset or class of assets, but varies with time; losses are bunched, so that historical experience is of limited use.

I believe that there is a new approach to supervision that can overcome this reliance on historical experience. This is based on computer simulation, and research is being carried out in the Institute of European Finance to see how this instrument can best be applied to the problems of supervision. The approach being explored goes one stage back, and focuses attention on the use of computer simulation by individual banks to assess the risks involved in projected plans; the role of the supervisor is then to conduct a 'risk audit', to satisfy himself that the bank has adequately assessed and can cover from its capital resources the risks inherent in its operations over the next year or so.

The sort of simulation envisaged is mechanical simulation of the effects of certain hypothetical circumstances (abrupt and severe changes in interest rates, exchange rates, equity prices and the rate of inflation, for instance) and not simulation within the framework of an econometric model of the financial sector. The use of an econometric model, which is built up from the observed relationships between certain financial magnitudes over the recent past, would be merely the importation of historical experience through the back door. The first suggestion for the use of computer simulation in bank regulation was made by G. J. Vojta,[8] but his was only a halfway house towards the system that we are suggesting: the main element in the assessment of capital adequacy by simulation was historical loss experience.

Such an approach is not without its problems, quite apart from the need to gain acceptance for a major innovation. The main problem is to determine the severity of the hypothetical tests to which a bank is to be subject. Computer simulation offers the possibility of simulating the conditions necessary for a bank to become insolvent – testing to destruction – without causing any damage to the bank and without alerting the market to its weaknesses, but it would be pointless to do this. It can be assumed that as soon as the banking system gets into general difficulties or threatens to do so, the central bank would intervene as lender of last resort and, requiring banks to cover all eventualities, would raise the cost of intermediation to an unwarranted level. The level of safety to be maintained must be a matter of judgement by the regulatory authorities. Unfortunately, this may well upset the European Community, whose doctrine of 'transparency' requires that the rules of the game must always be specified in detail and must be the same for everybody.

The second problem is suggested by the mention of the market in the previous paragraph. The more sophisticated the method of supervision becomes the less can the market make its own assessment of the safety of different banks. The supervisors will be working with information that is not available to the market; indeed, the availability of more detailed information to the supervisors is perhaps the strongest justification for superimposing a public system of regulation on top of the policing conducted by the market. Although the safety of the system may come to depend entirely on the risk audit of the supervisors, some provision must be made for the market to receive sufficient information for it to make a reasonable assessment of banking risk.

NOTES

1. L. V. Chandler (1938).
2. D. R. Hodgman (1963).
3. See M. J. Flannery and D. M. Jaffee (1973) for the United States and D. Hopton (1979) for the United Kingdom.
4. For recent expositions, see H. P. Minsky (1975) and (1977).
5. C. P. Kindleberger (1978).
6. C. R. Barclay (1978).
7. E. P. M. Gardener (1978).
8. G. J. Vojta (1973).

REFERENCES

Altman, E. I. and A. W. Sametz (eds) (1978) *Financial Crises: Institutions and Markets in a Fragile Environment* (New York: Wiley–Interscience).
Barclay, C. R. (1978) 'Competition and financial crises – past and present', in J. Revell (ed.), *Competition and Regulation of Banks* (Cardiff: University of Wales Press, Bangor Occasional Papers in Economics, 14).
Chandler, L. V. (1938) 'Monopolistic Elements in Commercial Banking', *Journal of Political Economy*.

Cox, A. M. Jr. (1966) 'Regulation of interest on demand deposits', *Michigan Business Studies*, vol. 17, no. 4.

Edwards, F. R. (ed.) (1979) *Issues in Financial Regulation* (New York: McGraw–Hill).

Flannery, M. J. and D. M. Jaffee (1973) *The Economic Implications of an Electronic Monetary Transfer System* (Lexington, Mass.: Lexington Books).

Gardener, E. P. M. (1978) 'The philosophy of capital adequacy', in J. Revell (ed.), *Competition and Regulation of Banks* (Cardiff: University of Wales Press, Bangor Occasional Papers in Economics, 14).

Hodgman, D. R. (1963) *Commercial Bank Loan and Investment Policy* (Champaign, Ill.: University of Illinois).

Hopton, D. (1979) *Electronic Fund Transfer Systems: the Issues and Implications* (Cardiff: University of Wales Press, Bangor Occasional Papers in Economics, 17).

Kindleberger, C. P. (1978) *Manias, Panics, and Crashes* (New York: Basic Books; London: Macmillan).

Minsky, H. P. (1975) 'Financial resources in a fragile financial environment', *Challenge* (July-August) pp. 6–13.

Minsky, H. P. (1977) 'A theory of systematic fragility', in E. I. Altman and A. W. Sametz (eds), *Financial Crises: Institutions and Markets in a Fragile Environment* (New York: Wiley–Interscience).

Revell, J. (ed.) (1978) *Competition and Regulation of Banks* (Cardiff: University of Wales Press, Bangor Occasional Papers in Economics, 14).

Vojta, G. J. (1973) *Bank Capital Adequacy* (New York: First National City Bank, privately circulated).

Comment on Revell

DIRK HEREMANS

In his highly interesting contribution, Revell raises a variety of issues in the debate of competition and regulation in the financial sector. Due to the comprehensiveness of the chapter it is impossible to comment upon all the interesting points that are developed.

In particular, the author opens fascinating perspectives concerning the application of technological breakthroughs in the financial sector. Electronic funds transfer systems are described as enhancing new prospects for competition and regulation in the financial sector. However, are these not part of a more general phenomenon? Will the new information and communication technology not have strong repercussions on the functioning of markets in general, especially on the relationship between government and the market system in general? The question remains to what extent this will raise problems that are specific to the financial sector.

Nevertheless, I shall concentrate my comments around the main theme of the chapter, the issue of competition and financial regulation. Revell plays down the need for financial deregulation in Europe on the following grounds. He argues that, on the one hand, there exists already a great deal of competition and that competition will anyway be enhanced in the future; on the other hand, aggressive competition will inevitably lead to financial crises. Regulation can be distinguished in structural and prudential regulation, and the latter is complementary to competition, so that more competition requires more regulation.

First, the author stresses that competition increases risk taking and that this leads to financial crises. However, as the empirical evidence he puts forward refers to recent periods of high inflation, the increased financial difficulties could also be attributed to unstable monetary policies to fight inflation.

At the analytical level, the association of a high degree of competition with a high degree of risk in banking requires further investigation into the microeconomic foundations of the behaviour of the banking firm. The thesis that competition leads to bad banking practices rests upon a too narrow short-run view of profit maximisation by the firm. It does not take into account the typical nature of bank products relying upon confidence. Bank products are not homogenous but tend to be differentiated by the brand name of the bank, even if product segmentation in the financial sector is increasingly being eroded. Hence, it pays off for banks to invest in their brand name capital by confidence-creating expenditures such as keeping stocks of reserves, deposit insurance, advertising .... A major method by which a bank invests in brand name capital is by past successful performance; that is, by monitoring its risks.[1] Along the same lines, F. Hayek has argued that the concept of competition should be broadened: 'In actual life the fact that our inadequate knowledge of the available commodities or services is made up for by our experience with the persons supplying them – in fact that competition is in a large measure competition for reputation or good will – is one of the most important facts which enables us to solve our daily problems. The function of competition is here precisely to teach us who will serve us well.'[2]

From this analysis, it is clear that the issue of financial regulation must be stated differently. As confidence will also be produced in a competitive banking system by the individual financial institutions, the proper question, not dealt with, becomes whether confidence can be more efficiently produced by governments.

Another observation is that in the whole literature on financial regulation much emphasis is laid upon the stability of the financial system. Also Revell, in investigating the purposes that a system of financial regulation ought to serve from the point of view of society, points to the paramount importance of safety of the financial system. However, there remains a general need in the literature to clarify what is understood by financial stability, safety, soundness ..., also why for the financial sector, compared with other sectors in the economy, stability is so important. The answers to these questions may be crucial to the type of regulation that should be envisaged.

This requires further investigation into macrodynamic theory along the lines set forth by R. Clower and A. Leijonhufvud. Efficient financial intermediation is a crucial condition for a stable aggregate demand function and for the operation of the self-regulatory capabilities of the market economy. The income-determination process is seen as a cash-constrained process in which financial intermediation is crucial to the permanent reshuffling of cash balances from surplus units to deficit units. Liquid buffer stocks then maintain expenditures when receipts fall off. If the financial system fails, these liquid buffer stocks are squeezed out of the system and effective demand failures lead via negative multiplier effects to major macroeconomic instability.[3]

From this analysis, one could derive that what matters is the maintenance of these liquid buffer stocks, not necessarily the protection of individual financial institutions. Hence, this widens the scope for the role of deposit insurance and the central bank as the lender of last resort.

Finally, the complementarity between competition and regulation, as Revell wants to emphasise, rests crucially upon the distinction between prudential and structural regulation. Although the distinction is interesting at the analytical level, its usefulness in practice may be questioned. Where to draw the line (for example, prudential regulation) may involve barriers to entry in the financial sector, so that structural regulation is brought in through the back door. Hence the issue of competition *versus* regulation remains relevant.

NOTES

1. B. Klein (1974) 'The Competitive Supply of Money', *Journal of Money, Credit and Banking*, vol. vi, pp. 423–53.
2. F. A. Hayek (1948) 'The Meaning of Competition', in *Individualism and Economic Order* (University of Chicago Press) pp. 92–106.
3. A. Leijonhufvud (1973) 'Effective Demand Failures', *The Swedish Journal of Economics*, vol. 75, pp. 27–48.

3. Deregulation of Deposit Rate Ceilings in the United States: Prospects and Consequences[1]

ROBERT A. TAGGART

1. INTRODUCTION

Interest rates paid by depository financial institutions on demand, savings and time accounts have been limited by law for more than forty years now in the United States. Although these rate ceilings have frequently been attacked by economists on grounds of both equity and efficiency, efforts to dismantle them have so far met with little success. Quite recently, however, prospects for change appear to have brightened. President Carter has urged Congress to do away with all deposit rate ceilings, and administration officials have expressed optimism that this change may be implemented.[2]

The purpose of this chapter is to explore some reasons why the removal of deposit rate ceilings may now face improved prospects. As a background for the discussion, Section 2 of this chapter briefly summarises the history of rate ceilings in the United States, and notes the arguments that have been invoked for and against them. One reason that removal of the ceilings may currently face a better chance is that experience in the financial markets, as documented in a number of recent studies, has proven the case in favour of ceilings to be quite weak. Results of these studies are surveyed in Section 3. A second and more important reason is that the regulatory system itself may no longer be capable of sustaining the ceilings. Making use of recent work on the theory of economic regulation, Section 4 analyses the response of regulators, financial institutions and consumers to changing technological and competitive conditions, and concludes that pressures against rate ceilings have increased enormously.

2. EVOLUTION OF THE DEBATE OVER RATE CEILINGS

The original impetus for deposit rate ceilings in the United States rested on the argument that excessive competition for deposits promoted instability of the banking system by raising the cost of funds and by encouraging banks to make higher-risk loans. This argument surfaced repeatedly following the periodic banking panics of the late nineteenth and early twentieth centuries, but the federal government was not spurred to take action until the Great Depression.[3] Under the Banking Acts of 1933 and 1935, interest payments were prohibited on demand deposits for all federally insured commercial banks, and federal regulators were empowered to set ceiling rates on the time and savings deposits of these banks.

This structure of ceilings remained intact and stirred little controversy until the 1960s, by which time, non-bank thrift institutions, whose rates were unregulated, were paying significantly higher deposit rates than banks and had made large inroads into banks' share of the savings deposit market.[4] In retaliation, banks began to compete more aggressively for savings funds and succeeded in inducing regulators to raise the ceiling rates on time deposits four times between 1961 and 1966. Thus when interest rates rose rapidly during the 'credit crunch' of 1966, thrift institutions faced stiff competition for funds from commercial banks as well as money market instruments.

Again, as in 1933, calls were heard for legislative action to limit competition, but it should be noted that the essential focus in this episode was far different. Since thrift institutions had become a chief source of mortgage credit by this time, the housing sector was seen as the primary victim of the competition for funds. Regulations and tax incentives had long dictated that savings and loan associations and, to a lesser degree, mutual savings banks, allocate large proportions of their portfolios to residential mortgages.[5] While borrowing short-term funds and lending in long-term markets created no problems under the upward sloping yield curves of much of the post-Second World War period, the thrift institutions were peculiarly vulnerable to liquidity crises during periods of tight credit and inverted yield curves such as occurred in 1966. Because of the thrift institutions' position as mainstays of the mortgage market, it was thus felt that they needed protection from competition during such periods not only to ensure their own solvency, but also to prevent mortgage credit and residential construction from being sharply curtailed. Congress responded to these concerns with the Interest Rate Act of 1966, empowering the Federal Home Loan Bank Board and the Federal Deposit Insurance Corporation to set ceiling deposit rates for all thrift institutions under their jurisdiction.

Although the prohibition of interest on demand deposits had as yet aroused little controversy,[6] the years following 1966 saw several attacks against rate ceilings on savings deposits. Both the 1971 President's Commission on Financial Structure and Regulation (the so-called 'Hunt Commission') and the 1975 FINE (Financial Institutions in the Nation's Economy) Study, for example, recommended the eventual elimination of all ceilings on time and savings deposits on the grounds that they were ineffective and discriminatory in their treatment of small savers. Despite these recommendations, little in the way of legislative change has been accomplished. Intensive lobbying efforts by a coalition of thrift institutions, homebuilders and organised labour, relying on arguments that ceilings are necessary to moderate competition for funds and thus channel an adequate supply of credit to the housing market, have been successful in blocking reform proposals. At the same time, however, new evidence has been accumulating that the arguments are invalid and that the true effects of the ceilings have been greater inefficiency and inequity for savers. It is to this evidence that we now turn.

3. RECENT EVIDENCE ON THE EFFECTS OF RATE CEILINGS

3.1 Rate ceilings and the supply of funds to the housing sector

Since rate ceilings have been most frequently defended of late in terms of their ability to maintain the supply of funds by thrift institutions to the housing sector, evidence on this issue will be discussed first. A key tenet of the argument is that ceilings will be effective in preventing thrift deposit outflows, but analysis of tight credit periods occurring during and subsequent to 1966 suggests that this is not the case.

P. Fortune investigated the tight credit period of 1966, focusing on the thrift institutions' claim that competition from commercial banks was a primary cause of their deposit losses in that year.[7] His model of the allocation of household savings flows among commercial bank time and savings deposits, thrift institution deposits and US Treasury bills indicates that intensified commercial bank competition following the increase in savings deposit ceilings in December 1965 was not the major cause of the decline in savings inflows experienced by thrift institutions in 1966. By fixing the yield on commercial bank time deposits at its fourth-quarter 1965 level, Fortune estimated that only 22 per cent of the decline in inflows into thrift deposits during 1966 could be attributed to higher rates paid by commercial banks. The remaining decline was apparently caused by competition from Treasury bills.

In an attempt to curb such competition, the Treasury in early 1970 instituted a $10,000 minimum purchase requirement for bills, up from the previous $1000. To test the effectiveness of this move, Fortune estimated his model using data through the end of 1969 and then predicted 1970 household portfolio allocations. These predictions indicated that, in the absence of the Treasury's action, household purchases of bills would have been 8 billion dollars more than actually occurred and thrift deposit inflows would have been 6.6 billion dollars less. Thus it appears that the thrift institutions were helped far more by actions designed to curb open market competition than by those to curb competition from banks.[8]

A similar conclusion was drawn by E. J. Kane, who studied the behaviour of banks and savings and loan associations during the so-called 'Wild-Card Experiment' of 1973.[9] In July of that year, authorities declared that a new category of 'Wild-Card' Certificates of Deposit, having a minimum denomination of $1000 and a minimum maturity of four years, would be exempt from rate ceilings. The experiment lasted only three months and was ended in response to outcries from the thrifts about ruinous competition from commercial banks. Kane, however, found that only 11.4 per cent of these wild-card deposits at commercial banks were paying rates in excess of the eventual ceilings imposed, and that their magnitude was not nearly sufficient to account for the decline in thrift deposit inflows during this period. At the same time, there was a large increase in non-competitive bids for Treasury bills (that is, bids that are usually entered by individual purchasers) despite the $10,000 minimum denomination, so again it appears that open market competition posed the most serious threat to thrift deposit inflows.

In view of the evidence that deposit rate ceilings are insufficient to maintain the supply of funds to thrift institutions during periods of tight credit, it is not surprising that studies of the mortgage market have likewise found ceilings to be ineffective in maintaining the supply of mortgage credit. R. C. Fair and D. M. Jaffee, for example, have conducted simulation experiments with the large-scale FMP (Federal

Reserve MIT-Pennsylvania) econometric model of the United States economy which indicate little effect on the housing and mortgage markets from removing all deposit rate ceilings. Had ceilings been absent during the 1969–70 period, the simulation predicts that the stock of mortgages would have been 3.1 billion dollars lower (relative to a total stock of 829.3 billion dollars) by the end of 1970 than their levels with ceilings.[10]

3.2 Rate ceilings and the safety of depository institutions

Since the studies cited above point to the poverty of the argument that ceilings aid the housing sector, the case on their behalf seems to rest on their ability to enhance the safety of depository institutions. Evidence on the latter point indicates that ceilings engineer a sizeable regressive wealth transfer from savers to the institutions and are thus capable of bolstering the institutions' net worth positions. The ceilings do not appear to induce more conservative portfolio behaviour, however, and substantial portions of the potential net worth increase may be competed away by non-price means. Furthermore, a recent experiment with interest-bearing checking accounts in the New England states suggests that these may be offered by both commercial banks and thrift institutions without calamitous consequences.

The ability of rate ceilings to reduce interest expenses for depository institutions and thus transfer wealth from savers was first estimated by D. H. Pyle.[11] Arguing that ceilings did not significantly constrain deposit rates until after 1967, he fitted three regression equations on data for the years 1952–67 to explain the normal relationship (without ceilings) between the savings deposit rates paid by commercial banks, savings and loan associations and mutual savings banks. Projecting the fitted equations over the 1968–70 period, he then estimated that the total loss in interest income to savers, relative to what institutions would have paid without ceilings, came to slightly more than 5 billion dollars. Likewise, a recent update of these estimates through 1975 indicates that total compound interest forgone as a result of ceilings from 1968 through 1975 was close to 22 billion dollars.

Pyle's estimates of unregulated deposit rates have been used by C. Clotfelter and C. Lieberman to obtain a measure of the impact of this loss to savers on the US income distribution.[12] Assuming that the percentage distribution of time and savings deposits among households in different income deciles is the same as reported in a Federal Reserve study of consumer asset holdings for 1963, they argue that the deposit rate ceiling 'tax' has been highly regressive. Relative to losses that would have occurred had all deciles borne the 'tax' proportionately, they estimate rate ceilings to have 'transferred' 420.6 million dollars in 1970 from the bottom half of the income distribution to the top half.

A tax of this type might still be defensible if it could be demonstrated that depository institutions used the resulting transfer to bolster their net worth positions and hence reduce the chances for financial difficulty. While there appears to be some merit to this position, it is not as clear-cut as proponents of ceilings might hope.

One element of the allegedly salutary influence of ceilings is their effect on portfolio behaviour, but N. B. Murphy has presented evidence that casts doubt on this effect.[13] A special regulatory situation that existed in the state of Massachusetts between 1966 and 1971 allowed him to observe both regulated and unregulated thrift institutions operating simultaneously. By state law, all thrift institutions in Massachusetts are required to subscribe to state-administered deposit insurance, and many thus felt no need to obtain federal insurance in addition. But since the imposition of rate ceilings in 1966 operated through the Federal Home Loan Bank Board and the Federal Deposit Insurance Corporation, a large number of Massachusetts institutions, being members of neither, were not reached. Murphy compared twenty-four co-operative banks,[14] some of whom were regulated and some not, and found no significant differences in portfolio behaviour. In fact, during the 1969–70 period, both types of institutions tended to shift funds away from mortgages and into higher-yielding open market securities, thus casting further doubt on the hypothesis that ceilings help maintain the supply of funds to the mortgage market.

Further evidence on the ability of ceilings to bolster the net worth of thrift institutions has been developed by R. A. Taggart and by R. A. Taggart and G. Woglom.[15] Economists have often argued that price controls will simply channel competition into non-price forms and, in the case of household savings, thrift institutions can try to attract deposits by offering special gifts, by advertising more intensively and by offering extra convenience in the form of longer hours, free ancillary services and additional branch office locations.

To examine this proposition empirically, Taggart estimated a model of deposit rates, branch offices, advertising, wage and other expenses, deposit flows and gross income for Massachusetts' mutual savings banks and then simulated the model over the period 1970–5, during which ceilings were in effect. On the basis of the simulations, it was predicted that average deposit rates were about 125 basis points lower by 1975 than they would have been without ceilings and that, of 370 branch offices in existence by that time, ninety would not have been opened had ceilings not been instituted. Operating expenses were also estimated to have totalled 128 million dollars more than they would have without ceilings so that, over the six-year period, the savings banks dissipated about one-quarter of the extra profits conferred upon them by regulation. Similar findings were reported for Connecticut savings banks by R. A. Taggart and G. Woglom.

Although a sizeable fraction of the savings in interest expense from rate ceilings appears to be competed away by other means, a cautionary note stemming from these studies is that they do increase thrift institution net income to some extent. Taggart's study indicates that total savings bank net income in Massachusetts, while still positive, would have been substantially reduced in 1972 and 1973 had ceilings not been in effect, and this raises the possibility that at least some institutions would have experienced financial difficulty. Moreover, to the extent that non-price competition tends to transform variable interest expense into fixed costs through branching, an abrupt removal of ceilings may cause considerable distress for those institutions with extensive branch office networks.

A final item of evidence on the safety issue comes from the NOW account experiment in the New England states. NOW accounts bear interest, but entitle their holders to write 'negotiable orders of withdrawal' against them; in effect, they are interest-bearing cheque accounts. Both commercial banks and thrift institutions in these states may offer these accounts and thus have been competing recently on an equal footing for household cheque balances.[16]

The fact that the experiment has proceeded without widespread financial turmoil lends support for both removing the prohibition against interest on demand deposits and allowing thrift institutions broader powers. It cannot be denied, however, that the combination of interest expense on these deposits and competition from thrift institutions has had an adverse effect on bank earnings in New England. R. C. Kimball has documented a decline in profitability for commercial banks in New England relative to those in the rest of the United States between 1970 and 1977, and he concludes that about one-third of New England banks' poorer profit performance may be attributed to the increased expense of NOW accounts.[17]

To summarise the results of this section, there appears to be no reason to fear that removal of all rate ceilings will have disastrous consequences for the nation's depository institutions. Unregulated rate-setting does not seem to provoke unusually risky portfolio behaviour nor lead to ruinous competition, and the removal of ceilings may bring significant reductions in the institutions' operating expenses. Nevertheless, it must be conceded that lifting ceilings will reduce depository institution profits and, although widespread failures are highly unlikely, smaller institutions and those with extensive numbers of branch offices may face a difficult transition to a more competitive environment. To allow for orderly adjustment, a gradual withdrawal of ceilings thus seems more prudent than their abrupt abolition.

4. RATE CEILINGS AND THE REGULATORY PROCESS

If the case against deposit rate ceilings is such a strong one, the reader may understandably wonder why they don't simply crumble in the face of overwhelming logic and evidence. Ceilings have been shown to be at best marginally successful in accomplishing their alleged purposes and to be unfair to small savers besides. After years of such wonderment on this and other regulatory issues, however, economists have only recently begun to examine the regulatory process itself to try to understand its resistance to change. The hypotheses advanced as a result of these studies offer some clues as to why proponents of rate ceilings have successfully blocked the opposition this long and at the same time why the current climate may be more favourable to change.

4.1 The public interest versus the capture theory of regulation

It was formerly common to view government regulation of private business as an attempt to correct 'market failures'. Intervention in the market system is justified under this view in situations of extensive economies of scale, externalities or lack of perfect information, since the usual efficiency properties of competition may not hold in their presence. Furthermore, since regulation is designed to promote the public interest, reform should be forthcoming if initial regulatory attempts fail to improve market performance.

Deposit rate ceilings might be rationalised on two grounds under this 'public interest' theory of regulation: first, financial distress among banks is thought to entail the externality of loss of confidence by the public and consequent macroeconomic disruption, so efforts to curb competition and stabilise the banking system are justified; second, housing has beneficial externalities to communities, but information failures lead to credit rationing in the mortgage market, so it makes sense to try to ensure a steady flow of credit to the housing sector. In view of the evidence cited in the preceding section, however, this form of regulation has not been successful, and it is hard to explain under the public interest theory why attempts to change the current system of deposit rate ceilings have been largely frustrated to date.

A contrary view of the regulatory process is the 'capture' theory, according to which regulators are captured by and operate in the interest of the industries they regulate rather than in the public interest.[18] The capture theory's interpretation of deposit rate ceilings is that they are a cartel-like device, designed to stifle competition and enhance profits, that operates for the benefit of a coalition of commercial banks, thrift institutions and housing industry interests.[19] According to this view it is not at all surprising that rate ceilings have survived attempts to dismantle them, and the capture theory has even led some economists to despair over the prospects for reform. In a recent discussion of the regulation of depository institutions, for example, A. Phillips follows up a long list of pro-competitive reform proposals with the pessimistic conclusion that both the industries and their regulators would feel threatened by such changes and could probably mount a successful campaign against them.[20]

4.2 Dynamic theories of regulation

One element that seems missing from either the public interest or the capture theory, however, is the dynamic nature of the interaction between regulators, regulated industries and consumers. Several scholars in recent years have focused their attention on regulatory procedures and their response to external pressures, and they have cited numerous examples of adaptive behaviour on the part of both regulators and regulated firms. When such behaviour is taken into account, specific regulatory forms no longer have the air of finality that they seem to have under the capture theory, nor do reform prospects appear as bleak as that theory would suggest.

P. L. Joskow, for example, argues that regulators typically exhibit two distinct modes of behaviour.[21] The first is an equilibrium mode in which regulators will behave passively as long as they feel that pressures upon them from both firms and consumers are in satisfactory balance. Periodically, however, imbalances in these pressures may cause the regulators to switch to an innovative mode, whereby they search for new techniques and procedures to restore equilibrium. In the case of deposit rate ceilings, Joskow's concept of an innovative mode of regulation is useful in describing recent Federal Reserve system behaviour. Consumer groups have been exhibiting heightened awareness of the discriminatory treatment accorded small savers by rate ceilings. As interest rates have risen in 1978 and 1979, they have exerted increasing pressure on public officials for a change in policy. The Gray Panthers, an elderly persons' lobbying group, has impressed upon Congress the importance of rate ceilings and called for more equitable treatment of savers.[22] In response to such pressures, banking authorities have recently raised the ceilings on savings accounts by 25 basis points, eliminated minimum denomination requirements for most savings certificates and eased the required penalties for early withdrawal of funds from time accounts.[23]

At the same time, inflation and high interest rates have encouraged ever greater competition for savings, particularly from money market mutual funds, and depository institutions have been forced in self-defence to weaken their resistance to change. Instead of shielding them from competition, rate ceilings have often become a hindrance to these institutions, and they have had to accept and even encourage regulatory change to maintain their ability to raise funds.

Another feature that lends an element of dynamism to the regulatory process is the interplay between firms' attempts to strategically manipulate the process and the consequent reactions to these strategies by regulators. This feature has been emphasised in different ways by E. J. Kane and by B. M. Owen and R. Braeutigam.[24]

Kane refers to what he calls a 'regulatory dialectic', whereby regulators impose some constraint on firms, firms alter their behaviour to get around the constraint, and then regulators respond by imposing a new constraint. The process continues, and to keep up with the innovations by firms that their own constraints have induced, regulators must extend their control over an ever-expanding set of activities.

Owen and Braeutigam argue that one of the primary purposes of the regulatory process is to slow down or mitigate the changes imposed on economic agents by market and technological forces. The formal administrative set-up of regulation allows for an adjustment to changing conditions that is generally viewed as fairer and more orderly, they contend, than the impersonal process of the market. At the same time, however, the administrative framework affords firms opportunities to try to further other economic ends. Thus, the regulated firms may strategically use information and innovations, lobbying efforts and conflicting objectives of different regulatory agencies to try to enhance their own profits.

Both descriptions of the interaction between strategic behaviour by firms and the regulator's response appear to have relevance to the case of deposit rate ceilings. Kane himself provides numerous examples of the regulatory dialectic at work in cheque and savings deposit markets. Authorities have had to restrict the payment of non-money gifts to depositors, and attempts have even been made to restrict competition for depositors' funds from the open market, as in the increase in the minimum denomination on Treasury bills to $10,000. These efforts, however, have not been sufficient to stem the tide of financial innovations designed to circumvent rate ceilings. Authorities have not been able to restrict payment of implicit interest through services to depositors or automatic repurchase agreements, whereby depositors' funds above a specified minimum are invested in government securities for short periods, nor have they been able to curb open market competition from money market mutual funds.

Evidence can also be found of the type of behaviour described by Owen and Braeutigam. One form of strategic behaviour they discuss is the attempt by firms to prey upon regulators' fears of chaotic conditions in the industry and to thereby induce them to act as cartel managers. The lobbying efforts by thrift institutions, discussed above, to extend deposit rate ceilings to themselves and maintain them surely come under the heading of this type of strategy.

Ironically, however, the fragmented nature of regulatory authority over US depository institutions renders any cartel in this industry inherently unstable. Various segments of the industry are subject to the authority of the Federal Reserve system, the Comptroller of the Currency, the Federal Deposit Insurance Corporation, the Federal Home Loan Bank System and the different state regulatory agencies. Since there is no unified policy to which all these agencies necessarily adhere, there is an incentive for different segments of the industry to follow a strategy of playing one agency against another and of trying to get looser regulation for itself while other segments remain bound by more stringent regulation. Furthermore, since each regulatory agency is responsible for the welfare of its own particular segment of the industry, it may be responsive to pleas for action that will enhance the welfare of that segment even at the expense of others. This in turn can provoke a series of retaliatory moves by other agencies until the effectiveness of regulatory control in general is seriously undermined.

Illustration of this point may be found in the savings deposit market and to a larger extent in attempts by thrift institutions to offer the equivalent of interest-bearing cheque accounts. In the savings deposit market, as stated above, commercial banks succeeded in inducing the Federal Reserve to raise ceiling rates on savings deposits several times in the early 1960s to counter competition from thrift institutions. This was followed by the extension of ceilings to thrift institutions and the establishment of the 25 basis point differential between commercial bank savings deposits and those offered by thrift institutions. At this point, all major segments of the industry had been brought under effective control, but competition from the open market has prompted the regulatory agencies to loosen their grip somewhat. The short-lived 'Wild Card' experiment was tried in 1974, for example, and in 1978 'money market certificates', with ceiling rates tied to the average rate on six-month Treasury bills, were authorised. Thrift institutions were at first allowed to maintain a 25 basis point differential over commercial banks on money market certificates, but the banks were able to get this ruling reversed in 1979.

In the battle for the household cheque deposits, thrift institutions have won favourable rulings from their regulatory bodies, allowing them to take advantage of advances in electronic funds transfer technology, and commercial bank regulators have been forced to follow suit by allowing the banks broader powers. The effect of this sequence of moves has been to erode the prohibition against interest on demand deposits as well as some of the distinctions between banks and thrift institutions.

In 1970, for instance, savings and loan associations were permitted to make pre-authorised non-negotiable transfers from savings accounts for household-related expenses such as utility bills. The Federal Reserve countered by allowing its members to make transfers from savings to cheque accounts upon telephone orders from customers, but only nine days later the Federal Home Loan Bank allowed its members to make pre-authorised third-party transfers for any purpose. Similar authority was then extended to commercial banks and, in late 1978, they were authorised to offer automatic transfers of funds from savings accounts to cover cheques drawn on demand accounts. Although this latter ruling was later struck down by the courts, pending further Congressional action this year, the trend towards allowing interest-bearing savings accounts to act like cheque accounts is clear. A similar pattern has occurred in the development of remote electronic service machines, whose use was begun in 1972 when a savings and loan association in

Nebraska installed terminals in two supermarkets, allowing customers to withdraw funds on the spot to pay for groceries. To allow banks to meet this form of competition, the Comptroller of the Currency ruled in 1974 that these remote terminals would not be considered branches, but this ruling was disallowed by the courts in the following year. Thrift institutions currently have the upper hand in deployment of these terminals since they are not subject to comparable restrictions of their use.

On numerous occasions, then, both banks and thrift institutions have taken advantage of the fragmented nature of financial regulation in the United States to gain additional powers at one another's expense.[25] Such moves, and the responses to them made by other regulatory agencies, have weakened rate ceilings on savings and especially demand deposits.

5. CONCLUSIONS

Deregulation of deposit rate ceilings in the United States appears to be an idea whose time has come. Although long argued to have a public interest rationale in terms of ensuring bank safety and protecting the housing industry, this form of regulation has been shown in recent research to be ineffective in attaining these ends. Because they are unable to prevent competition from the open market, deposit rate ceilings do not maintain the supply of funds to depository institutions during tight credit periods and hence, by themselves, do little to bolster the housing and mortgage markets. Ceilings do appear to enhance financial institution profits and, consequently, to some degree, their potential stability, but this comes at the expense of a highly regressive transfer from low-income savers, and a sizeable proportion of this transfer is dissipated through non-price competition.

Economists have learned enough from other deregulation efforts, however, to know that the fate of deposit rate ceilings will not rest solely on these research results. Perhaps a more important factor pointing to the ceilings' ultimate demise is that the regulatory authorities' ability to maintain them has been undermined, both from within and without. From without, the open market continues to find new ways to lure savings funds in ever-smaller denominations away from depository institutions; this competition has in turn forced regulators to loosen the bonds on depository institutions. From within, thrift institutions particularly have won regulatory backing for such innovations as electronic funds transfer mechanisms and NOW accounts, and in many cases are currently offering the equivalent of interest-bearing cheque deposits. As banking regulators have countered these moves by offering more freedom to commercial banks, the elaborate control mechanism supporting the ceilings has begun to show signs of crumbling. It thus appears that even cartels with regulatory sanction are not immune from external and internal competition.

NOTES

1. I would like to thank Stuart I. Greenbaun for helpful comments on an earlier draft.
2. See, for example, *Wall Street Journal* (23 May 1979).
3. For a review of the early history of arguments for rate ceilings, see C. M. Linke (1966).
4. In 1950, for example, commercial banks were the issuers of 48 per cent of savings deposits in the United States with thrift institutions, consisting of savings and loan associations, mutual savings banks and credit unions issuing the rest. By 1960, the commercial bank share had fallen to 39 per cent. Savings and loan associations in particular had experienced spectacular growth, moving from a 19 per cent market share in 1950 to 36 per cent by 1960. During this period, interest rates on time and savings deposits averaged about 150 basis points higher at savings and loan associations than at banks. See US Savings and Loan League (1977).
5. In 1970, for example, real estate loans comprised 85 per cent and 73 per cent of the total assets of savings and loan associations and mutual savings banks, respectively. See *Report of the President's Commission on Financial Structure and Regulation* (1971).
6. The privately-sponsored National Commission on Money and Credit, for example, which undertook an extensive investigation of the US monetary system between 1958 and 1961, recommended retention of this prohibition in the interest of bank safety (*Money and Credit*, 1961).
7. P. Fortune (1975).
8. Fortune's conclusions are supported in an analysis of the Treasury bill market by D. J. Mullineaux (1973).
9. E. J. Kane (1978).
10. R. C. Fair and D. M. Jaffee (1972).
11. D. H. Pyle (1974).
12. C. Clotfelter and C. Lieberman (1978).
13. N. B. Murphy (1977). In earlier studies on bank failures during the Great Depression also, no relationship was found between interest rates paid by commercial banks on deposits and the likelihood of failures. See G. J. Benston (1964) and A. H. Cox Jr. (1966).
14. Co-operative banks in Massachusetts are akin to state-chartered savings and loan associations.
15. R. A. Taggart Jr. (1978); R. A. Taggart Jr. and G. Woglom (1978).

16. NOW accounts are not held by businesses. The NOW account experiment has been extensively documented by the Federal Reserve Bank of Boston. See K. Gibson (1975); R. C. Kimball (1976, 1977, 1978); D. Basch (1976).
17. R. C. Kimball (November/December 1978).
18. For expositions on the capture theory, see G. J. Stigler (1971) and S. Peltzman (1976).
19. For an interpretation along these lines, see D. D. Hester (1977).
20. See A. Phillips (1975).
21. P. L. Joskow (1974).
22. See *Wall Street Journal* (21 March 1979) p.1.
23. *Wall Street Journal* (31 May 1979).
24. E. J. Kane (1977); B. M. Owen and R. Braeutigam (1978).
25. These studies are chronicled in more detail in Board of Governors of the Federal Reserve System (1977), A. Broaddus (1978) and J. M. Lovati (1975).

REFERENCES

Basch, D. (1976) 'The Diffusion of NOW Accounts in Massachusetts', *New England Economic Review* (November/December) pp. 20–30.

Benston, G. J. (1964) 'Interest Payments on Demand Deposits and Bank Investment Behavior' *Journal of Political Economy* (October) pp. 431–49.

Board of Governors of the Federal Reserve System (1977) 'The Impact of the Payment of Interest on Demand Deposits' (Washington, D.C.: Staff Study, January).

Broaddus, A. (1978) 'Automatic Transfers From Savings to Checking: Perspectives and Prospects', *Federal Reserve Bank of Richmond Economic Review* (November/December) pp. 3–13.

Clotfelter, C. and C. Lieberman (1978) 'On the Distributional Impact of Federal Interest Rate Restrictions', *Journal of Finance* (March) pp. 199–214.

Cook, T. Q. (1978) 'Regulation Q and the Behavior of Savings and Small Time Deposits at Commercial Banks and the Thrift Institutions', *Federal Reserve Bank of Richmond Economic Review* (November/December) pp. 14–28.

Cox, A. H. Jr. (1966) 'Regulation of Interest on Bank Deposits', *Michigan Business Studies*, vol. 17, no. 4.

Fair, R. C. and D. M. Jaffee (1972) 'The Implications of the Proposals of the Hunt Commission for the Mortgage and Housing Markets: An Empirical Study', in *Policies for a More Competitive Financial System* (Conference Series No. 8, Federal Reserve Bank of Boston, June) pp. 99–148.

Fortune, P. (1975) 'The Effectiveness of Recent Policies to Maintain Thrift-Deposit Flows', *Journal of Money, Credit and Banking* (August) pp. 297–315.

Gibson, K. (1975) 'The Early History and Initial Impact of NOW Accounts', *New England Economic Review* (January/February) pp. 17–26.

Hester, D. D. (1977) 'Special Interests: The FINE Situation', *Journal of Money, Credit and Banking* (November) pp. 652–61.

Joskow, P. L. (1974) 'Inflation and Environmental Concern: Structural Change in the Process of Public Utility Price Regulation', *Journal of Law and Economics* (October) pp. 291–327.

Kane, E. J. (1970) 'Short-Changing the Small Saver: Federal Government Discrimination Against the Small Saver During the Vietnam War', *Journal of Money, Credit and Banking* (November) pp. 513–22.

Kane, E. J. (1972) 'Proposals for Rechanneling Funds to Meet Social Priorities Discussion', in *Policies for a More Competitive Financial System* (Conference Series No. 8, Federal Reserve Bank of Boston, June) pp. 190–8.

Kane, E. J. (1977) 'Good Intentions and Unintended Evil: the Case Against Selective Credit Allocation', *Journal of Money, Credit and Banking* (February) pp. 55–69.

Kane, E. J. (1978) 'Getting Along Without Regulation Q: Testing the Standard View of Deposit-Rate Competition During the "Wild-Card" Experience', *Journal of Finance* (June) pp. 921–32.

Kimball, R. C. (1976) 'Recent Developments in the NOW Account Experiment in New England', *New England Economic Review* (November/December) pp 3–19.

Kimball, R. C. (1977) 'Impacts of NOW Accounts and Thrift Institution Competition on Selected Small Commercial Banks in Massachusetts and New Hampshire, 1974–75', *New England Economic Review* (January/February) pp. 22–38.

Kimball, R. C. (1978) 'The Maturing of the NOW Account in New England', *New England Economic Review* (July/August) pp. 27–42.

Kimball, R. C. (1978) 'Commercial Bank Profitability in New England: A Comparative Study', *New England Economic Review* (November/December) pp. 5–24.

Linke, C. M. (1966) 'The Evolution of Interest Rate Regulation on Commercial Bank Deposits in the United States', *National Banking Review* (June).

Lovati, J. M. (1975) 'The Changing Competition Between Commercial Banks and Thrift Institutions for Deposits', *Federal Reserve Bank of St Louis Review* (July) pp. 2–8.

Lovati, J. M. (1977) 'The Growing Similarity Among Financial Institutions', *Federal Reserve Bank of St. Louis Review* (October) pp. 2–11.

Money and Credit: The Report of the Commission on Money and Credit, Their Influences on Jobs, Prices and Growth (1961) (Englewood Cliffs, N J: Prentice Hall).

Mullineaux, D. J. (1973) 'Deposit-Rate Ceilings and Noncompetitive Bidding for U.S. Treasury Bills', *Journal of Money, Credit and Banking* (February) pp. 201–12.

Murphy, N. B. (1977) 'Removing Deposit Interest Ceilings: An Analysis of Deposit Flows, Portfolio Response and Income Effects in Boston Co-operative Banks', *Journal of Bank Research* (Winter) pp. 256–65.

Owen, B. M. and R. Braeutigam (1978) *The Regulation Game: Strategic Use of the Administrative Process* (Cambridge, Massachusetts: Ballinger).

Peltzman, S. (1976) 'Toward a More General Theory of Regulation', *Journal of Law and Economics* (August) pp. 211–40.

Phillips, A. (1975) 'Competitive Policy for Depository Financial Institutions', in A. Phillips (ed.), *Promoting Competition in Regulated Markets* (Washington, DC: The Brookings Institution) pp. 329–66.

Pyle, D. H. (1974) 'The Losses on Savings Deposits from Interest Rate Regulation', *Bell Journal of Economics* (Autumn) pp. 614–22.

Pyle, D. H. (1977) *Interest Rate Ceilings and Net Worth Losses by Savers* (University of California, Berkeley: Working Paper 57, Research Program in Finance, Institute of Business and Economic Research, February).

Report of the President's Commission on Financial Structure and Regulation (1971) (Washington, DC).

Stigler, G. J. (1971) 'The Theory of Economic Regulation', *Bell Journal of Economics* (Spring) pp. 3–21.

Taggart, R. A. Jr. (1978) 'Effects of Deposit Rate Ceilings: the Evidence from Massachusetts Savings Banks', *Journal of Money, Credit and Banking* (May) pp. 139–57.

Taggart, R. A. Jr. and G. Woglom (1978) 'Savings Bank Reactions to Rate Ceilings and Rising Market Rates', *New England Economic Review* (September/October) pp. 17–31.

US Congress, House Subcommittee on Financial Institutions Supervision, Regulation and Insurance of the Committee on Banking, Currency and Housing, *Financial Institutions and the Nation's Economy (FINE) Discussion Principles* (Hearings, 94th Congress, 1st and 2nd Sessions, December 1975).

US Savings and Loan League, *Savings and Loan Fact Book* (Chicago, Ill.).

Wall Street Journal (1979) 'Consumer Groups Complain that Rules on Interest Rates Injure Small Savers' (21 March).

Wall Street Journal (1979) 'Carter Calls For End to Federal Controls on Interest Rates, Citing Inflation Impact' (23 May).

Wall Street Journal (1979) 'Agencies Lift Lid on Interest Rates at Banks, S & Ls' (31 May).

Comment on Taggart

MARCEL MAES

Interest rate ceilings constitute an actual problem in the Belgian financial scene. Although there is actually no regulation comparable to regulation Q, the interest rates of the Belgian financial intermediaries of the three main sectors (commercial banks, savings institutions and financial institutions of the public sector) are embedded in agreements the monetary authorities (National Bank of Belgium and Banking Commission) are not opposed to. Those agreements did not imply, however, the practice of one single interest rate for a given type of financial asset; on the contrary. Furthermore, it appeared that this system was far from being waterproof. No wonder that consumer organisations not so long ago even published score lists illustrating important rate differentials from one institution to another.

Recent efforts to replace these agreements by a more rigid system were opposed by the smaller financial institutions.

The behaviour of Belgian interest rates is characterised by hectic changes in the short-term market interest rates, which are mainly reflecting tensions brought about by the monetary authorities in order to discourage a switch of Belgian francs into foreign currencies. For this reason, money market interest rates may rise to high levels (two or even three times as high as corresponding small deposit interest rates in financial institutions).

This leads us to the item of the discrimination of small savers. In my opinion, the abolition of all ceilings or agreements will never result in a rise of interest rates of small deposits, bringing them to the interest rate level of big deposits. A big deposit is a financial input you only need a telephone for, without expensive branches and elaborate electronic data-processing services. In other words, the channels through which big and small deposits flow in and out are quite different and so are their handling and administration costs. The spread in interest rates is therefore the reflection of these costs differences. The abolition of

52

nterest rate ceilings will multiply the number of these spreads. This means that increasing interest rates will be granted to deposits of increasing importance: market forces will inevitably lead thereto. So the relevancy of the social discrimination argument strongly needs to be overhauled, at least if the discussion has to be pursued within the general framework of competition.

And by the way, differences between interest rates on big and small deposits are not always that important. When we look, for instance, to the interest rate evolution in the last three turbulent monetary years of Belgium, it appears that at several periods the spread between market interest rates and the small deposit interest rates was not exceeding 1.5 per cent, which represents a spread that is not exceeding that prevailing inside some of the small deposit interest rates.

Another official concern for interest rate behaviour in Belgium is due to the circumstances that the Belgian Treasury competes aggressively for small savers' funds through recurrent public issues of bonds in order to finance the budget deficits. In doing so, the Treasury agency must face the dilemma of offering competitive rates and minimising the debt-service burden for the tax payer.

Turning to another point now, I must admit it intrigues me that it is invariably being alleged by every author that deposit rate ceilings always end up in windfall profits for the financial institutions and that this extra profit is finally disposed off in less interesting directions (overbranching, extra opening hours, services and so on). No mention at all is made of possible reductions of the cost of credit. I personally feel that the credibility of this approach would gain by refining the research in that direction. More attention should go to the revenue transfer processes involved.

These processes probably differ from commercial banks to savings institutions. In the last type of financial intermediaries, for instance, the identity between deposit-owners and debtors is far more current than in the commercial banks.

As to branching, extra opening hours and other services, one can only hope that their respective merits will soon be determined with the aid of appropriate techniques. It means a lot to people to find a branch open on Friday 6 p.m. or once or twice a month on a Saturday morning, especially in societies with high employment ratios and a high propor-tion of working women.

As to the phenomenon of regulation itself, returning to the Belgian scene I would say that there is far less regulation in financial matters compared with the US situation. On the contrary, nationalised enterprises in the financial sector are very important in Belgium.

Furthermore, structural regulation, as opposed to prudential regulation (using here Professor Revell's terminology), tends to decline in Belgium. The Mammoth law of 1975 not only entrusts the supervision and regulatory task in savings institutions to the Banking Commission but constitutes the framework wherein further erosion of regulation differences between the two financial sectors involved can be realised. In practice, attention has gone in the first place to the complicated regulations regarding savings institutions. Recently, for instance, a number of asset restrictions have been abolished.

4. Concentration and Economies of Scale in the Belgian Financial Sector[1]

JOZEF PACOLET and
ALBERT VERHEIRSTRAETEN

1. INTRODUCTION

There exists a close relationship between the financial market structure on the one hand and the behaviour of intermediaries and the market performance on the other. Therefore one important aspect of financial market structure is analysed hereafter for Belgium: its degree of *concentration*. In addition, for the banking sector we will try to explain the observed degree of concentration by studying a main determinant of it: the possible existence of *economies of scale*.

The first part on concentration will start with a short description of the delineation of the financial markets and submarkets for which the structure will be studied. Different concentration measures are then calculated for the main items of commerce of the financial intermediaries. In the following part of the study, cost functions are estimated, testing the relation of the costs to output. However, prior to that, some general information is given on the Belgian financial sector.

The study covers three important groups of intermediaries: deposit banks, private savings institutions and public financial institutions that belong to the government sector. Not considered are among others insurance companies and specialised mortgage and credit associations.

The empirical analysis is based on cross-section data contained in the published financial statements of these institutions for 1976. The balance sheet will be the main research instrument for the concentration analysis,

TABLE 4.1 Size and relative importance of the considered groups of financial institutions in 1976

Subgroup	Number of institutions	Balance sheet total			Total of deposits, bonds and notes				Revenues–expenses account		
		Amount (billion BF)	% of group total	% of overall total	Amount (billion BF)	% of own balance sheet	% of group total	% of overall total	Amount (billion BF)	% of group total	% of overall total
A. Banks											
Four largest	4	1 379.3	64.4	36.0	807.6	58.5	77.7	33.8	118.2	46.8	38.9
Total	86	2 140.3	100.0	55.8	1 040.0	48.6	100.0	43.6	182.5	100.0	60.0
B. Savings banks											
Four largest	4	260.8	67.3	6.8	240.1	92.1	68.3	10.1	20.0	61.5	6.6
Total	33	387.7	100.0	10.2	351.7	90.7	100.0	14.7	32.5	100.0	10.7
C. Public financial institutions											
Four largest	4	1 163.9	89.2	30.4	890.6	76.5	89.5	37.3	85.9	96.3	28.2
Total	7	1 304.5	100.0	34.0	995.8	76.3	100.0	41.7	89.2	100.0	29.3
D. Overall total	126	3 832.5	–	100.0	2 387.5	62.3	–	100.0	304.2	–	100.0

SOURCE Bankcommissie, *Balansen, afgesloten tussen 1 juni 1976 en 31 mei 1977* (Brussels: Banking Commission, 1977); also *Belgisch Staatsblad* and annual reports of the institutions.

s each asset and liability can be studied as a market (or submarket) for
any group or for all financial institutions together. The revenues–
expenses account contains the additionally needed information to study
some of the performance aspects.

In 1976 there were eighty-six deposit banks in Belgium, of which
twenty-seven had a considerable foreign participation and twenty-three
were completely owned by foreigners.[2] The second group, private
savings banks, is composed of thirty-three institutions, seven of which
have a co-operative form, including the two largest Belgian private
savings banks.[3] Finally, the sample encloses seven public institutions
whose activities are related with those of the deposit banks and private
savings institutions; they include the largest Belgian savings institution,
the postal deposits office and five other institutions mainly typified
according to their credit activities.[4]

In Table 4.1 the size is given of the three mentioned groups of financial
intermediaries, showing that in Belgium the deposit banks are the most
important group, followed by the public financial institutions and finally
by the private savings banks.[5] The ranking is the same when one uses as a
measure either the size of balance sheet total or the total of deposits.
However, the relative figures are different, mainly due to the considerable
international activities of the Belgian commercial banks, whose activities
are only included in the balance sheet total. Finally, as another
alternative indicator of output, Table 4.1 also includes the
revenues–expenses account total.

2. CONCENTRATION IN THE FINANCIAL MARKETS

After some thoughts on the delineation of financial markets, different
measures of concentration will be calculated for the whole group of
Belgian financial intermediaries and for the separate subgroups of
deposit banks, private savings banks and public financial institutions.

2.1 The definition of financial markets

As other markets, financial markets are 'made up of a group of buyers
and sellers that freely interact with each other in such fashion as to effect
a unique price net of transportation costs, at which a particular good, say
money or banking services, is exchanged'.[6] Therefore the attention will
be focused hereafter on the financial intermediaries as the buyers and
sellers of financial products.

Before being able to analyse the performance of a concrete market (prices and so on) or its competitive structure as determined by the number of market participants, it is necessary to define the borders of the market and to identify the firms operating in it.

A first criterion of market delineation is a geographic one, as it allows identification of the participating buyers and sellers. This constitutes the problem of defining the *relevant market area*, which clearly depends on the nature of the goods and services exchanged. For some financial products, like safety boxes, only the local area is important, for supply as well as demand. For large deposit accounts, the relevant area is usually larger than for small accounts, and even the international market has to be considered also. The latter is especially the case in small open economies as the Belgian one.

A second problem of market delineation is that of the definition of the *line of commerce* (*or relevant product line*), based on the product exchanged. Since one does not observe one single financial price or interest rate, this implies that – except for the case of monopolistic price discrimination – there are different financial products each with their own market.

In this study we take the approach that the lines of the balance sheet of financial firms can be treated as different financial markets. A financial firm is indeed a multiproduct firm, operating simultaneously in several markets. The balance sheet total can thus be considered as the overall market, although a very heterogeneous one. Defining in that way the lines of commerce and the kinds of activity allows the establishment of the number of financial institutions competing in the relevant market area.[7] In doing this, it is important to include all possible competitors, the actual market participation being dependent on the level of the interest rate.[8]

For some financial assets and liabilities, considered as lines of commerce, commercial banks, private savings banks and public financial institutions are competitors. The question remains if these three groups are also competitors for their overall activities, expressed by their balance sheet total: are deposit banks, savings banks and public credit institutions constituting one industry, or are they rather separate financial industries, with or without interindustry competition? Considering the existence of still marked differences in the balance sheet composition of the three groups, but also considering an increasing tendency to despecialisation, we have chosen – for each disaggregated line of commerce as well as for the overall one – to approach the three groups of financial institutions not only as financial industries on their own, but also as an aggregate, taking the hypothesis of the existence of interindustry competition.

On these grounds, we distinguished several financial markets. Clearly, there may be substitution between them, but only a study of substitution elasticities can clear the matter on how sharp the boundaries are.

2.2 Applied measures of concentration

As an important determinant of the competitive structure of the markets thus distinguished, we study hereafter their degree of concentration, depending on the number of financial firms and on their market shares.[9] A list of the symbols used is given in Appendix 4.1.

A first, very rude indicator of concentration is simply the *number of firms n*; for an individual item of commerce, the actual number of firms having it on their balance sheet is indicated by n_A.

A second indicator, the *concentration ratio* C_n, contains already more information as it measures the share of the n largest firms in total output. Often used are the C_3 and C_4 ratios for the three respectively four largest firms.

These two measures do not, however, tell anything on the size distribution of the institutions. The latter is graphically represented by the *Lorenz curve* and, in addition, can be expressed in one number, the *Gini coefficient G*, this coefficient measuring in fact the difference between the Lorenz curve actually observed and the one observed in the case where all firms would have equal market shares. To adjust for differences in the number of firms in the market, it is also useful to calculate a relative or adjusted Gini coefficient as a ratio to the maximum value of G, this being equal to $(n - 1)/n$.[10]

$$GA = \frac{G}{G_{\max}} = \frac{G}{(n - 1)/n}$$

The number of firms as well as the inequality of the distribution of market shares is also taken into account by the *Herfindahl index H*, which results from the weighting of the market share m_i of the different firms with their own value.

$$H = \sum_{i=1}^{n} m_i^2$$

As in the Herfindahl index, the largest firms also get the highest weights. It can be argued that this index gives a somewhat overestimated picture of the market concentration, although the largest firms may indeed have the greatest market power. This objection is met by weighting the market share of each firm with the logarithm of the inverse of it, as is done in the calculation of the so-called measure of *entropy E*

$$E = \sum_{i=1}^{n} m_i \cdot \log_2 \frac{1}{m_i}$$

To make industries with different numbers of firms comparable, here also the relative entropy is calculated and adjusted for its maximum value.

$$EA = \frac{E}{E_{max}} = \frac{E}{\log_2 n}$$

The meaning of the Herfindahl index as well as of the entropy can be made fairly understandable by calculating in addition the *numbers equivalent NE*. This is the number of equally-sized firms showing the same value as the Herfindahl index or the entropy measure computed for the actual number and size dispersion of the firms in the market. As said by I. Horowitz, the numbers equivalent allows easy analysis of an industry by means of the traditionally used theoretical concepts of monopoly, oligopoly or polyopoly.[11] For the Herfindahl index and the entropy respectively, the numbers equivalents are obtained as follows.

$$NE_H = 1/H$$
$$NE_E = \text{antilog}_2 E$$

Although all those different indicators are often applied, the question can be raised *which measure should be preferred* in quantifying the market concentration. In that respect, it has first to be remembered that the different concentration indicators may refer to different characteristics of market structure, as the number of firms, the share of the dominant firms and the distribution of the shares of all firms over the market. Comprehensive measures like the Herfindahl index and the entropy cover all those aspects but, as a consequence, differences in their values are less easy to interpret. Simple measures like the C_4-ratio reflect only one aspect, but are more convenient to calculate as they need less information.[12] These different aspects are a first explanation why it has often been proposed to calculate several concentration indicators simultaneously.

Further, it has to be taken into account that the concentration measures have an important field of application in structure–conduct–

performance studies, where they may have a different explanatory power. Therefore the choice of the optimal measure should be based on the theory of industrial economics as well as on the empirical evidence. Again this points to the usefulness of calculating different concentration measures in order to discover whether the results of any particular study are influenced by the measures used.[13]

However, a high degree of correlation has been observed between the ranking of markets according to different measures of concentration. For instance, A. P. Jacquemin and H. W. de Jong have found a high rank correlation of the C_4 with the H- and E-measure, but a lower one with the Gini coefficient.[14] This correlation has led some authors to the conclusion that 'the choice of index is not of critical importance'[15] and that the easily computable C_4 can be used as well as more complex ratios that require a lot more information.[16]

Indications on the correlation between the different concentration measures calculated for the banking sector and for the overall group of financial intermediaries in Belgium are given in Table 4.2. The figures given refer to the Spearman rank correlation coefficients between the different measures of concentration classified according to value. They have been calculated for the markets of the individual balance sheet components of the Belgian financial intermediaries, the results of which will be analysed hereafter.

The measures are calculated, however, taking into account the total number of firms in each group of intermediaries, and not the actual number operating on each submarket, considering all firms as potential competitors. As a consequence, there is no reason to include adjusted G-

TABLE 4.2   Spearman rank correlation coefficients for different concentration measures calculated for several financial submarkets

Measure	Deposit banks				All financial intermediaries			
	C_4	G	H	E	C_4	G	H	E
C_4	1				1			
G	0.919	1			0.940	1		
H	0.942	0.901	1		0.974	0.956	1	
E	0.966	0.978	0.958	1	0.966	0.989	0.974	1

and E-measures in Table 4.2. In addition, the ranking with respect to the numbers equivalents NE_H and NE_E on one hand and with respect to the H- and E-measures themselves on the other are identical.

From Table 4.2, it follows that with respect to the Belgian financial sector all concentration measures show very high rank correlations, the highest being found between the Gini coefficient and the entropy.[17] In addition, the easily computable C_4-ratio shows a rank correlation higher than 0.90 with all other concentration measures; an exception is found, however, when the small group of public financial institutions is considered separately, the related rank correlation coefficients then decreasing to about 0.70.

It can be concluded that the C_4-ratio, which is computable with very limited information, already seems to discriminate markets according to concentration in a rather identical way as more complex indicators. However, in view of a thorough analysis of the concentration of Belgian financial markets, all the measures considered will be calculated hereafter simultaneously. This is certainly meaningful, taking into account the different aspects of market concentration and also the possible applications of the indicators in structure–conduct–performance studies.

In view of an easier interpretation of the empirical values obtained, we give in Appendix 4.2 the extreme values of the different concentration measures in the cases of monopoly, on the one hand, and of a size distribution which is perfectly equal, on the other. In addition, it is shown there how these values change when groups of intermediaries with a different number of firms are considered.

2.3 Concentration in total output of the Belgian financial intermediaries

We first analyse the concentration of *total* output assuming that the individual lines of commerce can be aggregated. This total output will be considered for the sector of deposit banks, private savings banks and public financial institutions and finally for the overall sector as if all the intermediaries were operating in one market with 126 participants. Two general measures of output are used: the balance sheet total and the revenues–expenses account total, the latter being comparable with a value-added variable in the industrial sector.[18]

Objections are sometimes raised against using these totals as output measures. It is argued, indeed, that the real output of financial firms is the number of accounts or of loans made; if large intermediaries have a lot of small accounts, using amounts as a measure leads to an underestimation of concentration, as the share of these intermediaries in the number of accounts would be even higher. A similar problem is that using amounts can lead to an overestimation of per unit cost; in this case, costs would be a decreasing function of the number of accounts.[19] Due to a lack of data, using amounts is therefore to be considered as a second best solution for measuring concentration. In addition, the balance sheet total has the advantage that it can be disaggregated afterwards for studying the markets for the different assets and liabilities.

The results of the concentration calculations for total output are given in Table 4.3. Remarkable is the great similarity of the values of nearly all concentration indicators for the two measures of output considered, except for the private savings banks who show a somewhat lower concentration when considering the revenues–expenses total.

From Table 4.3, it can be seen that the share of the four largest firms range from 64 per cent of total output in the banking sector, to 67 per cent in the sector of the private savings banks and to 93 per cent in that of the public financial institutions.[20] When all intermediaries are considered together as operating in one overall financial market, there still remains a C_4-ratio of 50 per cent.

The high values of the C_4-ratio in the sectors of the deposit banks and of the private savings banks indicate that, as these are sectors with a considerable number of firms, the distribution of market shares must be very unequal. Especially, the (relative) Gini coefficient and the relative entropy are adequate indicators to express this size inequality, a higher value pointing to a more unequal market structure.

The size dispersion is also clearly shown by the Lorenz curves depicted in Figures 4.1 to 4.4. From these graphs one can derive that the sector of the deposit banks, when compared with the other groups, is characterised by the greatest departure of the curve from the diagonal and thus by the largest inequality, although the distribution for the overall sector of all financial intermediaries is nearly as unequal. For more detailed information on the size distribution, we indicate on each graph the market share of the four largest intermediaries as well as the number of firms of which the output has to be cumulated to reach 1 per cent and 5 per cent of the market total. For the overall sector of 126 intermediaries, it can be observed that the output of fifty firms has to be cumulated to reach 1 per cent of the market, and of seventy-eight firms to arrive at 5 per cent.

Table 4.3, in addition, contains some concentration indicators depending on both the number of market participants and the distribution of their market shares: the Herfindahl index and the entropy. As explained, the meaning of their values can be easily interpreted by looking at their corresponding numbers equivalents. For the public financial institutions, the oligopolistic market structure

TABLE 4.3 Aggregate concentration measures for the banks, private savings banks and public financial institutions – 1976

Category of institution and output measure	n_A	C_4	G	GA	H	NE_H	E	EA	NE_E
Banks									
Balance sheet total	86	0.64	0.82	0.82	0.14	7.2	3.96	0.62	15.5
Revenues–expenses account total	75	0.65	0.81	0.82	0.14	7.0	3.90	0.63	14.9
Private savings banks									
Balance sheet total	33	0.67	0.75	0.78	0.14	7.2	3.42	0.68	10.7
Revenues–expenses account total	32	0.62	0.73	0.75	0.12	8.3	3.56	0.71	11.8
Public financial institutions									
Balance sheet total	7	0.93	0.51	0.59	0.27	3.7	2.14	0.76	4.4
Revenues–expenses account total	6	0.96	0.49	0.58	0.30	3.3	1.94	0.75	3.8
All institutions									
Balance sheet total	126	0.50	0.83	0.84	0.08	13.1	4.60	0.66	24.4
Revenues–expenses account total	113	0.50	0.81	0.82	0.08	12.7	4.60	0.67	24.1

obtained conforms with the expectations because of the small number of market participants, although the concentration measures may be less meaningful as indicators of competition because all institutions belong to the government sector and because their activities are often rather differentiated. A marked observation, however, is the high concentration

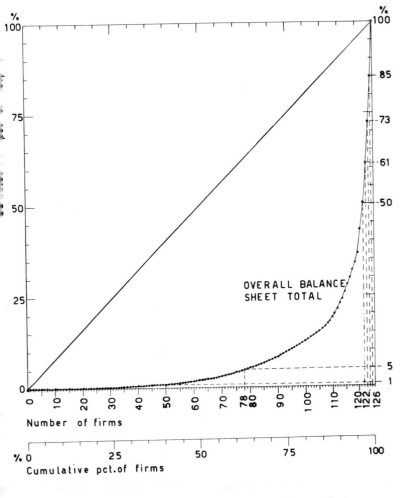

FIGURE 4.1 Lorenz curve for all Belgian financial intermediaries

SOURCE Published financial statements

values for the banking sector, in spite of the higher number of firms than in the sector of the private savings banks. Finally, for all financial intermediaries together, the NE_H points to a share distribution as if the overall market was divided over thirteen equally sized firms, including only the largest firms of each group of intermediaries. However, Table

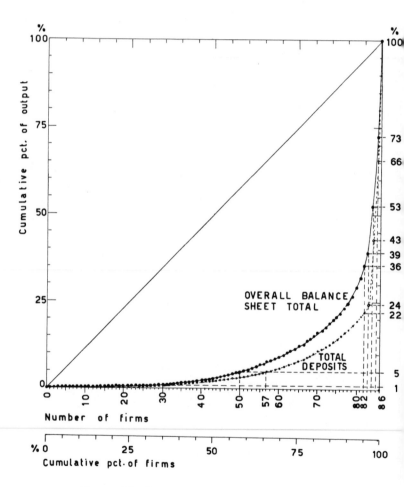

FIGURE 4.2   Lorenz curves for the banking sector

SOURCE   Published financial statements

4.3 shows clear differences between the number equivalents of the Herfindahl index and the entropy. Although the NE_H may induce some overestimation of the market concentration by giving heavier weights to the largest firms, as already said it can be defended that those firms indeed have proportionally more power, so that the NE_H can be regarded as a better indicator for the monopolistic influences in the market.[21]

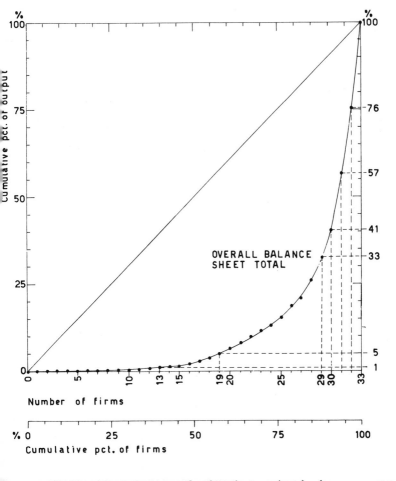

FIGURE 4.3   Lorenz curve for the private savings banks

SOURCE   Published financial statements

From this analysis of total output concentration we conclude that, especially in view of the observed inequality in size distribution and the considerable number of firms with a minimal market share, there are reasons for serious concern about the degree of competition in the Belgian financial sector.

This conclusion contrasts with the argument put forward that

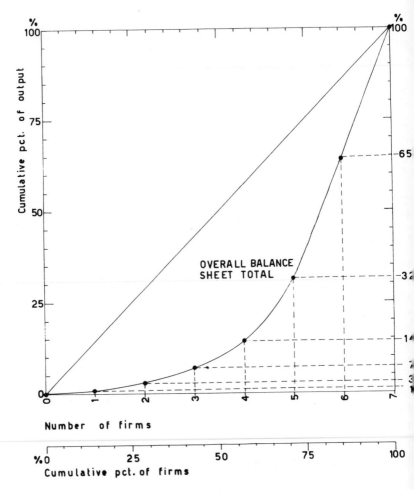

FIGURE 4.4   Lorenz curve for the public financial institutions

SOURCE   Published financial statements

specifically in the Belgian banking sector there is no lack of competition, considering the number of banks – being, for example, greater than in a comparable country as the Netherlands – and considering the important entries and exits on the market. These entries are mostly by foreign banks, while the exits often take the form of a merger of smaller institutions 'in order to increase competitive power'.[22] In addition, it is said that the continuous entries show that there are no barriers to entry (except the official chartering and minimal capital requirements).

The foregoing evidence on market share distribution raises, however, the question whether all those movements are not mainly taking place in a marginal area of the sector, that of the smaller banks.[23] This challenges whether, in fact, there is no *barrier to significant entry*; that is, entry that would affect the market position of the larger banks. The same issue may concern the group of private savings banks. As another conclusion, one can derive that actually competing the few larger banks seems only possible from a minimal scale, which up to now is not reached by the great number of small firms. Finally, a lot of new entries occur in specialised markets, especially for international transactions.

2.4 Concentration on the markets for the individual assets and liabilities

As financial intermediaries are typical multiproduct firms, the balance sheet total and revenues–expenses account total are only very rude indicators of output. Therefore, we calculated the concentration measures for the different lines of commerce that can be distinguished on the aggregated balance sheet of the three groups of intermediaries considered and of all of them together. In the case of specialisation – possibly even within one group – higher concentration values are indeed to be expected for the individual submarkets.[24] Further, it is remarked that the concentration measures are calculated taking into account the total number of firms in the sector, including the firms with a market share of zero, the latter thus being treated as potential market participants. For expenses–revenues account total and current profits, however, the actual number is taken for which data are available.

Table 4.4 gives the value of the concentration measures for the main assets and liabilities of the eighty-six Belgian *deposit banks*. Taking the balance sheet total as a point of reference, we observe some lines of commerce with a lower degree of concentration: capital – partly explainable by the lower capital requirements imposed on the larger

TABLE 4.4 Concentration measures for the main financial statement items of commercial banks in Belgium – 1976[a]

Lines of commerce (percentage of balance sheet total)		n_A	C_4	G	GA	H	NE_H	E	EA	NE_E
Assets										
Bankers	(24.2)	86	0.62*	0.85	0.86	0.14	7.4*	3.86	0.60	14.5
Government bills	(2.9)	32	0.79	0.93	0.94	0.23	4.4	2.87	0.45	7.3
Commercial paper	(9.5)	76	0.83	0.91	0.92	0.22	4.6	2.98	0.46	7.9
Acceptances	(2.6)	59	0.78	0.91	0.92	0.21	4.8	3.12	0.49	8.7
Other debtors	(24.6)	85	0.61*	0.79*	0.80*	0.12*	8.2*	4.23*	0.66*	18.8*
Government bonds	(18.5)	84	0.86	0.92	0.93	0.25	4.1	2.76	0.43	6.8
Other bonds	(2.4)	60	0.90	0.94	0.95	0.23	4.4	2.59	0.40	6.0
Liabilities										
Bankers	(36.4)	79	0.56*	0.84	0.85	0.10*	9.6*	4.10*	0.64*	17.1*
Deposits ⩽ 30 days	(32.9)	86	0.82	0.89	0.90	0.22	4.5	3.05	0.47	8.3
Deposits > 30 days	(12.2)	85	0.68	0.84	0.85	0.17	6.1	3.76	0.59	13.6
Bonds and notes	(3.5)	34	0.94	0.96	0.97	0.28	3.5	2.19	0.34	4.6
Capital	(1.5)	86	0.43*	0.68*	0.69*	0.06*	16.4*	5.03*	0.78*	32.7*
Current profits	(0.3)	72	0.67	0.82	0.83	0.14	7.0	3.81	0.62	14.1
Total balance sheet	(100)	86	0.64	0.82	0.83	0.14	7.2	3.96	0.62	15.5
Expenses–revenues account total		75	0.65	0.81	0.82	0.14	7.0	3.90	0.63	14.9

[a] Values marked with * indicate a lower degree of concentration than the balance sheet total.

banks[25] – bankers' liabilities, bankers' assets and other debtors, the last two items, however, only showing small differences. Only slightly higher than the average is also the concentration of the current profits. But for the rest, several markets for items with an important share in the balance sheet total show a degree of concentration higher than the average. This is especially the case for government bonds and commercial paper at the asset side, and for the bonds and notes and the deposits at the liability side (for the latter, see also the corresponding Lorenz curve in Figure 4.2). According to the NE_H indicator, these submarkets are no longer to be characterised as polyopolistic but as clearly oligopolistic, as if there were three to four equally sized market participants.

Concerning the measures used, it may be remarked that the C_4-ratio in Table 4.4 gives the share of the four largest firms in that submarket, which are not necessarily the same as the overall four largest banks with respect to the balance sheet total or total deposits. A more detailed analysis, however, shows that the overall four largest banks have in general a higher share on the markets of the assets and liabilities which are the most important in their 'product mix' or balance sheet structure – what, in fact, is statistically to be expected.

A more general remark concerns the relevant geographic market to be considered, as Belgium represents typically the case of a small open economy. More specifically, for banking activities the importance of *internationalisation* is very clearly shown by the fact that, in 1976, of the overall balance sheet of banks in Belgium not less than 38 per cent was held towards foreigners. To be sure that the calculated concentration measures are meaningful there is a strong need to identify the transactions most exposed to competition by banks located outside the country, thus belonging in fact to the international market, which is much more competitive.[26]

As a first approximation of this problem, we disaggregated the assets and liabilities of the banks in Belgium according to the nationality of the bank clients as well as to the currency used (Belgium versus foreign).

Table 4.5 gives a picture of the change in the C_4 ratio for the most important bank assets and liabilities as a consequence of differences in the market delineation. Some interesting conclusions can be derived from it: (i) the C_4 is nearly always higher for transactions in BF than for those in other currencies (a notable exception is the line 'Bankers' at the asset side; (ii) in the same way, the C_4 is higher for the total transactions with Belgian residents versus those with foreign residents. Among the individual lines of commerce, an exception is again constituted by the interbank market, not only at the asset side but now also at the liability

TABLE 4.5 Changes in the C_4 ratio for some important bank assets and liabilities corresponding to differences in market delineation (31 December 1976) – Market share of the four largest banks with respect to total deposits

Lines of commerce	Transactions in BF			Transactions in foreign currency			Transactions in BF and other currencies		
	Towards Belgian residents (1)	Towards foreigners (2)	Subtotal (3)	Towards Belgian residents (4)	Towards foreigners (5)	Subtotal (6)	Towards Belgian residents (7)	Towards foreigners (8)	Total[a] (9)
Assets									
Bankers	0.33	0.66	0.41	0.41	0.65	0.61	0.37	0.65	0.58
Commercial paper	0.83	0.93	0.85	0.58	0.38	0.43	0.83	0.81	0.83
Other debtors	0.66	0.49	0.65	0.33	0.35	0.34	0.63	0.36	0.55
Government bonds	0.85	—	0.85	0.92	—	0.92	0.85	—	0.85
Other bonds	0.92	0.95	0.93	0.67	0.50	0.50	0.92	0.65	0.73
Total assets	0.74	0.75	0.74	0.41	0.44	0.44	0.71	0.48	0.62
Liabilities									
Bankers	0.36	0.61	0.53	0.29	0.48	0.46	0.32	0.50	0.47
Demand deposits	0.84	0.67	0.83	0.71	0.42	0.60	0.83	0.58	0.81
Savings books	0.90	0.82	0.89	1.00	1.00	1.00	0.90	0.82	0.90
Total deposits	0.82	0.69	0.81	0.72	0.42	0.51	0.81	0.52	0.77
Bonds and notes	0.89	—	0.89	—	—	—	0.89	—	0.89
Total liabilities	0.76	0.59	0.74	0.42	0.43	0.43	0.73	0.47	0.62

[a] The C_4 for the overall four largest banks is not comparable with the one in Table 4.4, where the C_4 is referring to the four largest firms on each submarket.

SOURCE Based on aggregated data for the four largest and all banks obtained from the Banking Commission.

ide. One can also observe that the C_4 for the total assets and liabilites in foreign currency is slightly higher for the transactions with foreign residents than for those with Belgian ones; (iii) Without decreasing the importance of the disaggregation, one can observe that the overall C_4-ratio shows the highest concentration for mainly domestic markets and lower values for those markets most exposed to competition from abroad. These last C_4-values are, in addition, less significant as they relate to markets that in fact are parts of the broad international market. The lower C_4 for the more internationally oriented markets can be explained by the relatively larger share in those markets of foreign bank subsidiaries.

Turning next to the *private savings banks*, we observe in Table 4.6 that while the results for current profits are again close to those for the balance sheet total, several lines of commerce show concentration values that are slightly lower, as bonds of corporations, mortgage credits, savings deposits on more than two years, and capital. More concentrated han the output total are, however, at the liability side the savings deposits on less than two years – including the considerable amounts on savings books – and at the asset side government bonds and non-mortgage loans (the NE_H-indicator even pointing for the latter to a nearly duopolistic market).

With respect to the third group of *public financial institutions*, it has already been said that it includes specialised intermediaries which in addition do not publish their financial statements in a uniform way. A disaggregated analysis therefore leads to the consideration of numerous detailed items for which – not surprisingly – often highly concentrated structures are found, even monopolistic ones. However, sometimes this corresponds to the actual situation, as for loans to the lower public authorities which are only granted by the Municipal Credit Institution. For this sector, we add in Table 4.6 only one individual line of commerce, which is very important for nearly all these intermediaries: bonds and notes at the liabilities side. Due to the low number of firms in the group we, of course, obtain high concentration values again, the relative Gini coefficient GA pointing, however, to a somewhat less unequal market distribution than for most items of the deposit banks and private savings banks.

As a generally accepted characteristic of the Belgian financial sector is its despecialisation, especially in the collecting of funds and also in its regulation, concentration is finally calculated for the main lines of commerce for the *overall group of* 126 *financial intermediaries*, as if commercial banks, private savings banks and public institutions were all

TABLE 4.6 Concentration measures for the main financial statement items of private savings banks and public financial institutions—1976[a]

Lines of commerce (percentage of the balance sheet total)		n_A	C_4	G	GA	H	NE_H	E	EA	NE_E
		A. Private savings banks								
Assets										
Claims on other financial institutions	(2.76)	32	0.75	0.80	0.83	0.17	6.0	3.10	0.61	8.6
Advances and loans (without mortgage)	(7.96)	26	0.90	0.90	0.93	0.42	2.4	1.99	0.40	4.0
Bonds of the government sector	(31.86)	32	0.71	0.79	0.81	0.17	6.0	3.19	0.63	9.1
Bonds of corporations	(3.74)	29	0.64*	0.77	0.79	0.13*	7.7*	3.37	0.67	10.3
Mortgage credit	(42.99)	32	0.63*	0.74*	0.77*	0.12*	8.2*	3.50*	0.69*	11.3*
Liabilities										
Savings deposits ≤ 2 year	(65.96)	32	0.74	0.79	0.81	0.16	6.1	3.18	0.63	9.1
Savings > 2, ≤ 5 year	(6.36)	26	0.62*	0.76	0.78	0.13*	7.6*	3.42	0.68	10.7
Savings > 5 year	(18.41)	28	0.65*	0.75	0.77*	0.13*	8.0*	3.46*	0.69*	11.0*
Capital	(1.97)	33	0.65*	0.73*	0.75*	0.13*	7.5*	3.55*	0.70*	11.7*
Current profits	(0.33)	32	0.67	0.75	0.77*	0.14	7.3*	3.41	0.68	10.6
Balance sheet total	(100)	33	0.67	0.75	0.78	0.14	7.2	3.42	0.68	10.7
Revenues—expenses account total		32	0.62*	0.73*	0.75*	0.12*	8.3*	3.56*	0.71*	11.8*

TABLE 4.6 (Contd.)

B. Public financial institutions

Bonds and notes (liabilities)	(39.6)	6	0.96	0.60	0.70	0.35	2.9	1.85	0.66	3.6
Total balance sheet	(100)	7	0.93	0.51	0.59	0.27	3.7	2.14	0.76	4.4
Revenues–expenses account total		6	0.96	0.49	0.58	0.30	3.3	1.94	0.75	3.8

[a] Values marked with * indicate a lower degree of concentration than the balance sheet total.

operating on each submarket. Due to the larger number of market participants, the picture obtained in Table 4.7 points to less concentration – see, for instance, the number equivalents – but at the same time one observes different markets remaining very unequally distributed. Compared with the aggregate measure of total output, all main items considered (except the capital stock and current profits) show higher concentration values. For the assets, Gini coefficients are even found of more than 0.90, with only one exception being the heterogeneous item miscellaneous debtors. Compared with Table 4.4 for the commercial banks and Table 4.6 for the private savings banks, some concentration measures do not really change, such as for commercial paper and mortgage credit. This confirms that the tendency of de specialisation of the financial intermediaries remains rather weak at the assets side. At the liabilities side, unfortunately, the lack of harmonisation in the published financial statements only allows consideration of broad categories of funds collected. Aggregated deposits remain, however, characterised by high inequality values, this being even stronger the case for the financing by means of notes and bonds.

3. ECONOMIES OF SCALE IN THE BANKING SECTOR

A highly concentrated structure like we observed for the Belgian financial market may be under certain conditions economically justifiable, especially if there exist substantial economies of scale. This will be examined hereafter for the important sector of the deposit banks.

3.1 Economies of scale, cost functions and their relationship with concentration

Economies of scale can be derived from *cost functions*, relating total, average and/or marginal costs of a firm to its output. These cost functions depend on the technical production function, and also on behavioural hypotheses such as cost minimisation.[27] According to the time period considered, a distinction is made between *short* and *long run cost functions*, the latter presuming that there is enough time to adjust all inputs to output, including the physical capital stock. Long run cost functions can be estimated for a single firm on the base of data for a sufficiently long time period, allowing the scale to vary over a wide range. An alternative way of estimating long run cost functions is using cross-section data, with respect to scale covering a range as large as possible

TABLE 4.7 Concentration measures for some important lines of commerce of the overall group of Belgian financial intermediaries – 1976[a]

Lines of commerce (percentage of balance sheet total)	n_A	C_4	G	GA	H	NE_H	E	EA	NE_E
Assets									
Treasury bills	(2.3)	42	0.78	0.94	0.95	0.18	5.7	3.18	0.46	9.1
Commercial paper	(7.0)	90	0.82	0.93	0.94	0.17	5.7	3.19	0.46	9.1
Miscellaneous debtors	(42.9)	125	0.55	0.85	0.86	0.10	10.5	4.38	0.63	20.8
Government bonds[b]	(18.6)	120	0.66	0.90	0.90	0.12	8.1	3.82	0.55	14.1
Private bonds and shares	(2.6)	30	0.65	0.92	0.93	0.13	7.3	3.65	0.52	12.6
Mortgage credits	(6.1)	34	0.61	0.93	0.94	0.12	8.4	3.56	0.51	11.8
Liabilities									
Deposits[c]	(44.4)	123	0.62	0.87	0.88	0.11	9.2	4.14	0.59	17.6
Notes and bonds	(17.9)	68	0.72	0.94	0.95	0.20	5.0	3.17	0.45	9.0
Deposits, notes and bonds	(62.3)	125	0.54	0.87	0.88	0.10	11.0	4.25	0.61	19.0
Capital	(9.1)	123	0.32*	0.69*	0.70*	0.04*	24.7*	5.57*	0.80*	47.6*
Current profits	(0.2)	110	0.49*	0.81*	0.82*	0.08	12.7	4.62	0.68*	24.6*
Balance sheet total	(100)	126	0.50	0.83	0.84	0.08	13.1	4.62	0.66	24.5
Revenues–expenses account total		113	0.50	0.81*	0.82*	0.08	12.7	4.60	0.67*	24.1

[a] Values marked with * indicate a lower degree of concentration than the balance sheet total.
[b] Includes investment of legal reserve.
[c] For the private savings banks, including deposits up to two years; deposits with longer maturity are added to 'notes and bonds'.

and, in addition, making the hypothesis that each firm is operating on its short run efficiency border. This is the approach taken here. *Economies of scale* appear when total costs are proportionally increasing less than output or, in other terms, when average costs are decreasing.

The general accepted form of a long run total cost function is a cubic one, relying on the laws of initially increasing and afterwards diminishing returns. This implies a U-shaped average cost function, the minimum point of this curve representing the *optimal scale*. As is well known, under competitive conditions this is the scale where profit-maximising firms in the long run should operate on. An alternative form often considered is that average costs, after having decreased significantly to a certain scale, arrive in a phase where they remain stable over a certain range of output. The explanation for this rather L-shaped curve is that the upswing in average costs is delayed to a larger scale as eventual diseconomies of scale are compensated, for example, by better managerial techniques.[28]

The minimum size at which this optimal scale is reached is referred to as the *minimal optimal scale* (*MOS*). From there on, and as long as average costs remain on the same minimal level, the firm is characterised by *operational efficiency*.[29]

It is now clear that in the case where the optimal scale is large relative to the size of the market, there is only room for a small number of firms being operationally efficient. If, on the contrary, the optimal scale is small, then there is no economic justification for a concentrated market. If, finally, there is a minimal optimal scale, this means that each firm on that scale has realised all economies; when the scale increases further, however, competition decreases while the operational efficiency remains the same.

Consequently, the relation of costs to scale is an important element to judge the structure of a market as well as changes in it. It is also particularly relevant for the regulating authorities in the case of an *eventual merger*. If the merger would go beyond the optimal scale, it is becoming operationally inefficient. If the merger remains in the range of economies of scale, the ultimate welfare effect depends on the gain in operational efficiency compared with the loss of competition.[30] Finally, one has to notice that a merger increasing the size of a firm to the minimal optimal scale, although it reduces the total number of possible competitors, may increase the number of *significant competitors*. 'Competition among the few' between larger and more efficiently operating firms may indeed be as vigorous as pure competition, but enhancing a greater danger of collusion.

Arguments with respect to efficiency gains and competition losses seem to be important with respect to the jurisdiction concerning bank mergers in the United States, where one is trying thus to define concretely the public interest.[31] Those arguments are, however, used less in Europe and also in the reports of the Belgian regulating authority, the Banking Commission.[32]

3.2 Specification of cost functions and identification of economies of scale[33]

To analyse the existence of economies of scale or of an optimal scale, total costs (TC), average costs (AC) and marginal costs (MC) are related to output (Q). Output homogeneity measures or dummies (Z) may be included to capture differences in the organisational structure. We first specify the main theoretical forms of those cost functions, indicating briefly the implied characteristics when the scale is changing.

The most simple specification is a *linear total cost function*, implying a reciprocal relation between average costs and output, while marginal costs are constant.

$$TC = a.Q + b + c.Z.Q$$
$$AC = a + \frac{b}{Q} + c.Z$$
$$MC = a + c.Z$$

Depending on the value of b, average costs are constant $(b = 0)$, increasing $(b > 0)$ but at a decelerating rate, or finally decreasing $(b < 0)$ asymptotically, approaching the constant marginal costs. This last specification implies economies of scale, where the gains in efficiency from a certain scale may, however, become very small.

A second generally used specification is a *log linear total cost function*, implying also a log linear form of average and marginal costs.

$$TC = a.Q^b.Z^c \quad \text{or} \quad \log TC = \log a + b.\log Q + c.\log Z$$
$$AC = a.Q^{b-1}.Z^c$$
$$MC = a.b.Q^{b-1}.Z^c$$

This function is characterised by a constant elasticity of costs to scale whose value is given by the output coefficient b. If $b = 1$, average and marginal costs have no relation with output and are constant and equal, if $b > 1$ there are diseconomies of scale and if $b < 1$ this points to economies of scale. The advantage of this specification is that one can derive the importance of the (dis) economies of scale immediately from the scale factor as $(1 - b)$, which is a percentage. This percentage is however, constant over the whole range of output.

Finally, we consider the more complex *cubic total cost function* corresponding to the total cost equation as it is generally depicted in standard microeconomic theory.

$$TC = a.Q^3 + b.Q^2 + c.Q + d.Z.Q$$
$$AC = a.Q^2 + b.Q + c + d.Z$$
$$MC = 3.a.Q^2 + 2.b.Q + c + d.Z$$

Under the condition that $a > 0$ and $b < 0$, average and marginal costs then show the well-known pattern of U-shaped curves. The optimal long run scale is found in the minimum of the average costs, where also the elasticity of total costs with respect to output is equal to 1 or $AC = MC$. Therefore, by constraining average and marginal costs to be equal, one can derive as a root the optimal scale Q^*.

$$Q^* = -\frac{b}{2a}$$

3.3 Testing economies of scale in the Belgian banking sector

In order to test the existence of economies of scale in the Belgian banking sector, we use hereafter as a measure of output the balance sheet total since physical indicators (for example, the number of accounts or loans are lacking. In addition, this balance sheet total is highly correlated with an alternative measure of output: the revenues – expenses account total ($r = 0.998$ for all banks).

Cost data are not available for individual banking operations as loans or deposits, but only with respect to the overall activity. Several cost components are to be considered. For the Belgian deposit banks, the best results were obtained by using the most broad cost concept: *gross overall costs*. These include: general costs and wages, other welfare expenses for employees, advertising expenses, taxes, depreciation allowances with respect to buildings and equipment as well as to the portfolio and, finally, reserve funds, partly consisting of effective precautionary reserves and partly of provisions for predictable risks.

The main empirical results of the cost calculations are included in

Tables 4.8 and 4.9. To avoid problems of heteroscedasticity, we only tested average cost functions from which, however, the total cost function is easily derived.[34] In Tables 4.8 and 4.9, we give (in brackets) the t-values; the standard error of estimation (SEE) is expressed as a ratio to the mean value of the explained variable, that is average costs. The output variable is measured in billions of Belgian francs (BF). Finally, the structural variables included in the cost functions are Z_1: the share of bankers' and group accounts (assets side) to the balance sheet

TABLE 4.8   Regression results of cost functions for the banks in Belgium – 1976

A. All banks

(1) AC $= 0.048 - 0.0001\,Q + 0.00000018\,Q^2 - 0.053\,Z_1$
         (21.8) (−1.7)   (1.6)   (−10.1)

$R^2 = 0.62$ $SEE = 0.40$ $F(3, 70) = 38.12$
$Q^* = 279$ billion BF

(2) Log $AC = -2.82 - 0.11 \log Q - 2.34\,Z_1$
              (−32.5) (−3.7)   (−11.9)

$R^2 = 0.73$ $SEE = 0.11$ $F(2, 71) = 95.86$
$E_{TC} = 0.89$

(3) Log $AC = -4.2 - 0.10 \log Q - 0.34 \log Z_1$
              (−27.8)(−2.4)   (−6.7)

$R^2 = 0.50$ $SEE = 0.16$ $F(2, 71) = 35.8$
$E_{TC} = 0.90$

B. All banks except three largest

(4) AC $= 0.05 - 0.00097\,Q + 0.000011\,Q^2 - 0.048\,Z_1$
         (23.0) (−4.1)   (3.2)   (−9.3)

$R^2 = 0.69$ $SEE = 0.36$ $F(3, 67) = 50.74$
$Q^* = 45$ billion BF

(5) Log $AC = -2.80 - 0.18 \log Q - 2.18\,Z_1$
              (−34.1) (−5.2)   (−11.3)

$R^2 = 0.77$ $SEE = 0.11$ $F(2, 68) = 111.9$
$E_{TC} = 0.82$

(6) Log $AC = -4.02 - 0.19 \log Q - 0.30 \log Z_1$
              (−27.0) (−4.0)   (−6.2)

$R^2 = 0.57$ $SEE = 0.15$ $F(2, 68) = 45.4$
$E_{TC} = 0.81$

TABLE 4.9   Regression results of cost functions for subsamples of banks in Belgium – 1976

A. *Large banks except three largest* (> 20 *billion BF*)

(7) $\text{Log } AC = \quad -7.08 + 0.33 \log Q + 5.59 Z_2$

             $(-10.7) \quad (2.1) \qquad\quad (10.4)$

             $R^2 = 0.95 \qquad\qquad SEE = 0.05 \qquad\qquad F(2, 7) = \ 64.4$

             $E_{TC} = 1.33$

(8) $AC \qquad = \ -0.009 + 0.00012\, Q + 0.073\, Z_2$

             $(-2.4) \quad (2.4) \qquad\quad (9.5)$

             $R^2 = 0.94 \qquad\qquad SEE = 0.21 \qquad\qquad F(2, 7) = \ 52.49$

B. *Small and medium-sized banks* (< 20 *billion BF*)

(9) $AC \qquad = \quad 0.043 + 0.0061 \left(\dfrac{1}{Q}\right) - 0.050\, Z_1$

             $(17.6) \qquad (4.4) \qquad\quad (-9.3)$

             $R^2 = 0.68 \qquad\qquad SEE = 0.33 \qquad\qquad F(2, 58) = \ 63.03$

(10) $\text{Log } AC = \quad -2.79 - 0.18 \log Q - 2.19\, Z_1$

             $(-34.8) \ (-4.7) \qquad\quad (-11.4)$

             $R^2 = 0.76 \qquad\qquad SEE = 0.11 \qquad\qquad F(2, 58) = \ 93.43$

             $E_{TC} = 0.82$

---

total, and Z_2: the share of total deposits, notes and bonds (liabilities side) to the balance sheet total.

In Table 4.8, the overall group of banks is considered first.[35] The cubic total cost function as estimated in equation (1) delivers output parameters that are not very significant. It would point to an optimal scale of 279 billion BF, the three largest Belgian banks all being bigger (with a scale in 1976 of respectively 587, 430 and 283 billion BF). Introducing a dummy to take into account that the three main banks in Belgium would be structurally different from the other banks results in a larger optimal scale (442 billion BF), the estimate, however, being dominantly influenced by the dummy variable.

More significant coefficients are, however, found when log linear total cost functions are estimated, implying a constant elasticity of total costs to scale and declining average and marginal cost curves, asymptotically approaching the *x*-axis. Both equations (2) and (3) indicate that when the scale increases by 1 per cent, total costs of the banks grow by about 0.9 per cent, thus pointing to economies of scale. The R^2 of the logarithmic estimate, however, decreases considerably when also the output homogeneity measure Z_1 is expressed in logarithms.

Since it is often argued that the three largest banks in Belgium are haracterised by structural differences compared with other banks, we ested the same equations excluding them. The results are given in the ower part of Table 4.8. When omitting those three largest banks, a quadratic, U-shaped average cost function is obtained that is statistically acceptable, showing an optimal scale of 45 billion BF. Only four of he seventy-one banks considered have a larger scale, but representing 2 per cent of this subgroup's balance sheet total. However, still better esults are obtained with a completely logarithmically specified average ost function. Both equations (5) and (6) reveal an elasticity of total osts to scale of about 0.8, the economies of scale thus being larger than n the case where the three main banks were included.

Although for the group of Belgian banks exclusive of the three largest nes two different specified cost functions seem to perform well, an mportant common conclusion can be derived. All estimates, indeed, ndicate that there exist economies of scale up to a certain point. There is o clear evidence only if average costs are decreasing continuously – but perhaps with minimal gains from a certain scale – or if, after having lecreased, they show an upswing, this last seeming less endorsed by the esults of the estimates. Therefore one can derive from the regressions he probable existence of a *minimal quasi-optimal scale*, although light economies of scale may still occur after that point of ninimal efficiency.[36] The gains in costs with larger scales may in addition be compensated by the loss involved with decreasing ompetition.

More evidence regarding whether average costs in the Belgian panking sector are U-shaped or rather L-shaped can be obtained by considering different subsamples of banks with respect to scale and by esting if they are characterised by a different relationship of costs to output. Therefore, in Table 4.9 regression results are given for two separate subgroups: one of ten large banks (balance sheet total > 20 pillion BF) with the exception of the three main ones, and another group of sixty-one small and medium-sized banks (balance sheet total < 20 pillion BF). The results for both groups are indeed remarkably different.

For the group of larger banks (except the three main ones), equation 7) indicates *dis*economies of scale, even important ones, because the coefficient of output – being equal to $b - 1$ – implies a scale elasticity of $b = 1.33$. A simple linear average cost function as equation (8) gives the same picture of increasing average costs. It has been remarked that when the three main banks are added to this group, the estimated relations become less significant and also unstable.

For the group of small banks, on the contrary, the average cost function (9), derived from a linear total cost function, shows a positive coefficient for the inverse of scale, thus pointing to decreasing average costs. Equation (10) for the same group supposes, on the other hand, a constant elasticity to scale: the value of it amounting to 0.82. This result again reveals economies of scale being, in addition, considerable.

The estimates for subsamples of banks of different size in this way confirm that economies of scale in the Belgian banking sector are not unlimited, and that an U-shaped average cost function even looks more realistic than thought on the base of the regressions for the overall banking sector in Table 4.8. When distinguishing subgroups according to size, it was also observed that in a cost analysis the three largest banks seem to take a special position.

The foregoing analysis of economies of scale is closed with a brief comparison with two earlier studies. Starting from a classification of the banks in subgroups according to size, M. Maes also affirmed the existence of long run U-shaped average cost functions, with still decreasing costs for each subgroup of banks except for that of the three largest ones. The diseconomies of scale for the largest banks were, however, considered as only apparent, taking into account the strong differences in the structure of the three largest banks.[37] F. R. Edwards, in another study, also proved the existence in the Belgian banking sector of a minimal optimal scale which he placed in 1970 at 10 billion BF, from which the gains in cost efficiency were very small, these minimal gains going together with the disadvantages of decreasing competition.[38]

4. CONCLUSIONS

This study has shown that the financial sector in Belgium is highly concentrated, not as a consequence of a limited number of firms but primarily due to a pronounced inequality in the size distribution. A striking characteristic is the considerable number of deposit banks, also of private savings banks, having only a minimal market share. In spite of some tendencies towards despecialisation, also for the overall group of deposit banks, private savings banks and public financial institutions, we found a similar picture of a strongly concentrated market with a very unequal size dispersion. In addition, for important individual lines of commerce even higher concentration values have been observed than for total output. An interesting observation was also that by further distinguishing according to the currency used and the nationality of the arket participants, clearly higher concentration values were found for ose markets least exposed to international competition.[39]

A possible explanation for this concentrated financial structure could e sought in the large scale of firms in the industrial sector. However, of venty-four industrial sectors, only six show a C_4 higher than the one in ie banking sector.[40]

Therefore, as an economic rationale for the high concentration in the nancial sector, we examined the existence of economies of scale, oncretely with respect to the banking sector. When relating average osts to output, decreasing L-shaped functions were found, as well as the aditional U-shaped ones. It follows from this that in the Belgian anking sector there exists a (quasi-)optimal scale. Small firms can thus ealise economies of scale up to a certain point, from which the gain in ost may become minimal or even negative.

An identification of this point of minimal (quasi-)optimal scale equires further research to take into account structural differences (for xample, for the three main banks and the foreign banks in Belgium) and lso to quantify more accurately the gains of increasing scale together ith the losses due to decreasing competition.

However, the derivation of important initial economies of scale raises a any case new critical questions about the existence in Belgium of the onsiderable number of very small banks as was revealed by the oncentration analysis. Why are mergers not changing the market tructure to such an extent that a financial sector emerges with more *ignificant* competitors? Those small banks, indeed, seem to be haracterised by operational inefficiency, unless the higher costs are elated to special services they are providing.

Finally, we draw the attention to the significance of the results of this oncentration and cost analysis from the point of view of the regulatory uthorities. The large scale of the main banks may be important for perating in the international markets, such as the Eurocredit and 'urobonds market. It may, however, imply serious problems con- erning the degree of competition in more typical domestic market reas, asking eventually for countervailing measures. The question also :mains as to how far the existence of concentration is partly resulting om the actual regulation and the attitude of the financial authorities.

APPENDIX 4.1 LIST OF SYMBOLS AND ABBREVIATIONS

AC	Average costs
BF	Belgian franc
C_4	Share of the four financial institutions with the largest amount of the balance sheet item considered
G	Gini coefficient
GA	Adjusted Gini coefficient (relative to the maximum value)
E	Entropy
EA	Adjusted entropy (relative to the maximum value)
E_{TC}	Scale parameter, elasticity of total cost to output
H	Herfindahl coefficient
MC	Marginal costs
NE_E	Numbers equivalent with respect to the entropy measure
NE_H	Numbers equivalent with respect to the Herfindahl coefficient
n	Number of financial institutions
n_A	Number of relevant financial institutions having the considered item on their balance sheet
Q	Output
Q^*	Optimal scale
TC	Total costs
Z	Output homogeneity measure or dummy

NOTES

1. The authors thank Mr G. Gelders of the Belgian Banking Commission for providing information and P. Zonderman for computer assistance. The study has benefited from financial support of the National Fund for Collective Fundamental Research (FKFO).
2. For the criteria of classification and the list of banks according to ownership, we refer to M. de Smet, G. Martin and J. F. van der Straeten (1978) pp. 21–34. See also, Banking Commission, *Annual Report* (1975–6) Appendix 4; (1976–7) p. 147.
3. Centraal Bureau voor de Kleine Spaarder, *Annual Report* (1975) pp. 93– Banking Commission, *Annual Report* (1976–7) p. 174.
4. The seven public financial institutions covered by the study are in decreasing order of their importance:

   General Savings and Retirement Institution
   Municipal Credit Institution
   National Company for Industrial Credit
   Postal Office
   National Company for Professional Credit
   National Institute for Agricultural Credit
   Central Bureau for Mortgage Credit

5. A problem for deposit banks is that not all balance sheets are published on the same date (31 December 1976). Some were earlier, but for two of the

APPENDIX 4.2 EXTREME VALUES FOR THE CALCULATED CONCENTRATION MEASURES

Concentration measure	Theoretical values		Concrete values for the markets considered							
			Perfectly distributed market				Monopoly			
	Perfectly distributed market	Monopoly	Banks	Private savings banks	Public financial institutions	All intermediaries	Banks	Private savings banks	Public financial institutions	All intermediaries
C_4	$4/n$	1	0.05	0.12	0.57	0.03	1	1	1	1
G	0	1	0	0	0	0	1	1	1	1
GA	0	$(n-1)/n$	0	0	0	0	0.99	0.97	0.86	0.99
H	$1/n$	1	0.01	0.03	0.14	0.008	1	1	1	1
NE_H	n	1	86	33	7	126	1	1	1	1
E	$\log_2 n$	0	6.43	5.04	2.81	6.98	0	0	0	0
EA	1	0	1	1	1	1	0	0	0	0
NE_E	n	1	86	33	7	126	1	1	1	1

largest banks they were published on a later date, which may lead to som overestimation of their importance.

6. I. Horowitz (1977) p. 170.
7. Cf. D. V. Austin (1977) p. 185.
8. I. Horowitz (1977) p. 170.
9. See, for instance: M. A. Adelman (1969) p. 100; A. A. Heggestad (1979) p 457–65; I. Horowitz (1971) p. 376; A. P. Jacquemin and H. W. de Jon (1977) pp. 41–50; F. M. Scherer (1970) p. 50.
10. W. Buijink, B. de Brabander, G. Thiers and M. Vandoorne (1979) pp. VII 2–6.
11. I. Horowitz (1971) p. 369.
12. A. A. Heggestad (1979) pp. 469–70.
13. D. Needham (1974) p. 92.
14. A. P. Jacquemin and H. W. de Jong (1977) pp. 49–50.
15. A. A. Heggestad (1979) p. 470.
16. W. G. Shepherd (1979) p. 190; E. Vanlommel, D. Liebaers and B. D Brabander (1977) p. 15.
17. This high rank correlation with G is due to the special way of calculating th Gini coefficient taking into account all the firms. When computing the ran correlation between all the calculated concentration measures for the fou groups distinguished (that is, banks, savings institutions, public financi institutions and all intermediaries), then the G takes the same speci position as was found in A. P. Jacquemin and H. W. de Jong (1977) p. 5 Between the other measures there remains a very high rank correlatio especially between H and E, which is to be expected since they are both reflection of the total number as well as of the size distribution, where th different weighting schemes seem of less importance for discriminating thes markets. When the (relative) Gini coefficient and relative entropy a calculated with the actual number of firms (n_A), they even show a reverse ranking compared with other measures; it has to be kept in mind, howeve that they are then pure indicators of inequality among the actual mark participants.
18. F. W. Bell and N. B. Murphy (1968) p. 4; M. Maes used, in an earlier stud as an output measure the balance sheet total plus rediscounted bil M. Maes (1970) p. 199; see also G. J. Benston (1972) pp. 320–1.
19. G. J. Benston (1972) pp. 322–8.
20. It should, however, be observed that the group of public financi institutions includes the largest savings bank of Belgium; an alternativ procedure is to add the latter to the private savings banks, surely involvin higher concentration for typical savings banks activities.
21. Interesting to note is that in the United States, for the urban bankin markets (to so-called SMSAs, Standard Metropolitan Statistical Areas), a average numbers equivalent was found of 4.5, with only 20 per cent of th regional markets showing a higher NE_H than 7.0. This indicates that also i the United States, the banking sector is rather oligopolistic, in 80 per cent c the cases even more concentrated than the whole Belgian banking marke A. A. Heggestad (1979) p. 454.
22. M. de Smet, G. Martin and J. F. van der Straeten (1978) pp. 26 and 28.
23. The same opinion is expressed in F. R. Edwards (1970) pp. 8–9.

4. These items are thus considered as separate markets. In some cases, however, for example the items 'Bankers' and 'Bonds and Notes', we study in fact the concentration as well of the demand as of the supply side of one market. This illustrates also the problem that sometimes not all market participants are considered. A concentration measure – for each balance sheet item – can be a useful variable in structure–performance studies for different asset markets using, for example, as an indicator of performance the interest rate on the asset considered.

5. IBRO (ed.) (1978).

6. The issue is still more complex for Belgium, taking into account the economic union (with one currency) with the financial centre of Luxembourg.

7. J. Johnston (1960) pp. 4–25. See also F. W. Bell and N. B. Murphy (1968).

8. F. M. Scherer (1970) p. 77.

9. G. J. Benston and G. A. Hanweck (1977) pp. 158–61.

0. It can be argued that the regulating authorities should take care that the gains of cost reduction should be passed to the public, this implying eventually the need for taxing away monopoly profits in order to redistribute them afterwards. Cf. G. J. Benston and G. A. Hanweck (1977) p. 167.

1. See the content of the Bank Merger Act of 1960, quoted in D. V. Austin (1977) p. 187.

2. Cf. the attitude of the Banking Commission in the case of the merger in 1974 of the second and fourth largest banks in Belgium, increasing the share of the second largest bank from 19.5 to 23.8 per cent of total assets. In its yearly report, the Banking Commission mainly argued that this market share was still lower than that of the largest bank and that the share of the largest banks was also lower than it had been in the past. More relevant questions raised, however, were those of international competition and the increasing despecialisation, thus of the relevant market delineation. See Banking Commission, *Annual Report* (1974–5) p. 33.

3. F. W. Bell and N. B. Murphy (1968) 331 pp.; G. J. Benston (1965) pp. 285– 327; G. J. Benston (1972) pp. 312–41; G. J. Benston and G. A. Hanweck (1977) p. 160; J. E. Draper and J. S. Klingman (1972) pp. 176–7, 214–17 and 252–63.

4. G. J. Benston and G. A. Hanweck (1977) p. 160.

5. As eleven banks operating under the juridical statute of limited partnership do not publish revenue – expenses accounts, the overall group of deposit banks in the section on cost analysis contains only seventy-five institutions. This number is further diminished by one newly-established bank with exceptional high cost figures.

6. These results do also appear with other structural variables, or with dummies for the structure. The fits are similar to those represented in the table. Other structural variables were: bankers and group account (liabilities), total deposits, demand deposits, all as a share of the balance sheet total.

7. M. Maes (1970) pp. 226–8; M. Maes (1975) pp. 261–7.

8. F. R. Edwards (1970) p. 16.

9. It has to be mentioned also that the study does not take into account

participations of one bank in other ones, neither problems of possib collusion in management or interlocking directorship.
40. A. Jacquemin, E. de Ghellinck and C. Huveneers (1978) pp. 392–7.

REFERENCES

Adelman, M. A. (1969) 'Comment on the "H" Concentration Measure as Numbers-Equivalent', *Review of Economics and Statistics* (February) pp. 9 101.

Austin, D. V. (1977) 'The Line of Commerce and the Relevant Geograph Market in Banking: What Fifteen Years of Trials and Tribulations H Taught Us and Not Taught Us about the Measure of Banking Structure', *Proceedings of a Conference on Bank Structure and Competition* (Chicag Federal Reserve Bank of Chicago) pp. 185–209.

Bankcommissie (1978) *Balansen afgesloten tussen 1 juni 1976 en 31 mei 19.* (Brussel: Uitgave van de Bankcommissie) 283 pp.

Banking Commission, *Annual Report* (Brussels: 1974–5, 1975–6).

Bell, F. W. and N. B. Murphy (1968) *Costs in Commercial Banking: Quantitative Analysis of Bank Behavior and its Relation to Bank Regulati* (Boston: Federal Reserve Bank of Boston, Research Report 41, April) 331 p

Benston, G. J. (1965) 'Economies of Scale and Marginal Costs in Banki Operation', *The National Banking Review* (June); reproduced in F. W. B and N. B. Murphy (1968) *Costs in Commercial Banking* (Boston: Feder Reserve Bank of Boston, Research Report 41, April) pp. 285–327.

Benston, G. J. (1972) 'Economies of Scale of Financial Institutions', *Journal Money, Credit and Banking* (May) pp. 312–41.

Benston, G. J. and G. A. Hanweck (1977) 'A Summary Report on Bank Holdi Company Affiliation and Economies of Scale', in *Proceedings of a Conferen on Bank Structure and Competition* (Chicago: Federal Reserve Bank Chicago) pp. 158–68.

Buijink, W., B. De Brabander, G. Thiers and M. Vandoorn 'Inkomensverdeling binnen de bedrijven', in Vereniging voor economi *Inkomens-en vermogensverdeling* (Brussels: Vrije Universiteit Brussel, 197 pp. 1–16.

Centraal Bureau voor de Kleine Spaarder (1975) *Annual Report.*

Denayer, J. (1979) *Pleidooi tegen het kartel der creditinteresten in de financiè sector* (Gent: Europabank) 27 pp.

De Smet, M., G. Martin and J. F. van der Straeten (1977) 'Les banques au se du secteur financier Belge: quelques données comparatives', *Tijdschrift vo het bankwezen*, vol. 6, pp. 401–24.

De Smet, M., G. Martin and J. F. van der Straeten (1978) 'Familiealbum van h Belgisch bankwezen van 1960 tot 1977', *Tijdschrift voor het bankwezen*, no. pp. 21–34.

Draper, J. E. and J. S. Klingman (1972) *Mathematical Analysis, Business a Economic Applications* (New York: Harper and Row) 691 pp.

Edwards, F. R. (1970) 'Regulation and Competition in European Financi Markets – the Case of Banking in Belgium', *Recherches Economiques Louvain* (February) pp. 3–30.

dwards, F. R. (ed.) (1979) *Issues in Financial Regulation* (New York: McGraw-Hill) 526 pp.

eggestad, A. A. (1979) 'Market Structure, Competition, and Performance in Financial Industries: A Survey of Banking Studies', in F. R. Edwards (ed.), *Issues in Financial Regulation* (New York: McGraw-Hill) pp. 457–65.

orowitz, I. (1971) 'Numbers Equivalent in U.S. Manufacturing Industries: 1954, 1958 and 1963', *Southern Economic Journal* (April) pp. 396–408.

orowitz, I. (1977) 'On Defining the Geographic Market in Section 7 Cases', in *Proceedings of a Conference on Bank Structure and Competition* (Chicago: Federal Reserve Bank of Chicago) pp. 169–82.

RO (ed.) (1978) *The Regulation of Banks in the Member States of the EEC* (Alphen/Rijn: Sythoff & Noordhoff) xi + 323 pp.

acquemin, A., E. de Ghellinck and C. Huveneers (1978) 'Industriële concentratie in een open economie: de toestand in België', *Statistisch Tijdschrift* (May) pp. 389–415.

acquemin, A. P. and H. W. de Jong (1977) *European Industrial Organisation* (London: Macmillan) 269 pp.

hnston, J. (1960) *Statistical Cost Analysis* (New York: McGraw-Hill) 197 pp.

oots, R. S. (1978) 'On Economies of Scale in Credit Unions', *The Journal of Finance* (September) pp. 1087–94.

aes, M. (1970) 'Een statistische benadering van het verband tussen bankactiviteit en algemene onkosten', *Tijdschrift voor het Bankwezen*, no. 3, pp. 195–244.

aes, M. (1975) 'Les economies de dimensions dans le secteur bancaire Belge', *Tijdschrift voor het Bankwezen*, no. 4, pp. 261–7.

urphy, N. B. (1972) 'A Reestimation of the Benston–Bell–Murphy Cost Functions for a Larger Sample with Greater Size and Geographic Dispersion', *Journal of Financial and Quantitative Analysis* (December) pp. 2097–105.

eedham, D. (1974) *Economic Analysis and Industrial Structure* (London: Holt, Rinehart and Winston) 176 pp.

aelinck, J. P. (1976) *De bankconcentratie in de Europese Economische Gemeenschap. Een vergelijkende studie* (Gent: Faculteit Economische Wetenschappen) 358 pp.

cherer, F. M. (1970) *Industrial Market Structure and Economic Performance* (Chicago: Rand McNally) 576 pp.

hepherd, W. G. (1979) *The Economics of Industrial Organization* (London: Macmillan) 463 pp.

aylor, R. A. (1972) 'Economies of Scale in Large Credit Unions', *Applied Economics*, vol. 4, pp. 33–40.

anlommel, E., B. De Brabander and D. Liebaers (1977) 'Industrial Concentration in Belgium: Empirical Comparison of Alternative Seller Concentration Measures', *The Journal of Industrial Economics*, no. 1, pp. 1–20.

Comment on Pacolet and Verheirstraeten

MICHEL DE SMET AND GEORGES MARTIN

This is a very interesting study with important practical implication
We shall divide our comments into two categories: on the one hand
comments on the methodology and, on the other, on the main result
and conclusions.

We first pay some attention to the method and hypotheses of th
study.

As far as the section on concentration in the financial sector i
concerned, we remark that the calculations cover only one year: 1976.
would have been interesting to examine the sensitivity of the coefficient
calculated over several years, comparing certain results for two or thre
years, for instance 1975, when the monetary and economic climate wa
very relaxed and rates of interest were low; in other words, quite th
opposite of 1976. Besides, it might have been of particular interest t
compare two years at a certain interval from one another, for instanc
1970 or 1965 with 1976, in order to get an idea of the evolution c
concentration. We would then observe that, for example, the relativ
share of the three or four largest Belgian banks in the balance sheet an
deposit totals of the banking sector is diminishing quite significantl

With respect to the output measure used, in our view balance shee
totals are not the ideal factor for evaluating concentration in th
financial sector. Many services and activities do not appear in th
balance sheet. The most typical example is that of foreign exchang
operations, but there are also plenty of other examples.

In the study, also, more disaggregated calculations of the degree c
concentration have been made by considering each line of the balanc
sheet separately as representing an individual product or market. This i
a particularly theoretical approach, whose consequence is to accentuat
the degree of concentration. In fact, on both the deposit and the lendin

92

ide, several lines in the balance sheet often represent close substitutes, so that grouping together a number of lines would appear to us to be economically more meaningful in many cases, and this could result in a reduction of the concentration coefficients.

As regards the section which deals with the economies of scale, we may ask ourselves whether it would not be preferable to compare general expenses against net or gross total revenues rather than against the balance sheet total. Revenues certainly give a better indication of overall activity, not only for the reason already mentioned (that is to say, that numerous activities do not show up in the balance sheet), but also because the balance sheet juxtaposes items which are not always entirely comparable with one another: certain types of operation which achieve considerable volume but with very narrow profit margins, and others for which the opposite is true. In the end, total income is probably the best indicator of the turnover achieved by financial institutions.

Finally, we are in complete agreement with the authors when they complain of the lack of correspondence between the information published by the three sectors (banks, savings banks and public credit institutions), particularly with regard to balance sheets and profit and loss accounts. We are the first to deplore this state of affairs, and we note that once more, in this study as in many others before, this situation is reflected by the imbalance between on the one hand, the relative economic importance of the three sectors and, on the other, the disproportionate attention paid to the banks as opposed to the savings banks and the public credit institutions in the analysis and the commentary.

The following remarks relate basically to the substance and the conclusions of the study.

In their calculations on the financial market structure, the authors have not covered one important aspect of concentration: the relationships between various financial institutions which together make up groups or families and which at the same time often belong to several different sectors. We would then notice that certain institutions, considered in the context of this study as being very small are, when viewed in this manner, of a much more respectable size. From the point of view of concentration, as from the point of view of competition and economies of scale, this is an important question: is it preferable to have very large companies which do virtually everything or groups of legally separate companies each of which is a specialist in one or other part of the market?

We may also ask questions on the homogeneity of the different sectors. For instance, a large number of small banks certainly are muc closer to the private savings banks, as regards their activities, than to th large banks and foreign banks established in Belgium. Interesting result could be obtained by investigating along the lines of groupings of thi nature, which are perhaps economically more meaningful than group ings based on primarily legal and formal criteria.

An implicit assumption which comes across at a number of points in the study, as well as in the conclusions, is that a reduction of the numbe of businesses present on the market would be negative from the point o view of competition. Only once is the idea mentioned that a reduction in the number of possible competitors may well be accompanied by an increase in the number of significant competitors. This is an interestin, hypothesis which could usefully have been investigated in more depth Moreover, a rather important aspect has been left aside: even though th major institutions are relatively few in number, this does not preven them from indulging in fierce competition in certain areas, nor from being faced in certain segments of the market with rivals who ar perhaps much smaller than themselves, but very specialised and ver efficient, and who confront them with some problems.

Moreover, reference is frequently made to competition in genera terms, without it being specified whether this is always healthy an desirable in an area such as the financial sector and, particularly, in what form this manifests itself in this sector at different levels o concentration. Obviously, certain forms of competition are less de sirable than others. Moreover, the characteristics of the financial secto oblige qualification of one's judgement on the desirability of a more o less intensive competition. We do not propose to go into these subject further, due to lack of space, but we would just recall that the protectio of savings, the efficiency of monetary policy and the financing of th public sector – and this latter aspect is of particular importance in th Belgian context – are crucially important points when the question o the degree of competition desirable in the financial sector is bein, discussed in a concrete manner.

The authors dwell at length on the definition of the geographical are covered by the different markets. As far as this is concerned, we shoul like to make two remarks: in some cases, this geographical area may b purely local: in the field of retail banking, of the small saver, of the smal business, the market may represent a very restricted concept, and th local branch of a large public or private credit institution may hav hardly any competitive advantage, in fact quite the opposite in som cases, over the neighbouring branch of the local small bank or saving

ank. On the other hand, in some cases, and to an increasing extent, the
eographical area may extend far beyond the region and even outside
he country, not only in the area of credits but also as regards savings.
)ne example: when considering the collection of deposits, can one
issociate the Belgian market from the Luxembourg market, without
nentioning other neighbouring countries?

In similar vein, it would seem appropriate to distinguish clearly two
ypes of markets in which the competitors are not at all the same. On the
ne hand, in the area of retail banking it seems unrealistic to look
eparately at the degree of concentration in each of the three sectors.
'hey must be considered as a whole and together with a number of other
mall 'specialised' institutions. In fact, more than 150 institutions are
urrently competing against one another on this market in Belgium. On
he other hand, in the field of wholesale and corporate banking, the
narket is situated more and more at the European and even at a
vorldwide level. At this level there are only a few very large Belgian
nstitutions which play a significant role, and these have to face a large
umber of foreign competitors who, in most cases, are a great deal larger
han themselves.

We sometimes forget that the major Belgian financial institutions,
vhich appear of such mighty stature when viewed from a purely
ational viewpoint, are quite modest when compared to the competitors
hey must encounter in the international markets, including the major
nstitutions of countries whose size and economic structure are com-
»arable to Belgium's: we are thinking, for instance, of Switzerland and
he Netherlands. In 1978, the largest Swiss bank ranked 27th in the
vorld, the largest Dutch bank ranked 29th and the largest Belgian bank
vas number 49.

As regards the economies of scale, we should first of all mention that a
ew years ago, in the context of a broader study on the profitability of the
»anking sector, we made a few very rough calculations on the existence
»f economies of scale, which led us also to the clear conclusion that
nitially there were economies then, beyond a certain point, dis-
conomies of scale; in other words, a U-shaped curve, which in fact
tarted to move upwards again due only to the three largest banks.

As a consequence, we support the conclusion of this study that the
hree major banks occupy a position apart and are different in structure.
jiven certain essential aspects of their business, this is undeniable, and
»ne can even say that in certain respects these banks take upon
hemselves a sort of public service, which takes its toll on their
»rofitability and helps to give the impression that if they were smaller

they would be more productive and more profitable. That would, in fact, be the case, if they had limited their activities to certain sectors of the market as most other financial institutions have done.

This leads us to the problem of specialisation: can we still talk about economies of scale when the nature of an institution's activities alters drastically with its size? We should at least ask ourselves a few questions about the nature of these economies of scale: are the differences in productivity due to the fact that larger establishments can do the same things more efficiently, or to the fact that they can do other things, take on more profitable and less risky business?

Another question which remains unanswered is that of the optimal size. By excluding the three major banks, the authors' calculations lead them to the conclusion that this optimal size is relatively small: in the region of 45 billion BF. This brings to mind two questions: are there any comparable figures for other countries which would also indicate such a small optimal size? And how then can we explain the fact that so many financial institutions in other countries are considerably larger and apparently very competitive?

We should like to make another remark regarding the alleged inefficiency of the small banks. The authors, in fact, reach the conclusion that many institutions are smaller than the optimum size. We feel that in this area one should be very careful and that an individual approach is almost indispensable. Sometimes at the local level, sometimes in a specific segment of the market, certain small institutions demonstrate their efficiency and dynamism. Certain Belgian banks of very modest dimensions rank undeniably amongst the most profitable. This again puts the accent upon the lack of homogeneity within the sector and upon the fact that certain forms of specialisation apparently make small size compatible with efficiency and profitability.

Finally, the authors are amazed that there are not more mergers between small institutions, taking account of the importance of economies of scale as demonstrated by their calculations. In this regard we should like, however, to underline a trend which has not yet reached its end. Since 1960, about fifty banks have disappeared, the large majority due to mergers or takeovers. The cases of bankruptcy or simple closing down are, in fact, very rare. This figure represents over half the total Belgian banking population. In other words, over the last twenty years there has been an average of two or three mergers or takeover every year. We find these figures quite impressive, when you realise that there are about eighty-five banks in all.

5. Profitability and Risk of the Belgian Financial Sector: a Stock Market Analysis and a Comparison with Accounting Data[1]

1. INTRODUCTION

In this chapter the Belgian bank sector is analysed over the period 1970–8. Although most of the analysis is based on a sample of only seven individual banks,[2] they constitute a major share of the total Belgian financial sector.[3]

Some heterogeneity in the sample has to be pointed out: apart from the five private banks, there is the 'Nationale Bank van België', which is in fact the Belgian Central Bank. While this institution may be regarded as a public one, a non-negligible part of its equity is in private hands and its shares are regularly traded on the Stock Exchange. The 'Nationale Maatschappij voor Krediet aan de Nijverheid' (NMKN) on the other hand, that is, the 'National Company For Industrial Credit', is a semi-public institution.

The analysis is focused on the profitability and the riskiness of the sector and of the individual banks. An attempt has been made to confront market value-based estimates with accounting value-based estimates of risk and return.

Stock market data refer to monthly periods of observations, while accounting data are based on mostly year-end balance sheets and income statements.

2. A STOCK MARKET ANALYSIS OF THE BANK SECTOR

In this section the profitability of the bank sector is analysed over the period 1970–8. Returns of the bank sector are presented along with overall stock market returns.[4] Since we want to present some evidence on the question as to whether shares of banks constitute relatively good inflation hedges,[5] the corresponding evolution of the inflation rate is given as well.

In Figure 5.1 the evolution of the overall Brussels Stock Market Index is illustrated, as well as of the index of the bank sector[6] and of the Consumer Price Index. The one-month HWI interest rate[7] is shown at the bottom of Figure 5.1. Except for the interest rate, all data represent end of month observations.

The index of the bank sector appears to follow rather closely the evolution of the overall stock market index. This will be further substantiated *infra* when the risk aspect is analysed.

It can be noted that most of the time the index of the bank sector falls somewhat below the overall stock market index, although the relatively good performance of the bank sector in 1977 and 1978 explains why both indices are about equal again towards the end of 1978.

Shares of banks do not appear to be better inflation hedges than the

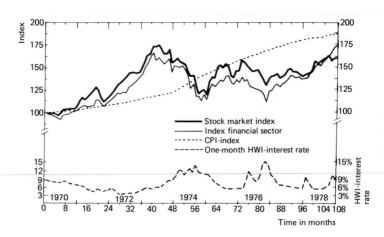

FIGURE 5.1   Evolution of the Brussels stock market index, the index of the financial sector, the consumer price index and the interest rate

overall stock market, contrary to some widespread belief that banks profit from inflation. The latter contention may be true in nominal accounting terms, but not in real market value terms.

In fact, over the period 1970-8 the consumer price index has risen somewhat faster than the bank and the stock market index. However, it should be pointed out that the period 1970-8 can be divided into two distinctly different subperiods. Before 1974, the bank sector index and the overall stock market index increased far more rapidly than the consumer price index. After 1974, the reverse phenomenon is observed.

As far as the relationship between inflation rates and bank sector returns is concerned, the overall impression suggests that there is a negative correlation, which is in line with previous results reported by E. F. Fama and F. Holvoet.[8] This will be confirmed *infra*.

Figure 5.1 further illustrates that the one-month HWI interest rate showed an overall high towards the end of 1976, when the inflation had already come down substantially.[9] The negative relationship between the bank sector and the stock market index, on the one hand, and the interest rate, on the other, is most clearly observed towards the end of 1974, 1975 and 1976.

In Table 5.1, some of the results discussed so far are illustrated more extensively.

Over the complete period of observations the average return of the bank sector slightly exceeds the average return on the overall market, and is about equal to the average inflation rate, resulting into an average real rate of return which is insignificantly different from zero. Moreover, the average bank sector return is almost identical to the average one-month HWI interest rate.[10]

It is hardly surprising that the worst stock market performance of the bank sector is situated in the period 1973-5, characterised by the highest inflation figures. The best stock market performance of the bank sector occurred in the period 1970-2, when inflation was lowest.

As far as the volatility of the various return variables is concerned, it can be concluded that it is lowest with respect to the interest rate, closely followed by the volatility of the inflation rate, and largely surpassed by the volatility of the bank sector returns and the stock market returns.[11]

Whereas this volatility remained relatively constant with respect to the interest rate and the inflation rate, it sharply increased in the period 1973-5 with respect to the bank sector and the stock market returns as an indication of the increased riskiness of the sector during that period.

In the following section, the return characteristics of the bank sector are more thoroughly analysed by looking at the individual banks.

TABLE 5.1   Stock market and bank sector returns[a]

Period	Stock market return	Bank sector return	Interest rate[b]	Inflation rate[c]
1970–8	6.25	7.09	7.16	7.08
	(42.5)	(39.8)	(2.7)	(4.4)
1970–2	14.44	12.86	5.50	4.88
	(32.1)	(28.2)	(1.7)	(2.8)
1973–5	0.73	− 0.79	8.18	10.63
	(55.3)	(52.1)	(2.7)	(4.2)
1976–8	3.57	9.22	7.82	5.72
	(35.0)	(34.1)	(2.7)	(3.6)
1970	8.21	4.02	7.58	3.06
1971	10.43	10.81	5.00	5.40
1972	24.69	23.74	3.93	6.18
1973	5.68	8.07	6.42	7.01
1974	− 26.33	− 26.44	11.45	14.47
1975	22.84	15.78	6.68	10.41
1976	− 3.74	− 6.15	10.12	7.26
1977	− 0.16	10.24	6.54	6.11
1978	14.60	23.55	6.80	3.78

[a] All returns are in percentages per year (averages of monthly rates of return). Standard deviations are given between brackets.
[b] The interest rate is the average HWI interest rate (one month) on bankers' non-rediscountable acceptances, as a proxy for the risk-free rate.
[c] Average of monthly percentages, based on the CPI index.

3. A STOCK MARKET ANALYSIS OF THE INDIVIDUAL BANKS

The return characteristics of seven Belgian financial institutions, all of which are quoted on the Brussels Stock Exchange, are analysed in Table 5.2.

Average return figures are given for the 1970–8 period, as well as for the three subperiods: 1970–2, 1973–5 and 1976–8. Yearly average return figures are shown as well.

Inspection of the figures in Table 5.2 reveals that in several years there is a considerable difference between the average returns of individual banks, despite the oligopolistic nature of the sector, for example Crédit Général performed far better than the other banks in 1973. Belgolaise appears to show some 'abnormal' behaviour as well, for example in 1971

TABLE 5.2 Average rates of return of individual banks (percentage per year)[a]

Period	GBM	KB	BBL	CG	BELG	NMKN	NBB
1970–8	7.51	8.97	3.20	8.34	7.20	7.13	7.56
	(42.7)	(52.1)	(58.6)	(77.8)	(57.3)	(49.2)	(38.2)
1970–2	8.42	17.59	15.31	19.51	4.72	16.02	11.21
	(32.0)	(34.1)	(39.4)	(48.6)	(40.3)	(41.9)	(41.6)
1973–5	2.04	0.25	−9.35	4.92	0.44	1.06	8.69
	(50.7)	(69.7)	(74.8)	(109.5)	(70.6)	(62.3)	(36.2)
1976–8	12.08	9.10	3.68	0.58	16.45	4.30	2.78
	(42.4)	(44.4)	(53.6)	(60.1)	(55.7)	(38.6)	(36.0)
1970	3.00	2.66	6.74	−8.05	4.53	5.18	4.00
1971	8.03	13.57	14.18	3.02	0.64	12.99	8.29
1972	14.26	36.48	25.00	63.58	8.99	29.90	21.33
1973	3.14	7.14	14.53	38.37	−7.88	0.73	14.34
1974	−9.92	−31.47	−49.77	−45.31	−20.71	−0.92	5.83
1975	12.91	25.10	7.16	21.70	29.93	3.37	5.90
1976	−0.77	−5.72	−20.46	−19.51	−8.32	−8.88	−11.37
1977	10.39	19.03	−0.43	14.85	27.91	9.24	11.06
1978	26.62	14.00	31.93	6.38	27.79	12.48	8.69

[a] Returns are averages of monthly rates of return. Standard deviations are given between brackets. For the names of the institutions, the following abbreviations are used:

GBM	= Generale Bankmaatschappij	BELG	= Belgolaise
KB	= Kredietbank	NMKN	= Nationale Maatschappij Voor
BBL	= Bank Brussel Lambert		Krediet aan de Nijverheid
CG	= Crédit Général	NBB	= Nationale Bank van België

and in 1973. Finally, the Bank Brussel Lambert performed poorly in 1977, while all the other banks showed a relatively high rate of return.

Considering the overall period 1970–8, the most profitable bank appears to be Kredietbank, closely followed by Crédit Général. However, the volatility of the returns on the much smaller Crédit Général exceeds substantially the volatility of the returns of Kredietbank.[12] The least profitable bank is the Bank Brussel Lambert which is, of course, heavily influenced by the 1974 event with respect to its foreign exchange problems, but also by the abnormal bad performance in 1977.

The volatility of the returns is lowest with respect to the Nationale Bank van België, closely followed by the largest bank, the Generale Bankmaatschappij.

It is evident that the return characteristics cannot be isolated from the corresponding risk dimensions. This will be further illustrated in the following sections.

4. THE RISKINESS OF INVESTMENTS IN THE BANK SECTOR AND IN INDIVIDUAL BANKS

A commonly accepted measure of risk, called 'systematic' or 'non-diversifiable' risk, is the so-called betacoefficient. This betacoefficient measures the degree of dependence (or covariation) between the variation of the returns on an individual security or portfolio and the returns of the overall market of risky assets.[13]

Betacoefficients as measures of the corresponding systematic risks have been estimated with respect to the bank sector as a whole and with respect to the individual banks over the period 1970–8. They are traditionally estimated using the so-called 'market model'.[14] In Table 5.3, these market model regression results are presented with respect to the bank sector as a whole. The results with respect to the individual banks are shown in Table 5.4.

On average, the betacoefficient of the bank sector appears to be approximately equal to 0.85, which is in line with previous results reported by L. Gheysens, B. Regidor and L. Vanthienen (1979a), and W. Van Grembergen.[15]

A marked increase in the riskiness of the bank sector is observed in the period 1973–5. On average, more than 60 per cent of the variations in the returns of the bank sector can be explained in terms of general market factors, which is a relatively high percentage.[16]

Looking at the betacoefficients of the individual banks, one observes a considerable dispersion. The Nationale Bank van België (NBB) has the lowest risk (beta = 0.557), while Crédit Général (CG) has the highest (beta = 1.176), considering the overall period. These results are not surprising: the NBB is in fact the Central Bank, being the lender of last resort for the other banks, and is backed by the government, while

TABLE 5.3   Estimation of the betacoefficients of the bank sector

Period	$\hat{\beta}_i$	$t(\hat{\beta}_i)$	R^2	D-W
1970–8	0.853	14.73	0.67	2.00
1970–2	0.703	8.18	0.66	2.58
1973–5	1.059	10.25	0.76	1.93
1976–8	0.693	6.84	0.58	2.05

TABLE 5.4   Estimation of the betacoefficients of individual banks[a]

Bank	$\hat{\beta}_i$	$t(\hat{\beta}_i)$	R^2	D-W	SE
Panel A: Period 1970–8					
GBM	0.799	9.44	0.46	2.20	2.43
KB	0.868	7.74	0.36	2.56	3.47
BBL	0.964	7.57	0.35	2.21	4.21
CG	1.176	6.69	0.30	1.75	5.30
BELG	0.922	7.33	0.34	2.14	3.94
NMKN	0.684	5.98	0.25	2.33	3.59
NBB	0.557	6.35	0.28	2.41	2.73
Panel B: Period 1970–2					
GBM	0.743	5.72	0.49	2.16	1.89
KB	0.782	5.62	0.48	2.09	2.35
BBL	0.547	2.69	0.18	2.25	3.14
CG	0.841	3.57	0.27	1.70	3.98
BELG	0.681	3.46	0.26	1.88	2.88
NMKN	0.771	3.91	0.31	2.60	2.65
NBB	0.559	2.58	0.16	2.72	3.25
Panel C: Period 1973–5					
GBM	0.719	5.33	0.46	2.06	2.70
KB	1.111	4.96	0.42	2.60	4.45
BBL	1.046	4.02	0.32	2.44	5.68
CG	1.785	5.17	0.44	1.84	6.30
BELG	1.148	5.13	0.44	1.96	4.78
NMKN	0.976	4.82	0.41	2.08	4.49
NBB	0.508	4.06	0.33	1.69	2.49
Panel D: Period 1976–8					
GBM	0.836	5.53	0.47	2.51	2.64
KB	0.584	3.02	0.21	2.70	3.38
BBL	1.113	6.16	0.53	1.52	3.16
CG	0.597	2.16	0.12	2.22	4.83
BELG	0.889	3.93	0.31	2.87	3.96
NMKN	0.305	1.93	0.09	2.02	3.26
NBB	0.639	4.60	0.38	2.74	2.43

In columns 1 to 5 are presented, respectively, the estimated betacoefficient, the t-ratio of the estimated betacoefficient, the coefficient of determination of the regression, the Durbin–Watson statistic and the standard error of the regression.

Crédit Général is a relatively small bank mainly operating in the French speaking part of Belgium.

Except for the Generale Bankmaatschappij and the Nationale Bank van België, betacoefficients of the individual banks appear to be unstable mainly showing a substantial increase in the second subperiod.

5. EVALUATING THE RISK-ADJUSTED RETURNS ON INDIVIDUAL BANKS

The returns on individual banks cannot reliably be compared without explicitly accounting for differences in risk. In fact, high rates of return

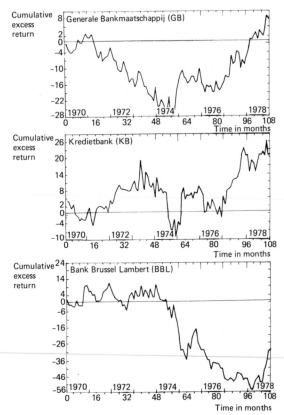

FIGURE 5.2   Cumulative excess returns for 'Generale Bankmaatschappij', 'Kredietbank' and 'Bank Brussel Lambert'

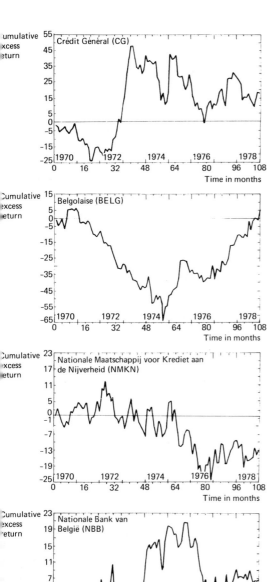

FIGURE 5.3 Cumulative excess returns for 'Crédit Général', 'Belgolaise', 'Nationale Maatschappij voor Krediet aan de Nijverheid' and 'Nationale Bank van België'

may simply reflect the high risk level of the corresponding bank, and vice versa.

One method to account for the appropriate risk level when evaluating the returns is to look at the 'excess return', being the difference between the total return and the return implied by the so-called 'Capital Asset Pricing Model'.[17] This model implies a rate of return given the systematic risk of the corresponding bank as measured by the betacoefficient.

Instead of just looking at these residuals or 'excess returns',[18] we prefer to look at the behaviour of the cumulative residuals (cumulative excess return). The evolution of these returns for each of the individual banks is illustrated in Figures 5.2 and 5.3.

From these graphs we conclude that the Generale Bankmaatschappij and Belgolaise show a rather poor performance throughout the 1970–8 period, except for the beginning and the end of the period. On the other hand, Kredietbank and Crédit Général perform well most of the time. The Bank Brussel Lambert's performance is deteriorating rapidly from October 1974 on, and it recovers just a little bit towards the end of 1978. The cumulative excess returns of the Nationale Bank van België have a distinct pattern, showing an abnormally good performance during 1974 and 1975, which were rather difficult years for the other banks. Only shareholders of Kredietbank and Crédit Général seem to have earned some 'abnormal' or 'excess' returns over the period 1970–8, amounting to an average of approximately 2 per cent per year over a period of nine years.

6. MARKET VALUATION VERSUS ACCOUNTING VALUATION

Some relevant accounting figures of the individual banks are presented in Tables 5.5, 5.6 and 5.7.

From the analysis of the ratio of the market value over the book value of equity, the following three conclusions can be drawn. On average, the market value of equity exceeds the book value of equity, especially so for Kredietbank and Crédit Général, being the most profitable banks in terms of the returns on their shares. The NMKN presents a notable exception, having a market value of equity far below its corresponding book value. For all banks there is a marked decrease in the market over book value ratio in the 1974–7 period, probably reflecting downward adjusted expectations of future earnings.

Let us now directly confront some of the market measures of
rofitability with some of the accounting measures of profitability. This
; illustrated in Table 5.5, while Table 5.6 illustrates some growth
neasures.

As for the ranking of the various profitability measures, there is a
lose correspondence between the two market measures of profitability.
However, the cumulative excess return measure makes a better and
nore pronounced distinction among the individual banks: no doubt
hat Kredietbank and Crédit Général are the most profitable banks, and
hat the Bank Brussel Lambert is the least profitable one.

There is a lack of a good correspondence between the market
neasures of profitability and the accounting measures; for example
Belgolaise ranks first based on the latter against only fifth according to
he former. For the Bank Brussel Lambert there is a better correspon-
ence in suggesting a relatively low profitability.

TABLE 5.5   A comparison of different profitability measures (percentage per
year)[a]

Bank	Average stock market return	Cumulative excess stock market return[b] 31 Dec. 1978	Average accounting return on equity	Average accounting interest margin[c]
GBM	7.51 (4)	7.43 (3)	11.46 (3)	3.59 (3)
BBL	3.20 (7)	−30.45 (7)	8.28 (6)	2.87 (5)
KB	8.97 (1)	20.96 (1)	14.32 (2)	3.79 (2)
CG	8.34 (2)	16.83 (2)	9.70 (5)	3.38 (4)
BELG	7.20 (5)	5.27 (5)	17.89 (1)	8.07 (1)
NBB	7.56 (3)	6.57 (4)	11.39 (4)	n.a.
NMKN	7.13 (6)	−13.29 (6)	7.99 (7)	n.a.

The ranking, in descending order of profitability, is given between brackets.
Derived from the 'market model' residuals. See above and Figures 5.2 and 5.3.
The interest margin is defined as the difference between the return on investments and the
average interest rate on debt. Cf. D. Wauters (1978) pp. 46–9.

TABLE 5.6   Some alternative growth measures (percentage per year)[a]

Bank	Total assets		Average rate of growth of			
			Net earnings		Equity (market value)	
GBM	15.84 (3.84)	3	6.51 (4.94)	4	5.10 (13.6)	3
BBL	15.74 (11.0)	4	7.39 (27.5)	3	−1.59 (21.64)	7
KB	17.67 (3.07)	2	14.06 (4.74)	2	10.31 (18.60)	2
CG	18.54 (11.78)	1	14.78 (10.59)	1	20.91 (44.81)	1
BELG	10.66 (12.77)	5	2.98 (10.78)	6	1.54 (18.12)	5
NBB	7.74 (6.37)	7	5.14 (2.25)	5	4.03 (7.74)	4
NMKN	7.81 (3.13)	6	−0.88 (13.00)	7	1.45 (11.34)	6

[a] Standard deviations are given between brackets. The ranking, in descending order of growth rates, is shown in the second column under each of the growth measures.

Interpreting the figures shown in Table 5.6, there is a relatively good correspondence between the two accounting measures of growth and the market measures of growth. Moreover, the very low ratio of the market value of equity over the book value of equity for the NMKN can be partially explained here: this bank has one of the lowest growth rates especially in terms of net profit. If this relatively low growth rate of net earnings has been extrapolated into the future, then the relatively low market value of equity can hardly be surprising. The most profitable banks, Kredietbank and Crédit Général, appear to be characterised by the highest growth rates.

Let us then finally have a look at the accounting measures of risk versus market measures of risk.[19] We first note that there is a rather good correspondence among the various market value-based estimates of risk, against a much less pronounced correspondence among the accounting value-based estimates, as shown in Table 5.7. The latter correspond best in the case of the Bank Brussel Lambert, and least in the case of the NMKN and the Nationale Bank van België.

The very high debt ratio (equity representing less than 5 per cent of

TABLE 5.7 A comparison of different risk measures[a]

Bank	Market value-based estimates				Accounting value-based estimates				
	$S(R)$	$BETA$	SE	$S(R)/\overline{R}$	$S(NP)$	$S(NP)/\overline{NP}$	$S(RE)$	$S(RE)/\overline{RE}$	$\overline{DR}$
GBM	42.7 (6)	0.799 (5)	29.16 (7)	5.69 (6)	0.214 (3)	0.161 (5)	0.707 (7)	0.062 (7)	0.972 (4)
BBL	58.6 (2)	0.964 (2)	50.52 (2)	18.31 (1)	0.253 (2)	0.410 (1)	3.576 (1)	0.431 (1)	0.976 (3)
KB	52.1 (4)	0.868 (4)	41.64 (5)	5.81 (5)	0.352 (1)	0.343 (2)	1.375 (4)	0.096 (5)	0.966 (5)
CG	77.8 (1)	1.176 (1)	63.6 (1)	9.33 (3)	0.018 (7)	0.323 (3)	1.062 (5)	0.109 (4)	0.961 (6)
BELG	57.3 (3)	0.922 (3)	47.28 (3)	7.96 (3)	0.021 (5)	0.143 (6)	3.412 (2)	0.191 (3)	0.937 (7)
NBB	38.2 (7)	0.557 (7)	32.76 (6)	5.05 (7)	0.073 (4)	0.125 (7)	0.894 (6)	0.078 (6)	0.984 (2)
NMKN	49.2 (5)	0.684 (6)	43.08 (4)	6.90 (4)	0.019 (6)	0.163 (4)	1.943 (3)	0.243 (2)	0.992 (1)

[a] The ranking in decreasing order of risk, is given between brackets. The following symbols are used:

$S(R)$	= standard deviation of return	$S(NP)$	= standard deviation of net profits
$BETA$	= betacoefficient	$\overline{NP}$	= average net profit
SE	= standard error of the market model regression	$S(RE)$	= standard deviation of return on equity
	as a measure of the diversifiable risk	$\overline{RE}$	= average return on equity
$\overline{R}$	= average rate of return	$\overline{DR}$	= average debt ratio

total assets) is of course typical of the bank sector. With the exception of the very high debt ratio of the NMKN in the last years and the relatively low debt ratio of Belgolaise, there are but small differences among the individual banks. In fact, the debt ratio of the individual banks is regulated by the Belgian Banking Commission, based on various subratios with respect to different categories of assets of the banks.

The debt ratio set apart, the association between accounting and market value-based estimates of risk appears to be relatively weak. The best correspondence is observed for the Nationale Bank van België and the Bank Brussell Lambert. On the other hand, the accounting measure of risk that best corresponds to the market measure of risk (the betacoefficient) appears to be the coefficient of variation of net earnings.[20]

7. CONCLUSIONS

The index of the bank sector follows rather closely the evolution of the overall stock market index. In fact, on average the betacoefficient of the bank sector is about 0.85, and approximately 60 per cent of the variations in its returns can be explained by general factors affecting the capital market as a whole.

Over the period of observation, the worst performance of the bank sector in market value terms is situated in the period 1973–5, characterised by particularly high inflation rates. The best performance has been observed in the period 1970–2, when inflation was lowest. There was a marked increase in the riskiness of the bank sector during the 1973–5 period.

The most profitable bank appears to be Kredietbank, closely followed by Crédit Général. The latter bank is significantly more risky though. Both banks are characterised by relatively high growth rates too. Shareholders of these banks appear to have earned some 'abnormal' returns in the order of approximately 2 per cent per year. The least profitable bank and, at the same time, one of the most risky banks appears to be the Bank Brussel Lambert.

On average, the market value of equity exceeds the book value of equity, and especially so for Kredietbank and Crédit Général. The NMKN presents a notable exception, having a market value far below its corresponding book value. For all banks there is a marked decrease in the market over book value ratio during the 1974–7 period.

There seems to be a weak correspondence between the market

measures of profitability and the accounting measures of profitability. On the other hand, there is a rather good correspondence among the various market estimates of risk, against a much more pronounced lack of correspondence among the accounting value-based estimates of risk. The association between accounting and market measures of risk appears to be relatively weak too. The accounting measure of risk that best corresponds to the market measure of risk is found to be the coefficient of variation of net earnings.

The seven individual institutions analysed in this paper constitute an important sample of the Belgian financial institutions. Further research, however, may be of interest in order to investigate various characteristics of a number of relatively smaller banks and savings institutions, the shares of which are less frequently traded or which are not quoted at the Brussels Stock Exchange.

NOTES

1. The author wishes to thank Professor H. Langhor and Professor L. Vanthienen for their helpful comments on an earlier draft of this paper.
2. The overall Belgian financial sector can be divided into banks, private savings institutions and public financial institutions. In 1978 there were eighty-five banks operating in Belgium. Only seven financial institutions have their shares regularly traded on the Brussels Stock Exchange (Corbeille): the Generale Bankmaatschappij (GBM), Kredietbank (KB), Bank Brussel Lambert (BBL), Crédit Général (CG), Belgolaise (BELG), the Nationale Maatschappij voor Krediet aan de Nijverheid (NMKN), and the Nationale Bank van België (NBB).

   It should be pointed out that Crédit Général is affiliated with the Kredietbank, and that Belgolaise is affiliated with the Generale Bankmaatschappij.
3. The market share of the seven institutions, in terms of their balance sheet total percentage of the overall balance sheet total of all financial institutions, amounts to approximately 50.
4. In this study, returns include capital gains (or losses) as well as dividend payments.
5. According to the contention that banks typically profit from inflation.
6. The indices are adjusted for dividend payments.
7. The interest rate refers to so-called 'niet-bankabel papier', that is, commercial paper accepted for rediscounting by the HWI, the 'Herdisconterings-en Waarborg Instituut' (Institut de Reescompte et de Garantie).
8. E. F. Fama and G. W. Schwert (1977), F. Holvoet (1978).
9. The vertical scale with respect to the interest rate variable is shown on the right side of Figure 5.1. The divergence between the HWI interest rate and the rate of inflation constitutes some counter evidence for the interest rate

being a good predictor of expected inflation, as shown by Van Eeckhoudt (1976) with respect to the Belgian case.

10. Some of these results do not hold as strictly when considering individual successive subperiods.

11. The corresponding coefficients of variation (standard deviation divided by the mean return) are 0.377 for the interest rate, 0.621 for the inflation rate, 5.613 for the bank sector returns, and 6.800 for the stock market returns considering the overall period of observations.

12. The coefficient of variation with respect to Credit General is 9.33 against 5.81 for Kredietbank.

13. The betacoefficient with respect to asset i is defined as:

$$\beta_i = \frac{COV\ (\tilde{R}_i, \tilde{R}_M)}{\sigma^2(\tilde{R}_M)}$$

with $\tilde{R}_i$ = return of asset i
$\tilde{R}_M$ = market return
$\sigma^2(\tilde{R}_M)$ = variance of the market return
Cf. E. F. Fama (1976) pp. 58–62.

14. This 'market model' can be expressed as:

$$\tilde{R}_{i,t} = \alpha_i + \beta_i \cdot R_{M,t} + \tilde{\varepsilon}_{i,t}$$

Cf. E. F. Fama (1976) pp. 63–98.

15. The market capitalisation of the bank sector, in fact of the seven individual institutions, in percentage of the total stock market capitalisation, was approximately equal to 10 per cent in 1975. See also L. Gheysens, B. Regidor and L. Vanthienen (1979a) and W. van Grembergen (1979).

16. Cf. L. Gheysens, B. Regidor and L. Vanthienen (1979b).

17. The Capital Asset Pricing Model (CAPM) implies that the expected rate of return on security i is a linear function of the systematic risk of security i:

$$E(\tilde{R}_i) = R_F + (E(\tilde{R}_M) - R_F) \cdot \beta_i$$

with R_F = risk-free rate
$E(\tilde{R}_M)$ = expected rate of return of risky assets
β_i = systematic risk of security i

18. The 'excess return' can be defined as:

$$e_{i,t} = R_{i,t} - (R_{M,t} \cdot \hat{\beta}_i + (1 - \hat{\beta}_i) \cdot R_{F,t})$$

with $R_{i,t}$ = observed rate of return on security i in period t
$R_{M,t}$ = observed rate of return on the market in period t
$R_{F,t}$ = observed risk-free rate in period t
$\hat{\beta}_i$ = estimated systematic risk of security i

Suppose that the estimated betacoefficient is equal to 0.8, that the market return is equal to 1 per cent per month, that the risk-free is equal to 0.5

per cent, and the rate of return on security i is equal to 1.2 per cent, then the excess return with respect to that period (month) becomes:

$$e_{i,t} = 1.2 - (1.0 \times 0.8 + (1.0 - 0.8)0.5) = 1.2 - (0.8 - 0.1) = 0.5 \text{ per cent}$$

9. This relationship is extensively discussed and documented in D. J. Thompson (1976), R. G. Bowman (1979), and W. van Grembergen (1979).

0. In a study by W. Beaver, P. Kettler and M. Scholes (1970), earnings variability was also the most significant variable in explaining the market betacoefficient.

REFERENCES

Beaver, W., P. Kettler and M. Scholes (1970) 'The Association Between Market Determined and Accounting Determined Risk Measures', *Accounting Review* (October) pp. 654–82.

Bowman, R. G. (1979) 'The Theoretical Relationship Between Systematic Risk and Financial (Accounting) Variables', *The Journal of Finance* (June) pp. 617–30.

Fama, E. F. (1976) *Foundations of Finance* (New York: Basic Books).

Fama, E. F. and G. W. Schwert (1977) 'Asset Returns and Inflation', *Journal of Financial Economics*, vol. 5, pp. 115–46.

Gheysens, L., B. Regidor and L. Vanthienen (1979a) 'Cost of Equity Capital of 185 Belgian Companies', *Tijdschrift voor Economie en Management*, no. 1, pp. 55–86.

Gheysens, L., B. Regidor and L. Vanthienen (1979b) 'Cost of Equity Estimation of Companies in Belgium, France, Germany, The Netherlands, Spain, Sweden and the UK: Some Empirical Results', *Tijdschrift voor Economie en Management*, no. 1, pp. 87–106.

Holvoet, F. (1978) *Inflation and Stock Returns, A Critical Look at the Belgian Stock Market in the Period* 1964–1977 (Leuven: Katholieke Universiteit, unpublished MBA thesis).

Thompson, D. J. (1976) 'Sources of Systematic Risk in Common Stocks', *Journal of Business* (April) pp. 173–88.

Van Eeckhoudt, M. (1976) *Inflatie en rentevoeten* (Leuven: Katholieke Universiteit, unpublished paper).

Van Grembergen, W. (1979) 'De raming van het systematische risico van Belgische ondernemingen' (Antwerp: UFSIA, working paper).

Wauters, D. (1978) *Studie van de winst-en verliesrekening van de Belgische Banken:* 1970–77 (Leuven, unpublished thesis).

Comment on Gheysens

HERWIG LANGOHR

The contribution of the Gheysens chapter consists in making a systematic exploration of the risk-adjusted investment performance from investing and holding shares of seven financial institutions actively trading on the Brussels Stock Exchange, and this for the period 1970 through 1978. Moreover, a description is given of several measures of accounting return and risk, and these measures are compared with market value measures. The author concludes that substantial excess returns were generated by five of the seven institutions involved (Table 5.5.), yet that the examined returns provided less of a hedge against inflation than would have been provided from a fully diversified portfolio in the stock market. Finally, little association is found between accounting and investors' measures of return and risk.

The issues addressed in the chapter are important ones. Do Belgian banks indeed earn quasi-rents and oligopoly profits? This is often being conjectured to be the case on the basis that Belgian banks profit from domestic regulatory protection (barriers to entry, officially sanctioned cartel agreements and condoned restrictive practices), subsidised refinancing opportunities at the central bank and loan demand, high concentration not demonstrated to be justified by economies of scale inhibition from effective domestic competition by the occasional freezing of market shares through quantitative controls, privileged position in the government securities market. Yet, little evidence exists to substantiate these statements from systematically analysing the Belgian banking industry return profile.

The author should be commended for the task he undertook in shedding more light on the profitability pattern of seven Belgian banks by using all available market information, but the reported findings about banking sector market risk reward relationships are less than convincing for reaching the affirmative conclusions on excess return put forward in the chapter. Our comments will further be focused on this

nore substantive part of the chapter, the author's evidence about bank
hares as inflation hedges and the relationship between accounting and
narket measures being highly impressionistic.

Two problems in method limit the validity of the chapter's main
conclusion. To the extent that the Brussels exchange is informationally
efficient (Fama sense), banking sector quasi-rents would have to
continuously, yet unexpectedly, increase to be manifested consistently in
stock market returns. On top of the unlikelihood that such a quasi-rent
generating process exists, its existence may not show up in stock market
returns if the quasi-rent is distributed among banking industry pro-
ducers and consumers in any form of economic income. Briefly, the
implications of stock market efficiency make the kind of market information typically used in application of the theory of finance a power-
ess test to discriminate between presence or absence of economic rents.

The method followed to assess the mere existence, magnitude and
significance of excess investor returns from investing and holding shares
in any of the seven institutions analysed is not convincing. Gheysens
correctly points out that the returns on individual bank shares (or for a
banking sector portfolio) cannot be evaluated without explicitly accounting for risk. He defines 'excess return' as the difference between
total return and the return implied by the "Capital Asset Pricing Model
(CAPM)" '. But how can this difference be estimated and its statistical
significance assessed?

Gheysens estimates it by the sum over t of the estimated residual
random error terms $\hat{e}_{it}$ of each i, obtained from the regression procedure
(same notation as Gheysens):

$$\tilde{R}_{it} - R_{Ft} = \beta_i (\tilde{R}_{Mt} - R_{Ft}) + \tilde{e}_{it} \qquad (1)$$

Unfortunately, he offers no statistical test about the null hypothesis that
$E(\tilde{e}_{it}) = 0$. Merely observing that the estimate of the mean, $\bar{\tilde{e}}$, is
different from zero says nothing about the statistical significance of this
result. Moreover, the statistical validity of this regression procedure rests
upon the assumption that this null hypothesis is, in fact, true. In
summary, either the null hypothesis is accepted, in which case no
systematic excess returns exist and valid inferences can be made from the
betacoefficients, as Gheysens did in various parts of the paper; or the null
hypothesis is rejected, in which case the coefficient and standard error
estimates reported in Table 5.4 are biased and the meaning of Gheysens'
'excess' returns is blurred. But, both propositions cannot simultaneously
hold.

Furthermore, as demonstrated by M. Jensen,[1] the economic meaning of the betacoefficients, estimated according to this procedure – as CAPM systematic risk factors – rests upon the empirical validity of the CAPM hypothesis, cast itself in expectational terms. What is the independent empirical evidence corroborating for the Brussels Stock Exchange the expectational CAPM hypothesis?

To test the hypothesis that a security yields investor returns significantly higher than the risk premium defined by the left-hand side of (1), several procedures have been proposed in the performance of mutual funds literature.[2] M. Jensen suggests to test the null hypothesis that α_i is zero:

$$\tilde{R}_{it} - R_{Ft} = \alpha_i + \beta_i[\tilde{R}_{Mt} - R_{Ft}] + \tilde{u}_{it} \qquad (2)$$

with $\tilde{u}_{it}$ having $E(\tilde{u}_{it}) = 0$ and being serially independent.[3]

We performed this test on the nine annual observations reported in Tables 5.1 and 5.2 with the result that none of the $\hat{\alpha}_i$, ranging from − 2.662 for BBL to 2.883 for the KB, are statistically significant at the 5 per cent level. Admittedly this evidence is not definitive because of the small number of observations. Yet, it appears to this commentator to be powerful enough to cast doubt about the significance of the 'excess returns' reported in Gheysens' paper, the more so in the light of our previous observations. To conclude, Gheysens made a noteworthy contribution to stimulate further research.

NOTES

1. M. Jensen (1968) p. 393.
2. M. Jensen (1968) p. 393; M. Jensen (1969) p. 205; I. Friend and M. Blume (1970) p. 562; E. F. Fama (1976) p. 380.
3. M. Jensen (1968, 1969).

REFERENCES

Fama, E. F. (1976) *Foundations of Finance* (New York: Basic Books).
Friend, I. and M. Blume (1970) 'Measurement of Portfolio Performance under Uncertainty', *The American Economic Review* (September) pp. 561–75.
Jensen, M. (1968) 'The Performance of Mutual Funds in the Period 1954–64', *Journal of Finance* (May) pp. 389–416.
Jensen, M. (1969) 'Risk, the Pricing of Capital Assets, and the Evaluation of Investment Portfolios', *Journal of Business* (April) pp. 167–247.

6. Bank Intermediation under Flexible Deposit Rates and Controlled Credit Allocation: the Italian Experience

MARIO MONTI and ANGELO PORTA

1. INTRODUCTION

The most striking feature of the Italian financial structure, compared to those of other industrial countries, is an extremely high and rising degree of liquidity. In the last two decades, and particularly in the 1970s, the process of capital formation has been associated with a very pronounced monetisation, money balances being by far the asset most largely accumulated by ultimate wealth-owners. This trend has been made possible, and to some extent stimulated, by a marked expansion of the intermediation performed by the commercial banking system.

Italy provides, therefore, an interesting case to students of financial markets and the development of financial structures. The peculiarity of the Italian case is increased by a regulation of the banking industry which, unlike in other countries, allows banks complete flexibility in setting interest rates on their deposits (including demand deposits) and, on the other hand, imposes strict controls on bank credit allocation.

At a time when there is a widespread trend in several countries towards deregulation of existing ceilings on deposit rates as well as some demand for the introduction of selective credit controls, it may be of interest to investigate the behaviour of a banking system actually operating under these conditions.

We first present data showing the level and growth of bank

intermediation and liquidity in the Italian economy (section 2). A picture emerges which has led Italian economists and public opinion recently to believe that the degree of liquidity and the scale of bank intermediation are not only very large, but also overoptimal and conducive to inefficiencies. An adequate analysis of the phenomenon however, is not yet available, perhaps also because the above-mentioned and other institutional peculiarities of the Italian system prevent a meaningful application of analytical schemes developed elsewhere.

As a contribution towards this analysis, we propose to identify the determinants of the growth of bank intermediation (section 3) with special emphasis on the role of the regulatory system (section 4). We will then discuss the main effects of the large scale of bank intermediation on the efficiency of the financial structure (section 5). Some criteria will be derived for a policy towards bank intermediation (section 6). A few concluding remarks will follow (section 7).

2. BANK INTERMEDIATION AND LIQUIDITY IN THE ITALIAN ECONOMY

In this section are reported a few data which may help the reader in appraising how high is the degree of liquidity of financial assets in Italy, and how important is the role of the banking system in the Italian financial structure.[1]

In Figure 6.1 is shown the trend of the share of liquid assets in total financial assets held by the economy. It may be noted that this ratio is quite high and has considerably increased from 1963 to 1978: at the end of 1963 the economy held about one-half of its total financial assets in liquid form; at the end of 1978 the share had almost reached 80 per cent. Out of the increase of the financial assets in the period considered, 85 per cent took the form of liquid assets.

Figure 6.1 shows also the high share of bank deposits in total financial assets. It may be observed that this share has substantially increased over the period considered: the ratio between bank deposits and total financial assets has gone from 34.5 per cent at the end of 1963 to about 61.4 per cent at the end of 1978, with 66.4 per cent of the increase in total financial assets being placed into deposits.

The data considered above give a first impression of the high importance which the banking system has assumed inside the Italian financial structure. The counterpart of the rise of the share of bank deposits in total financial assets consists obviously in an increasing

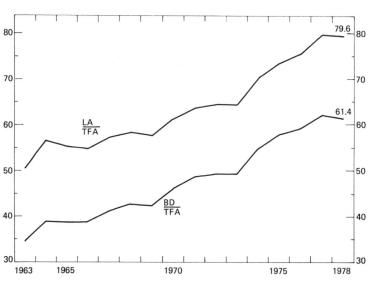

IGURE 6.1   Share of liquid assets and bank deposits in total financial assets in
Italy: 1963–78 (percentage) [a]

Symbols used:

FA: Total financial assets = total value of domestic financial assets held by
       the economy (household and business sectors), including shares.
A: Liquid assets = banknotes + bank and Post Office deposits + treasury
       bills held by the economy.
D: Bank deposits = demand and time deposits of the economy with the
       banking system.

OURCE   Banca d'Italia.

eight of the credit granted – in direct or indirect ways – by the banking
ystem over total domestic credit. In 1977, for example, 91 per cent of the
ow of total domestic credit extended by the credit system as a whole
banks *plus* special credit institutions) was financed by the flow of *bank*
eposits (82 per cent in the late 1960s).

   Another indicator of the high level of liquidity of the Italian economy
 the money stock/gross domestic product ratio (M2/GDP), the trend of
hich is shown in Figure 6.2 for Italy and six other industrial countries.
he data plotted are annual: they are not suitable for the analysis of

short-run fluctuations in monetary policies, but allow us to make som[e] considerations of a structural character.

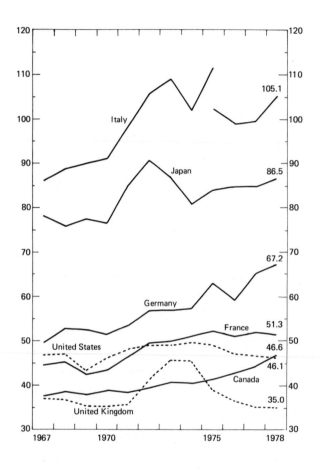

FIGURE 6.2   Money stock/GDP ratio in Italy and six other industria[l] countries: 1967–78 (percentage) [a]

[a] The gap at the end of 1975 for Italy is due to the adoption for the gros[s] domestic product as from 1975 on the new national accounting data. The ne[w] accounting procedure, which included in the calculation of GDP items whic[h] were not considered before, has implied an upward revision of the value o[f] gross domestic product and has therefore caused a decrease in the value of th[e] money stock/GDP ratio.

SOURCE   *International Financial Statistics* and National Bulletins.

It may be noted that, over the whole period considered, the M2/GDP ratio is much higher in Italy than in the other countries considered: its value at the end of 1978 was 1.05, a figure well above that assumed by the ratio for Japan (0.87) and nearly double the average value of the ratio for the other countries (0.55).

Figure 6.2 shows also that the M2/GDP ratio has in Italy a very strong upward trend (its value has increased from the end of 1967 to the end of 1978 by more than 30 percentage points).

The ratio exhibits a similar tendency only for Germany, where its level remains, however, much lower than in Italy. The ratio has also been rising, but comparatively to a much more limited extent, in Japan, France and Canada. It exhibits stability in the United States and in the United Kingdom.

In evaluating the degree of liquidity of the Italian financial structure it must finally be noted that, because of some peculiar characteristics of bank deposits which will be discussed in section 3.3 below, these are more liquid in Italy than in other countries. The higher liquidity of the Italian financial structure depends not only on the high value assumed by the ratios considered above, but also on the fact that the 'liquid assets' considered in these ratios are in fact more liquid in Italy than in other economies.

3. DETERMINANTS OF THE SCALE OF BANK INTERMEDIATION

The large and growing scale of bank intermediation observed in Italy, and the associated high and increasing degree of liquidity, can be explained in terms of several factors. Some of them are shared by most countries, while others may be regarded as peculiar to the Italian case, for their nature or the extent to which they operate.

For the purpose of exposition, these factors – although interrelated – can be classified into four categories concerning, respectively, (i) the supply of funds to banks; (ii) the demand for funds from banks; (iii) the behaviour of banks; (iv) the behaviour of public policy. In this section we will concentrate on the first three factors; we will deal more extensively with the fourth in the next section.

3.1 The supply of funds to banks

The Italian banking system faces a particularly large supply of funds both because (i) the savings-investment process is mostly dependent on external financing, as opposed to self-financing within economic units and (ii) the main share of such external financing is channelled throug banks. In other words, the financial 'superstructure' is peculiarly large i relation to the underlying economy's real 'structure', and the bankin system is the dominant component of it.

(i) The former phenomenon is due mainly to a particular distributio of savings formation among the sectors of the economy, which causes deep sectoral dissociation between savings and investment, and thu sectoral financial surpluses and deficits, of a magnitude unparalleled i other industrial countries. In recent years, households went as far a saving an amount *greater* than the nation's total net saving (141.3 pe cent of the latter on average in the period 1971–5), while the publi sector and the firms have actually been net dissavers (to the extent o 33.9 and 7.4 per cent respectively of net national saving). Among th determinants of this uncommon pattern have been a massive redistri bution of income from the business sector to labour, a decline in profi margins due to that redistribution and other factors, the fact that publi sector's revenues, although rapidly increasing, were unable to cove even the current part of public expenditures.

Associated with this peculiar distribution of savings formation (o destruction) among sectors is a more standard distribution o investment, where firms and the public sector account for most o national investment, also due to the relative decline of households investments in houses, partly caused by a discouraging rent-contro system. As a result, the dissociation between savings and investmen among sectors appears in Italy very high and more pronounced than i other countries, reflecting itself in a predominance of external financing

As shown by Table 6.1, at the end of 1977 the household sector' financial surplus (excess of savings over investment in real assets) was i Italy 16.6 per cent of GDP, while the financial deficits of firms and of th public sector were 6.0 and 9.7 per cent of GDP respectively. Both th household sector's surplus and the firms' and the public sector's defici stand up as particularly large in international comparisons. The forme is nearly three times as large, in per cent of GDP, as the average of group of other industrial countries, while the firms' deficit is almos twice as large and the public sector's deficit is about three times as larg (Table 6.1).

(ii) Not only is the flow of funds thus generated particularly large, bu most of it is channelled through the banking system, while relatively fe funds flow from surplus to deficit units directly in financial markets o are intermediated by non-bank financial institutions. From the point o

TABLE 6.1   Financial surpluses or deficits in Italy and six other industrial
             countries in 1977 *(percentage of GDP)*

Country	Households	Firms	Public sector	Foreign sector
Italy	+ 16.6	− 6.0	− 9.7	− 1.2
Average of countries indicated below	+ 6.3	− 3.7	− 3.2	+ 0.2
Canada	+ 3.5	− 4.9	− 2.0	+ 3.1
France	+ 5.8	− 5.5	− 1.2	+ 0.6
Germany	+ 7.1	− 4.6	− 2.6	− 0.6
Japan	+ 11.1	− 2.2	− 7.4	− 1.6
United Kingdom	+ 6.5	− 1.7	− 3.5	− 1.7
United States	+ 3.6	− 3.2	− 2.5	+ 1.2

SOURCE   OECD, *Financial Statistics* (1978).

view of the *supply* of funds, which concerns us directly here, the
predominant role of banks in attracting funds can briefly be explained as
follows.

Some of the causes pointed out above, which are responsible for the
peculiar sectoral pattern of savings and net financial positions, have also
determined a marked and increasing divergence of preferences between
surplus and deficit units, as to the liquidity and risk of the financial
instruments they respectively demand and supply.

In particular, the average propensity to liquidity and risk aversion of
the suppliers of funds have both substantially risen as funds have been
increasingly supplied by *households*, out of savings generated from
labour incomes and, to a growing extent, by low- and middle-income
classes. The unwillingness or inability to provide financial instruments
granting some protection from inflation – for example, private or public
indexed bonds – has also contributed to enhance savers' preferences for
liquid assets, in a country which since 1973 has been experiencing higher
than average inflation rates. Only a small portion of such demand for
low-risk liquid assets can be directly met by firms, the public sector or
non-bank financial intermediaries.

Firms – besides being hampered in their direct financing by the
institutional difficulties that will be mentioned in section 3.2 – are
characterised, as in other countries, by an increasing illiquidity in the
structure of assets (due mainly to the rising weight of fixed capital) and,
even more than in most other countries, by rigidity in factor

combinations. The latter is caused mainly by a set of regulations and pressures by trade unions and government authorities, aiming at preserving the existing level of employment, not only in the aggregate but also in specific firms and plants. Among other effects, this situation – which cripples large corporations mostly – increases the degree of risk of the financial instruments issued directly by firms and especially by the larger ones, that otherwise might be the only ones with an image notorious enough to attract direct financing by households.

The *public sector* and, particularly, the state, which can be considered safe as far as financial risk is concerned, have traditionally had postal deposits (accruing to the Central Post Office Savings Fund) as their principal form of short-term liability available to the public; but interest rates have been adjusted slowly to market trends and have usually been not competitive with rates paid on bank deposits. Only recently have the authorities issued bills of maturity shorter than one year (three and six months), modified the issuing methods of treasury bills and taken steps for a wider access of the public to the bills' primary and secondary markets.

As to *non-bank financial intermediaries*, they consist mainly of special credit institutions. As will be explained in greater detail below, these institutions may not issue short-term liabilities to the public. On the other hand, legal and institutional rigidities, coupled with a lack of aggressive trends to financial innovation, have prevented a large-scale insurgence of new types of intermediaries willing and able to provide the public with reasonably liquid and safe assets.

The joint operation of the circumstances mentioned above explains why Italian banks – virtually the only units able and willing to accommodate households' high propensity to low-risk and high-liquidity assets – have been facing a large and rapidly growing supply of funds from the household sector. Bank liabilities (mainly deposits), which represented 27 per cent of the sector's total financial assets at the end of 1963, went up to 54.6 per cent at the end of 1978. Measured on the increase of financial assets in 1976–8, the flow of funds supplied to the banks amounted to 60.2 per cent of the total (Table 6.2). For comparison, only 20.6 per cent of the same total went directly to the public sector (and yet this is by far a peak in the time series) and no more than 1.3 per cent reached the firms' sector directly!

We have tried so far to isolate the factors behind the large supply of funds to the banking system. It will be clear, however, that some of these factors depend, directly or indirectly, on the behaviour of public policy. It will also be clear that a crucial influence is exerted by the response of

TABLE 6.2 Households' financial assets by borrowing sector in Italy, 1963–78
(percentage of households' total financial assets)

		Claims on financial intermediaries					Claims on other sectors				
	Currency[a]	Banks	Special credit institutions	Insurance companies	Central Post Office Savings Fund	Total	Public sector	Firms	Foreign sector	Total	Total
Stocks at											
End 1963	9.0	27.0	8.5	2.8	9.2	56.5	9.3	28.7	5.5	43.5	100.0
End 1977	7.3	55.3	7.2	2.9	9.2	81.9	10.2	3.1	4.8	18.1	100.0
End 1978	7.1	54.6	6.2	2.8	9.4	80.1	13.2	2.7	3.9	19.8	100.0
Average flows in											
1964–65	8.5	39.4	11.2	4.6	10.9	74.6	9.6	4.1	11.7	25.4	100.0
1966–70	7.0	41.7	13.0	3.3	5.0	70.0	10.2	4.2	15.6	30.0	100.0
1971–75	7.2	59.7	8.3	2.9	9.2	87.3	5.4	2.9	4.4	12.7	100.0
1976–78	5.9	60.2	0.4	2.4	9.3	78.2	20.6	1.3	-0.1	21.8	100.0

[a] Currency consists of banknote and coin issues by the Banca d'Italia and the Treasury.
SOURCE   F. Cotula and P. de'Stefani (1979); our updating for 1978.

the banks themselves to exogenous factors, particularly as it concerns interest rates offered and other respects of policies pursued by banks to sell to the public their own deposits rather than alternative instruments for which they act as distributors. This subject, one where other peculiarities of the Italian case emerge, will be considered in section 3.3 below.

3.2 The demand for funds from banks

Several structural features identified above to explain the huge supply of funds to banks are also the cause of the high demand for funds faced by banks. As the latter is largely the mirror image of the former, it will not be necessary to add many remarks here.

Given the fact that households – the only surplus sector – place nearly two-thirds of the flow of their financial assets with the banking system, the public sector and firms have to rely heavily on the latter to finance their deficits. The ability of these sectors and, especially, firms to attract households' funds directly is impaired not only by the factors – set forth above – which have often prevented them from supplying liquid and low-risk liabilities, but also by factors that make it difficult to raise substantial funds in the stock and bond markets. Among these are the backward state of corporate laws, the insufficient amount and reliability of information made available by firms, the inadequate organisation of and supervision on the stock exchanges, and a tax treatment of financial instruments penalising direct issues of bonds and shares by firms, while ample subsidies are provided by the state and local authorities on loans that firms obtain from financial intermediaries.

These obstacles have been associated with, and to some extent have aggravated, a decline in firms' profitability over the 1970s of even greater proportions than has been generally observed in industrial countries. It is true that a decline in the profit rate is an impediment to providing adequate rates of return on financial instruments issued by firms, irrespective of whether they are purchased by households or by financial intermediaries. As such, therefore, it cannot explain a greater dependence of firms upon bank credit. It could explain it, however, if one assumed that the intervention of one (or more) stage(s) of intermediation, coupled with a particular behaviour of public policy towards the intermediaries, permitted an extensive loosening of the correspondence between the rate of return on investments and the rate of interest paid on households' savings. A similar explanation would also apply to the financing through bank intermediation of that part of he public sector's deficit which is generated by net public dissaving, rather than public expenditure on investments. On these aspects, we will dwell below.

The increasing requirements of firms for medium- and long-term finance, on the other hand, might be thought to limit the development of their demand for funds from the banks, given that the lending activity of the latter is mainly confined by law to the short term. However, since the special credit institutions are not allowed to gather short-term funds from the public, which is thus led by its strong liquidity preference to place most funds with the banks, these end up nevertheless by covering a large part of firms' requirements through an implicit or explicit maturity transformation. Implicitly, to the extent that banks continuously renew their nominally short-term credit extensions to firms. Explicitly, to the extent that banks purchase bonds issued by special credit institutions or finance them in other ways.

3.3 The behaviour of banks

The conditions identified above – concerning the supply of funds to banks and the demand for funds from banks – would stimulate the growth of bank intermediation under any given pattern of bank behaviour. Their stimulus, however, is magnified by the response of banks. These make full use of the ability to attract deposits through the offer of aggressive interest rates, and usually persuasively advise the public to prefer deposits over non-bank instruments, though distributed by banks themselves.

It is sufficient to note in this context that, throughout the 1970s, the average rates paid on demand and time deposits have not been much lower than the bond rate. The rate paid on large demand deposits has usually exceeded the bond rate, on two occasions (at the end of 1974 and the end of 1976) has reached 18 per cent and has frequently been almost as high as the prime rate on loans.

In the period 1972–8, the rate of interest on demand deposits, constrained by regulation to be zero in many countries, has on average been 8.2 per cent (12.1 per cent for large depositors).

Besides giving a high rate of return, bank deposits are characterised in Italy by a very high liquidity and a low risk.

As far as liquidity is concerned, it may be noticed that not only demand deposits, but virtually all bank deposits, can be considered as liquid assets. Unlike their counterparts in other countries, Italian banks are in fact not strict in requiring compliance with the maturity terms of time deposits or in applying penalties in case of withdrawals without advance notice. In fact, it can be said that Italian banks engage very actively in liability management. But they do so much more in the sense of expanding the size of their deposits than in seeking an appropriate composition of liabilities, as between capital and deposits, and an appropriate maturity structure of deposits. They do not seem to be too uneasy, in spite of a capital deposits ratio very low on international comparisons and an acute maturity disequilibrium between an increasingly illiquid asset structure and a liability structure concentrated on deposits of virtually perfect liquidity.[2] The reasons are probably to be found in the risk-reducing interventions of public policy and in the fact that the very liquidity of deposits co-operates in making them the dominant asset and thus makes a 'run' on deposits a rather unlikely event, at least under normal conditions.

Turning to risk, it may be noticed that bank deposits – though not protected by any explicit insurance scheme – have a very low *insolvency* risk, given the network of controls designed to achieve a high stability of the banking industry, as will be discussed in the next section. What is most relevant, depositors seem to behave as if there were a deposit insurance: either because they are simpleminded enough to deem bank insolvency an impossible occurrence, or because they are subtle enough to expect that public policy would intervene in one way or the other so as to protect depositors should an insolvency materialise. Turning to risks associated with *fluctuations in market interest rates*, not only demand deposits are free from them but also time deposits, whose interest rates can be renegotiated frequently as a consequence of bank tolerance mentioned above. By contrast, this form of risk fully hits fixed interest securities, whose market prices obviously reflect interest rate fluctuations (which over the 1970s have been even wider in Italy than in many other countries).

It can be concluded that the actual behaviour of banks, within the area allowed them by regulation, makes bank deposits a rather special financial 'product'. They are characterised not only by high *liquidity* and low *risk*, but also by a *return* which is either not much smaller or even greater than the return available on other financial or real assets, that are much less liquid and more risky. It is not surprising, therefore, if deposits 'dominate' – in the precise sense of portfolio theory – the spectrum of assets.

Given the circumstances under which the banks operate, the response now described is a rational one, from the microeconomic point of view, if their objective is – short-run or long-run – profit maximisation or

ome variant of it to take account of risks. It may be argued, however,
hat many Italian banks operate as if they were managed with an
objective of deposit maximisation under a profit constraint.[3]

This behaviour leads them to offer higher interest rates in order to
attract an extra amount of deposits, such that their marginal cost
exceeds the net marginal revenue from their use. A part of profits
otherwise obtainable is 'traded off' for a higher deposit volume.

The factors inducing banks to place more emphasis on deposit growth
than would be justified by profit maximisation may be summarised as
follows.

Some factors, put forth long ago by the theory of the managerial
firm,[4] apply particularly well to Italian banks, though certainly not to
them only. Management control is a frequent phenomenon, particularly
at large banks. Markets for bank assets and liabilities are often of
oligopolistic forms. The ratio of equity capital to total liabilities is
particularly low, a feature that makes financing of banking firms largely
independent of the market valuation of their profitability.

In addition, many large banks are owned by the state or local
governments. Their performance is likely to be gauged more in terms of
the expansion of credit and deposits achieved, leading – as is often
believed – to the growth of income and employment in the area of
operation, than in terms of profits. Such evaluation criteria are likely to
be used, in particular, by political authorities who appoint, and may
reconfirm, the top managers of public banks, who will therefore not
neglect these criteria in their activity. Also, the statutes of some public or
semi-public banks explicitly state that social objectives, which can better
be achieved with a growing scale, must prevail over profit
considerations. More generally, for a long period, Italian public opinion
has considered profits, and bank profits in particular, as socially
harmful.[5]

A proportion of the banks – mainly of medium or small size – are
privately owned and operated. These banks give more emphasis to
profit, to be sure. But here, too, there is some scope for deposit growth in
excess of the profit-maximising one, given the limited role played by the
market valuation by shareholders – very few banks are listed on the
stock exchanges – and the fact that the controlling interests often seem
to attach more weight to deposit size than to mere profitability, as
revealed on the occasion of several acquisitions.[6]

It will be clear, in conclusion, that a wide variety of factors co-operate
in making Italian banks particularly able and willing to expand their
deposits and thus to accommodate, and even further stimulate, the

demand for a fast-growing bank intermediation which has been shown
to be built into the Italian economy.[7]

4. A RECONSIDERATION OF THE REGULATORY SYSTEM AS A DETERMINANT OF BANKING EXPANSION

Some aspects of public policy have already been identified in the
previous section as determinants of the large scale of bank intermediation in Italy, through their influence on the supply of funds to banks or
on the demand for funds from banks.[8] It seems appropriate to consider
now more extensively the influence exerted by that part of public policy
which is particularly concerned with the *regulation of financial
institutions*.

The banking law which is now ruling in Italy has been in force since
1936. Unlike banking laws of many other industrial countries, which
have been extensively revised in recent years, the Italian law has
remained unchanged. One of the reasons which allowed Italian
authorities to avoid undertaking the reform of the law must be found in
the flexibility of the law itself, which in many important matters leaves to
the monetary authorities wide discretionary powers.

Especially in the 1970s, the authorities made on many occasions
ample resort to the use of these powers and, as a result, a considerable
evolution of the financial system's regulation has taken place without
any change in the banking law.

In order to assess the influence of regulation on the development of
bank intermediation we will first make a few remarks on the 'basic
philosophy' of the 1936 banking law and then discuss in some detail
the evolution of the system of controls on financial institutions which
has taken place in the last decade.

4.1 The banking law of 1936

It is impossible to give here an exhaustive account of the complex
structure of the Italian banking law.[9] We will therefore limit ourselves to
some remarks on its most important features.

It must first of all be pointed out that the law of 1936 was concerned
mostly with *stability* of the financial system, as in other countries at the
time. However, some important features which play an important role in
other regulatory settings are absent in Italy. First, as it has been recalled
above, payment of interest on demand deposits is not prohibited and

ιere are no legal ceilings on interest rates on time deposits. In the
:cond place, schemes of deposit insurance are completely absent in the
alian banking law. It must also be noted that the law – although it
οntains some incentives for banks to keep their capital at adequate
:vel – does not establish, in the form of a strict capital/deposits ratio or
ι other similar ways, the minimum amount of capital which banks are
:quired to have.

Two aspects of the Italian regulatory setting are particularly designed
ο ensure stability: strict *controls on entry* (and on the establishment of
εw branches) and the principle of *specialisation*, preventing banks from
οlding company shares and medium- and long-term loans, which are to
ε granted only by special credit institutions.[10]

In the principle of specialisation may be found, in our view, the 'basic
hilosophy' of the Italian banking law. For this reason, some remarks
n it seem in order.

According to this principle, the stability of the institutions operating
ι short term, issuing liabilities with a very high degree of liquidity, is
ssured by placing limits on the maturity of the loans they can grant.
hould these limits not exist, banks would tend to supply credit also on
οnger maturities: the asset side of the balance sheet would then become
ιuch less liquid than their liability side.

It is worth noting that the principle of specialisation protects
lepositors by controlling *directly* the asset side of the banks' balance
heets and may be considered a system of depositors' protection
ιlternative to the system, used in many countries, which is based on
ιrohibition of interest payments on demand deposits and regulation of
nterest rates on time deposits. The latter system influences only
ndirectly the assets side of banks' balance sheets: deposit rate controls
.re designed to avoid excess competition among banks which could
ιring them to extend credits with high level of riskiness.

Medium- and long-term credit, according to the principle, may be
;ranted only by special credit institutions, which collect funds not by
ssuing short-term deposits but with other instruments (medium- and
οng-term deposits and bonds).

It is worth noting that the principle of specialisation in the 1936
ιanking law is not supplemented by controls directed to channel funds
ο the two different kinds of institutions. Controls of this sort, as we shall
ιote, were introduced only subsequently, using the wide discretionary
ιowers granted by the banking law.

4.2 Bank regulation in the 1970s

The evolution of the Italian financial structure has taken place along lines quite different from those originally considered in the 1936 banking law.

The deep sectoral dissociation between savings and investment which, as we have noted in section 3.1 above, has also been connected with an increase in the demand for medium- and long-term loans by the deficit sectors and a strong liquidity preference of the surplus sector, has made it very difficult for market forces to operate, in the way outlined above in channelling funds directly towards special credit institutions.

The authorities have managed in various ways to cope with this situation and particularly with the scarce attitude of investors to take the higher risk and the smaller liquidity connected with medium- and long-term assets.

During the late 1960s, they intervened mainly by stabilising the yield on bonds with open market operations. This policy caused a remarkable increase in the demand for bonds by the public, by creating the illusion that they were exempt from capital losses and making it possible for special credit institutions to place their bonds largely with the public.

The policy of yield stabilisation was the main determinant of the development of the bond market in Italy, which increased consistently during the years in which the policy was conducted. It must be noted that the policy fostered the growth of the market in a very distorted manner. Bonds were not considered by investors as a medium- and long-term asset but instead as liquid assets, not very different from bank deposits. The policy did not, consequently, achieve the objective of reducing the liquidity preference of the economy: it just managed to satisfy it through nominally long-term instruments made, in fact, 'liquid' by central bank intervention. The great expansion of the bond market, fostered without promoting an increase in the public's propensity to (true) long-term investment, was going to cause great troubles to the monetary authorities when they were compelled to discontinue the policy.

This happened at the end of the 1960s when world interest rates began to move upward and the rate of inflation started to rise. The problem of financing special credit institutions and the public sector's deficit became, after the end of the policy of yield stabilisation, more and more difficult.

Monetary authorities were compelled in June 1973 to introduce a scheme of direct controls on bank credit which, as will be better

plained below, put limits on the rate of growth of bank loans and
orced banks to acquire medium- and long-term bonds. The controls,
hich in their original version extended only to a short period of time,
ere justified on the grounds of short-run considerations. The objectives
hich the controls intended to achieve, according to statements by the
ionetary authorities, were those of external equilibrium and of a
:duction in the rate of inflation. The structural character of the controls
as clearly emerged later on, when they have regularly been extended.[11]

It is now a widespread opinion that the main purpose of the controls is
iat of allowing the financing of special credit institutions and of the
ublic sector's deficit in a situation marked by a very low demand for
iedium- and long-term financial assets and by a very high liquidity
reference.

The controls are usually considered as a *consequence* of the high
iquidity preference of the Italian economy. This preference, it is argued,
as almost prevented the working of markets for medium- and long-
:rm financial assets and has forced monetary authorities to impose
onstraints on the portfolio composition of banks, which have become
lmost the sole collector of the households' financial savings.

We think that the controls on bank credit, which may certainly be
onsidered a consequence of the high liquidity preference of the country,
t the same time favour the maintenance of this high liquidity (and,
erhaps, also stimulate its growth). In this sense they may be considered
ot only as a consequence, but also in some way as a *cause* of the high
:vel of liquidity of the Italian economy.

Controls constitute, in our view, a complex mechanism by which the
nonetary authorities allow the banking system to expand to an extent
vhich, in their absence, would not be possible and assure the stability of
he financial system in a way which is very different from that originally
onsidered in the banking law.

To develop this point it is necessary to describe briefly the structure of
he controls which are under consideration. This structure is formed, as
t has been noted above, by two complementary instruments: a *ceiling on
vank loans* and a *portfolio requirement*. The ceiling does not apply to all
oans, but only to those extended to customers who already have a
onsistent debt position with the bank.[12] By the portfolio requirement,
vanks are requested to invest in bonds a specified percentage of the
ncrease in their deposits.[13]

From controls of the type now considered, one could have expected a
lepressing effect on the growth of bank intermediation. In our opinion,

as it has already been observed, the controls have instead led, throug
their effects on the stability of the banking system, to a further increas
in bank intermediation.

The way in which controls work in granting the stability of th
banking system may be analysed by considering their influence o
the composition of total credit extended by banks. This is, under th
working of the controls, divided into three different parts: loans nc
subject to ceiling, loans subject to ceiling and bonds.

Loans not subject to ceiling can be expanded freely. These loans ar
extended to small customers: the freedom of action left to banks i
granting them was officially justified with the necessity of avoiding a to
large incidence of credit restrictions on smaller enterprises. This freedor
can, however, be justified on a different basis when controls ar
considered from a structural point of view. A possible explanation has t
be found in the fact that in Italy smaller enterprises are much mor
profitable and flexible than bigger enterprises. Loans to smalle
enterprises are therefore probably more liquid than loans to the bigge
ones and constitute the form of investment which, according to th
philosophy of specialisation, has to be considered the more suitable fo
the banking system.

Loans to the bigger enterprises are instead less liquid. By the ceilin
placed on them, an excessive extension of this kind of loan by th
banking system is avoided.

By the portfolio requirement, banks are compelled to acquire bond
of special credit institutions. In an indirect way, banks have also ofte
been forced by the controls system to buy government bonds, which ar
not included in the portfolio requirement. Banks have been pushed t
this kind of behaviour by the existence of the ceiling which, preventin
them from expanding their loans, has often induced them to bu
government securities, besides the bonds of special credit institution
which they are forced to buy.[14]

The funds supplied by banks to special credit institutions through th
forced acquisition of their bonds are in the last instance used for th
financing of long-term investment. But banks do not bear directl
the solvency risk connected with this investment, which is taken b
special credit institutions.

With regard to government securities, it is worth noting that in the las
few years the size of the public sector's deficit has been largely influence
by transfers of funds made by the government to private and publi
enterprises.[15] These transfers have been directed mainly to enterprise
of large size and often operating in a very critical situation. Governmen

ransfers have the eventual effect of subtracting from the banking system hat part of the total demand for loans which is less liquid and more isky. Government transfers and the ceiling may be considered as two :omplementary instruments which, via their effects on the demand for oans facing the banking system (transfers) and on the amount of loans which the banking system is allowed to supply (ceiling), are designed to ivoid the direct extension by the banking system of loans with a too high legree of riskiness. As in the case of bonds issued by special credit nstitutions, funds collected by the banking system are finally channelled o the financing of credit requirements which are quite different from hose which, according to the 1936 banking law, could be satisfied by the anking system.

It is possible at this point to sum up briefly the way in which the stability of the system is now assured. Stability is not reached by preventing banks, whose liabilities are short term, to extend credit on onger maturities, as should have been done according to the principle of specialisation. There is instead a large intervention of the government by which, in the last instance, the risk connected with long-term investment s socialised.

The intervention has taken place, as explained above, mainly through controls imposed on the banking system. It is commonly argued that one of the reasons why these controls have been introduced has to be found n the high liquidity preference of the Italian economy. We have argued that controls are not only effects of the liquidity preference: their existence allows instead the permanence of this liquidity preference at a very high level.

Controls have not had the effect of discouraging the growth of bank ntermediation, which one could have expected from them. Our analysis suggests that the reason why this has happened has to be found in the fact that controls have not reduced the profitability of banking activity. According to many analyses of the effects of controls, this reduction should have taken place because controls impose on banks investment which are less profitable than those which they would otherwise freely choose. If one considers that in Italy a very large fraction of credit goes to the financing of activities which have a very low (and sometimes negative) profitability, it becomes apparent that the scope for profitable investment for the banking system is relatively limited. Therefore, in absence of the system of controls now ruling, the banking system would probably have ended up with a return lower than the one which it presently receives by granting credit according to the controls system.

We have drawn our attention in this section to the controls on credit allocation which, having been in force in a continuous way since 1973, may be considered as a permanent feature of the financial system's regulation during the 1970s.

It is worth noting that the monetary authorities' action to ensure the stability of the banking system did not limit itself to the imposition of controls on credit allocation. During the 1970s and especially in recent years, there have been on various occasions different types of interventions, which monetary authorities have conducted using the wide discretionary powers awarded to them by the Italian banking law.

Among these interventions, it is worth recalling a measure taken in January 1977 by which the total amount of short-term debts of local authorities *vis-à-vis* banks was consolidated through transformation into ten-year securities issued by the Central Post Office Savings Fund, a financial institution which acts as a government agency. The return on securities placed in bank portfolios was lower than that of the loans to local authorities which were substituted by securities. One could therefore argue that this substitution had an adverse effect on bank profitability. In fact, the effect was just the opposite. Since many local authorities were in financial difficulties and were unable not only to pay back their loans, but even to regularly make the interest payments on them, banks would have borne consistent losses on these credits in the absence of the intervention outlined above.

Similar types of intervention which are now about to be accomplished concern the transformation of part of the short-term loans extended by the banking system, often at very high rates of interest, to enterprises which presently have financial problems. These loans – which are authorised in spite of their breaching the principle of specialisation – are to be transformed in loans of longer maturities and with a lower rate of interest or in shares held by consortia to be formed by the banks.

The difference between the types of intervention just considered and the controls on credit allocation previously discussed (ceiling on loans and portfolio requirement) is not only the fact that the former have taken place occasionally whereas the latter have constituted a permanent feature of the regulation during the 1970s. They have also to be distinguished because of their different nature: controls on credit allocation have contributed to the stability of the banking system by acting *ex ante*; the other forms of interventions have, on the contrary, acted *ex post*.

One may conclude, therefore, that controls on credit allocation do not have the expected effect of reducing bank intermediation. On the contrary, these controls, supplemented by the order interventions considered above, have in fact operated as a 'subsidy' scheme increasing *ex ante* the return on bank assets and reducing *ex post* the losses on bad credits. They have thus been an incentive to the growth of bank intermediation.

Controls on credit allocation, being at the same time effect and cause of the high liquidity, give rise to a process of expansion of bank intermediation which feeds itself: the high liquidity preference makes controls necessary, this necessity is then strengthened by the favourable conditions for the maintenance of liquidity at a high level, which are created by controls. State interventions in situations of financial difficulties provide an even more favourable environment for this interplay.

5. BANK INTERMEDIATION AND THE EFFICIENCY OF THE FINANCIAL STRUCTURE

In the preceding sections we have considered the main causes of the growth of bank intermediation. We turn now to the analysis of the effects of bank intermediation on the efficiency of the financial structure. We will mainly deal with the effects on the allocative efficiency although, in addition, some concise remarks are made on the consequences of the Italian system for the flexibility of monetary policy and for the rate of inflation.

With regard to the problem of allocative efficiency, it can first be pointed out that in Italy a condition is fulfilled which by many students of monetary economics is considered as indispensable for the attainment of allocative efficiency. We refer here to the absence of prohibition to pay interest on demand deposits and of ceilings on interests paid on time deposits. According to the theory of the optimum quantity of money,[16] the payment of interest on deposits should foster an increase of the allocative efficiency of the financial structure in the form of a welfare gain to money holders which would be allowed by the payment of interest on money to hold money balances at the 'satiation level'.

In order for this level to be reached, the theory requires not only the payment of interest on deposits but also the existence of perfect competition. As has been noted in the previous sections, the Italian banking system is far from being perfectly competitive. According to the theory of the optimum quantity of money, one should therefore reach the conclusion that, notwithstanding the payment of interest on money, the level of liquidity of the Italian economy is below the optimum.

This conclusion, in our view, goes against the widespread opinion tha the Italian economy is over-liquid and induces us to think that the theory of the optimum quantity of money does not constitute a good tool for the evaluation of the allocative efficiency of the Italian banking system We think that the main reason must be found in the fact that the optimum is defined by the theory focusing on the market for bank deposits. The theory draws attention mainly to the function of providing a means of payment which is carried out by the banking system and doe not consider that the banking system also performs the other importan function of extending credit to economic units. Furthermore, the theory refers to a world where there is perfect foresight and there do not exis the various kinds of frictions which very much influence economi activity in real economies.[17]

If credit activity is considered and the risk connected with it is also taken into account, one can define an optimum condition for the banking system which differs from that of the theory of the optimun quantity of money. The new condition does not require, as the theory of the optimum quantity of money does, interest on deposits to equal th rate of return on capital. It requires instead that the interest rate paid on deposits equals the *net* rate of return on bank assets, calculated b subtracting from the rate of return on capital – assumed to equal th interest rate on bank assets – not only the operating costs but also a premium for insurance against the risk connected with credit operations.[18]

According to this new definition of optimality, one can reach the conclusion that the liquidity of the Italian economy is above the optima level. The reason for the overexpansion of the banking system has to b found, under this respect, in the behaviour of public policy and, i particular, in the system of controls discussed in section 4. Thes interventions increase the return of funds lent by the banking system over the value of their profitability, which in many cases is quite low o even negative (in part, also because of the behaviour of public polic itself), and thereby increase the volume of bank intermediation.

One could argue that, though it is by now clear that governmen intervention increases the volume of bank intermediation, this does no imply that bank intermediation becomes over-optimal. Allocativ inefficiencies would not exist if the higher return on credit granted b government intervention could be justified on the basis of externa economies associated with the investments financed by bank credit. I this case, government intervention would bring bank intermediatio from a situation below the optimal level to its optimal level. In othe words, government intervention would bring, using the condition considered before, bank intermediation from a situation where interest on deposits plus operating costs and the insurance premium equals the *private* return on capital to a situation in which it equals instead the *social* rate of return on capital.

We think that these circumstances are seldom met in the case of Italy, where a large fraction of credit is eventually channelled to the financing of activities (such as covering firms' current losses and the budget's current deficit) whose productivity is quite low, even when valued in social terms.

One could object that, if this is the case, a bad allocation of credit has to be considered a consequence of wrong government policies and not of the overexpansion of banking activity. We think that this objection is only partially relevant. In our opinion, a sizeable part of inefficiencies in credit allocation may in the present Italian situation be reconduced to the high scale of bank intermediation and to the necessity of maintaining the protection, accorded by government, to the liquidity created by the expansion of bank intermediation.

Had savers invested directly a larger fraction of their financial surplus instead of placing it with the banking system, it could have been more difficult to conduct the policies which have eventually led to a bad credit allocation. Savers would probably have paid more attention to the utilisation of their savings than they do in the present system where banks, acting to a large extent as a 'screen' between the deficit sectors (firms and government) and the surplus sector (households), make it difficult for the latter even to know the final utilisation of its saving.[19]

As far as protection of liquidity is concerned, it must be noted that, if the counterpart of loans and bonds which finance non-productive activities were not bank deposits, government would probably not be forced to intervene so extensively. These forms of government intervention have the effect – either deliberate or incidental – of ensuring the payment of interest on funds which, directly or indirectly, have gone through the banking system to the financing of non-productive activities. These interventions create conditions which allow these non-productive activities to continue: the allocative inefficiency of the high liquidity has to be found in the fact that it may to a large extent be a cause of the carrying on of these activities.

Other effects on allocative efficiency may be found if one considers the changes in banks' balance sheets caused by the system of controls which has been imposed on the banking system to ensure its stability.

In Table 6.3 is reported the percentage composition of the increases in

Table 6.3   Banks' assets and liabilities in Italy, 1968–72 and 1973–8
(percentage of increases in total assets and liabilities)

Assets	1968–72	1973–8	Liabilities	1968–72	1973–8
Liquidity	2.2	2.6	Deposits	96.0	96.7
Required reserves	11.2	13.3	Financing by Central Bank	2.8	−0.7
Loans	55.8	37.6	Foreign liabilities (net)	1.2	4.0
Bonds	29.0	52.1			
Other items (net)	1.8	−5.6			
Total	100.0	100.0	Total	100.0	100.0

Source   Banca d'Italia.

assets and liabilities of the banking system for the years 1968–72 and 1973–8. It can be noted that the composition of the asset side of the banks' balance sheet has changed considerably between the two periods considered. The ratio of the loans extended directly by the banking sector to its total assets has declined sharply (from 55.8 to 37.6 per cent). Loans have been substituted within the banking sector's balance sheet by bonds, in which banks have invested more than half of the total increase in their assets in the years 1973–8.

A very large fraction of these bonds is constituted by those issued by special credit institutions, which banks have to a large extent been *directly* compelled to buy (the banks' net supply of funds to special credit institutions has increased from 39.8 per cent of special credit institutions' total liabilities in 1973 to 62.4 per cent in 1978). But, as it has been noted in section 4.2, banks have also been *indirectly* forced by the system of controls to buy large amounts of government securities.

From the data which have been just considered, some conclusions may be drawn about allocative efficiency. They clearly show that the role plaid by the banking system in allocating funds according to market mechanisms is much less important than in the past, the main role of the banking system now being that of channelling funds towards other credit institutions[20] and the public sector.

We have already discussed the inefficiencies connected with this government intervention. It must be noted here that, in addition, inefficiency is not limited to the funds which are controlled by the government; it spreads out also to that part of funds over which banks exert directly their allocative powers, that is, bank loans to customers.

This happens mainly for two reasons. First, the system of controls, by limiting the amount of credit which can be directly extended by each bank, causes a decrease in the degree of competition among banks (though not among each bank's customers) in the market for this credit. In the second place, the permanence for a long period of time of the controls on credit, greatly limiting the area in which the banking system is allowed to perform its allocative function, may seriously reduce the ability of the system in the performance of this function. There are good reasons to think that this ability decreases if for a long time banks are prevented from freely exerting their allocative function and are compelled to act according to guidelines rigidly determined by the authorities; ultimately, they may even expect some form of implicit risk coverage to be provided by the government if bad credits materialise.

Aside from allocative efficiency, one can argue finally that the considerable growth of bank intermediation decreases also the efficiency of monetary policy and of the fighting of inflation. Although extending on this would lead us too far, the main arguments can succintly be summarised as follows.

The fact that a large part of the credit granted by the banks is influenced by the government may indeed raise heavy pressure against the manipulation of monetary instruments in the pursuit of the objectives of internal and external stabilisation of the economy, so that monetary policy loses its flexibility. Further, it has to be observed that the share of bank deposits in total financial assets of the public is in Italy quite high and that, as it has been noted in section 3, bank deposits are much more liquid in Italy than in other countries. One can therefore think that the risk of an acceleration of the inflation process, sustained by the very large amount of liquidity existing, is in Italy higher than in other countries.

5. CRITERIA FOR A POLICY TOWARDS BANK INTERMEDIATION

At the beginning of this chapter, commenting on the data on the high liquidity of the Italian economy, we observed that, although they showed an abnormal increase in the scale of bank intermediation, they did not by themselves constitute a sufficient basis for concluding that a policy aimed at reducing the volume of bank intermediation had to be considered desirable. We noted that an analysis of the main determinants and of the most important effects of the high scale of bank intermediation was necessary to assess the desirability of such a policy

The analysis made in the previous section allows us to draw some preliminary conclusions.

6.1 On the desirability of a relative decline of bank intermediation

The analysis of section 5 has led us to the conclusion that to the high scale of bank intermediation are connected various kinds of inefficiencies. An excessive expansion of the banking system may have considerable negative effects on the allocation of resources and, in addition, may decrease the efficiency of monetary policy and contribute to the inflation process.

A reduction of the scale of bank intermediation may therefore be considered desirable, but only if it is achieved in a way which leads to a reduction of the inefficiencies which are connected with a too high level of intermediation. From this consideration follows a first important conclusion: the policy directed to achieve a reduction of bank intermediation must be carefully designed. In order to be a good policy it not only needs to reach the objective of reducing bank intermediation; it is necessary that this reduction takes place by eliminating some of the inefficiencies which are connected with the high scale of intermediation.

As far as allocative efficiency is considered, the analysis of the previous section leads us to the conclusion that a reduction of the scale of bank intermediation should be realised by simultaneously reducing those assets of banks' balance sheets which are primary causes of inefficiency. These are, for the reasons which have been considered in the previous section, mainly bonds (issued both by special credit institutions and the public sector) and a large part of those loans extended to firms which, though being often formally at short term, end up to be long-term loans.

The assets now considered, because of their effect in increasing the degree of rigidity of banks' balance sheets, are also the main source of inefficiency, as far as the transmission of monetary policy is concerned. Through the effects on the volume and composition of output and on the public sector's deficit considered in 5.3, this same part of the banks' balance sheets may be a cause of inflationary pressures.

One can therefore reach the conclusion that under all the points of view here considered it seems desirable that the reduction of bank intermediation be carried on by a reduction of the weight on banks' balance sheets of bonds and loans of longer maturities.

One could argue that this would mean going back to the 1936 banking law's basic philosophy which has been considered in section 4.1. But it must be noted that it does not seem possible even to think that the changes desirable to increase the efficiency of bank intermediation may be accomplished over a short period of time, given the high liquidity preference of savers and the low profitability of funds in their final uses.

The desired changes must therefore be considered in a *long-run* perspective and it is worth noting that they require changes to be realised in the real sector of the economy leading to the removal of the distortions which, as explained in section 3, are to a large extent a cause of the inefficiencies of the Italian financial structure.

6.2 Feasibility in the short run

From the analysis made in this chapter, it does not follow only the conclusion that the problem of the scale of bank intermediation may be dealt with in a long-run context. Other conclusions can be drawn which may be of some help in designing the type of actions which can be taken in the short run.

First of all, our analysis suggests that short-run actions which are not in accordance with the desired evolution of the system in the long run are not desirable.

To clarify this point, let us consider one example. The promotion of a market for commercial paper in Italy is advocated by many students of financial problems, among other reasons, because of the effects it would have in discouraging the growth of bank intermediation.

We think that from the creation of this market – which certainly in other countries with institutional settings different from Italy contributes to raise the overall efficiency of the financial structure – could follow in the present Italian situation undesirable consequences. The reason has to be found in the fact that the reduction of bank intermediation would be realised without reducing the different kinds of inefficiencies which have been considered in the previous section. Bank intermediation would be reduced by a simultaneous decrease of deposits (which the public could divert to the market for commercial papers) and of the quantity of short-term loans to banks customers (who would issue commercial paper instead of recourse to bank credit). These changes would cause a decrease of the global value of banks' assets, but would at the same time worsen considerably their composition by increasing the share of those bank assets which contribute most to the 'rigidity' of the banking system and pose the greater problem for stability.[21] It seems to us that these changes do not contribute to movement towards that setting of the financial structure which in our opinion has to be considered desirable as a long-run objective.

In a different way has to be evaluated a reduction of bank intermediation achieved by a policy aimed at promoting the direct purchase of public sector's bonds from the public. A policy of this kind has to some extent recently been pursued by Italian authorities and it seems desirable because it does not contribute, as commercial paper does, to increase the rigidity of the asset side of banks' balance sheets. The scale of the banking system would be reduced by this policy, but in a way which will not subtract from banks that part of lending activity – consisting in the extension of short-term credit to firms – which seems more suitable for them.

While agreeing in principle on the desirability of a development of markets in which the public sector will be able to finance itself, drawing funds directly from the sector which has a financial surplus, it must be noted that, because of the high level attained by the public sector's borrowing requirement, this development seems to pose some relevant problems in a long-run perspective.

The development of the market for the direct financing of the public sector, if it were fully accomplished, would eventually result in a financial structure marked by a separation between the financial flows accruing to the private sector, which will in large part pass through the banking system, and the flows going to the public sector. This structure is quite different from that now existing, where almost all the funds are collected by the banking system, and in it will arise the problem of regulating the coexistence of the private and the public compartments.

The criteria worked out above and the examples just discussed show what kinds of relative reduction in the scale of bank intermediation are desirable and, at least to some extent, feasible in the short run. It will have been noticed that the discriminative features concern the type of instruments whose weight in the banks' asset structure is to be reduced. From the liability side, all kinds of relative reduction in the scale of bank intermediation require a more moderate growth of deposits. It is also desirable that deposits with a virtually perfect effective liquidity represent a declining share of the stock of deposits.

A necessary, though by no means sufficient, condition is thus a reduction in the peculiar concentration of the public's financial assets in bank deposits. One or the other of the following two solutions are often proposed to this effect: that the competing financial instruments be made more attractive; that ceilings be imposed upon deposit interest rates.

To be sure, it is highly desirable that instruments issued by non-bank intermediaries as well as by deficit units – in particular, by special credit institutions and firms, respectively – become more attractive than they presently are. In part, this requires a basic improvement in the performance of firms, enabling them to supply the public – directly or through the non-bank intermediaries – with instruments characterised by a higher return and/or smaller risk. A permanent improvement of this sort, however, can hardly be achieved in the short run. Even taking such underlying factors as given, on the other hand, there would be some scope also in the (relatively) short run for an increased attractiveness of instruments other than deposits; this may be obtained mainly through a change in those aspects of public policy which have so far penalised, in the various ways mentioned in section 3, the financial instruments issued by firms and have discouraged the emergence of new types of intermediaries. In particular, improvements should be made concerning corporate laws and the supervision on stock exchanges as well as the tax treatment of direct issues by the firms.

However, any increase in the attractiveness of assets other than bank deposits is likely to prove scarcely effective in containing bank intermediation, if there is no change in the other basic factors which have made bank deposits the dominant asset in the public's portfolio. Banks would respond to the increased appeal of those assets by raising deposit rates and by intensifying their deposit-promoting policies, since the factors which have been shown to have induced them to an expansionary behaviour so far would still be there. Their defeating response might even make use of the very instruments whose increased attractiveness would be meant to curb deposits, as banks might purchase those instruments themselves and finance them with a further deposit expansion.

Therefore, no desirable reduction in the role of bank intermediation can be achieved – however attractive alternative assets may become – unless bank deposits themselves become less attractive.

An intervention which is often suggested to this purpose – we come to the second solution mentioned above – is that of imposing ceilings on interest rates on deposits, possibly with the ceiling set at zero for demand deposits.

This measure – the practical implementation of which would in any case be far from easy, according to some past experiences – might lead to a decrease of the total volume of bank deposits. But if it were accomplished without a simultaneous action directed to channel the funds flowing out of the deposit market towards other markets, and particularly to medium- and long-term markets, it could have negative effects. The desire by savers to invest in assets denominated in foreign currencies, which is already quite high and has forced authorities to a policy of severe restrictions on capital movements, would be increased by a policy imposing rigid ceilings on deposit rates and would force the authorities to maintain and even strengthen these restrictions. Furthermore, the reduction in the return on bank deposits without a simultaneous creation of new financial instruments might induce a reduction in the propensity to save: funds flowing out of the deposit market could finance an increase in aggregate demand instead of being directed towards other markets, thereby contributing to a rise in the rate of inflation.

Furthermore, the introduction of the prohibition to pay interest on demand deposits and of ceilings on time deposit rates would provoke the inefficiencies noticed in countries where such controls exist and which have led many to propose a deregulation in this area.

It is worth remembering in this connection that our criticisms of the theory of the optimum quantity of money in section 5.1 were not addressed to the fundamental proposition of the theory, according to which interest should be paid on demand deposits, and that our analysis led to the conclusion that the main cause of allocative inefficiency had to be found, not in the payment of interest on deposits, but in various forms of government interventions directed to grant the stability of the banking system.

Rather than removing the feature of deposit rate flexibility by restricting the *freedom* of banks to pay interests as they like, it would seem appropriate to us to gradually remove those factors which *induce* banks to chase for deposits as aggressively as they do, also by offering interest rates as high (or higher) than are obtainable on less liquid and more risky assets. Many of these factors have been shown (sections 3 and 4) to be the direct or indirect result of public policy and of a regulatory system centred on controlled credit allocation. It would not seem consistent to us for public policy and the regulatory system to persist in a stance that artificially raises the banks' ability and willingness to pay high deposit rates and, at the same time, to prohibit banks from doing so.

A less distorted and more efficient financial structure – with less intermediation and less liquidity – would spontaneously be achieved, without resorting to controls on deposit rates, if public policy and the regulatory system refrained from contributing themselves to raising the marginal revenue – and reducing the risk – on bank assets in the ways iscussed above. This would reduce the optimal scale of intermediation nd the optimal deposit rate for profit-maximising banks. In addition, ublic policy should refrain from pushing bank managers, in the ways hat have been examined, to adopt deposit-maximising objectives and hus to increase deposits even above their profit-maximising level. ublic policy should also induce banks to seek changes in the maturity tructure of deposits and reduce the liquidity associated with deposits. n other words, it should gradually refrain from providing banks with an nvironment which encourages them *not* to prefer deposits of longer naturities and thus *not* to encourage a similar shift of preferences on the art of depositors.

Italian banks would probably move spontaneously towards the ehaviour indicated above if some flexibility is introduced in the resently rather rigid working of the economy and the financial system, uch as a more concrete possibility of failure of firms and of banks hemselves. They would then become more sensitive, as banks in other ountries seem to be, to the risks involved both in pursuing ex- ansionary policies at all costs and in financing with extremely short- erm liabilities an asset structure mostly composed of instruments that re in fact largely medium and long term. While the introduction of hose elements of flexibility may occur in a long-run perspective,[22] ublic policy and, particularly, the monetary authorities might induce anks, through appropriate measures, to make even in the short run ome initial steps in the direction indicated above.

The identification of the appropriate measures should follow from the nalysis of the ways in which public policy and the regulatory system resently contribute to induce banks to undesirable behavioural atterns. Besides removing some of those perverse influences, measures may be considered to introduce incentives towards the desired behaviour.

While the purpose of the present chapter was not to suggest specific policy measures but rather to identify a set of criteria which should inspire the measures, some concrete possibilities of this kind have been explored elsewhere.[23] They combine measures leading banks to shift the maturity structure of deposits – through a more marked distinction between demand and time deposits and incentives for banks to partly shift depositors towards the latter – and a restructuring of present forms of controls on credit allocation in such a way that the marginal revenue from deposits would decline more rapidly as deposits growth increases.

7. SUMMARY AND CONCLUSIONS

Italy's financial structure emerges from international comparisons a
one characterised by an outstanding degree of liquidity and o
commercial bank intermediation. The regulatory system, on the othe
hand, differs from that of many other countries, particularly in two
respects: interest rates on bank deposits – including demand deposits –
are allowed complete flexibility and the allocation of bank credit is
rigidly controlled. In addition, there is a rather peculiar extent and
nature of public policy intervention in the economy and in the financia
structure, so that Italy's mixed economy is indeed particularly 'mixed'

We have first presented empirical evidence on the level and growth o
bank intermediation and liquidity in Italy (section 2). These are so high
that economists and public opinion tend now to consider the degree of
liquidity and the scale of bank intermediation in Italy to be not only very
large, but also over-optimal and conducive to inefficiencies. An
adequate analysis of the phenomenon, however, has never been
provided, perhaps also because the peculiarities of the Italian regulatory
system and public policy – among which are those mentioned above –
prevent a meaningful application of analytical schemes developed
elsewhere.

This chapter is a contribution to such an analysis, which is needed also
as a basis for appropriate policy intervention. In addition, given the
present trend in several countries towards deregulation of existing
ceilings on deposits rates and towards consideration of selective credit
controls, our analysis of the behaviour of the Italian banking system
may also be viewed as a case study illustrating the behaviour of a system
actually operating under conditions similar to those that are proposed
elsewhere.

A systematic search for the determinants of the scale of bank
intermediation (section 3) has shown that the underlying real structure
of the Italian economy provides favourable conditions for the expansion
of intermediation. This, however, would not have been as large as it is
without the decisive influence of several features of public policy and of
the regulatory system and without a pattern of bank behaviour that has
made deposits a dominant asset, also as a result of the deposit-
maximising strategy pursued by many banks with the implicit en-
couragement of public policy itself.

The regulatory system, then, has been specially reconsidered as a
determinant of banking expansion (section 4). The original philosophy
of the 1936 banking law and, particularly, the subsequent controls

introduced during the 1970s, while they might have been expected to exert contractionary influences on the scale of bank intermediation, have in fact worked quite differently. Supplemented as they have been by a public policy often viewing the state as an 'insurer of last resort' of financial risks, the controls on credit allocation are shown to have operated as a sort of 'subsidy scheme'. Their net effect has been to increase the return and reduce the risk on bank assets, thus providing an incentive to the growth of bank intermediation. In this context, banks are both able and willing to pay high interest rates on deposits and to confer them a peculiarly high degree of liquidity. But only a very superficial consideration of the subject could identify the absence of ceilings as the *cause* of deposit rates being high and responsive to market conditions.

The consequences of large bank intermediation and liquidity on the efficiency of the financial structure have been subsequently investigated (section 5). As far as the allocation of resources is particularly concerned, several inefficiencies have been shown to result both from the existence of a bank-dominated financial structure and from the special protection that public policy feels necessary to accord to the banking system in view of the high liquidity of its liabilities. The scale of bank intermediation and liquidity seems to be excessive also for its effects on the transmission of monetary policy and on inflation.

It has been possible to derive from the analysis a set of criteria for a policy towards bank intermediation (section 6). A relative decline of bank intermediation is desirable, on the condition that the instruments whose weight declines within the banks' asset structure are those with which the inefficiencies identified above are associated – mainly bonds and loans of longer maturities. While a relative decline of bank intermediation of the type deemed desirable is only possible in the long run, some short-run progress in this direction is also feasible.

It will be beneficial, however, only if it can reduce some of the inefficiencies. This requirement would not be met by some measures which are often advocated. Among these is the proposal to impose ceilings on interest rates on bank deposits. Other measures by the monetary authorities that could instead prove effective are briefly outlined.

NOTES

1. For a detailed description of the Italian financial structure, see G. Carli (1978); G. Carli, M. Monti and T. Padoa-Schioppa (1977); D. P. Hodgman

(1974); Inter-Bank Research Organisation (1978); M. Monti and T. Padoa-Schioppa (1979); F. Vicarelli (1979).

2. If banks regarded the latter as a disequilibrium to be avoided, they would not be so accommodative as described above in the management of time deposit accounts and would offer a more substantive premium on time deposits over demand deposits in terms of interest rate than they presently do.

3. M. Monti (1971).

4. An analysis of such factors may be found, for example, in W. Baumol (1967).

5. F. Cingano (1978) pp. 245–6.

6. Also may act as an incentive to growth of the widespread belief among bank managers that the probability of some kind of rescue in case of solvency or liquidity problems is greater if the bank is a large one. For multi-branch banks, an additional factor induces a deposit expansionary behaviour, namely the practice of establishing targets for individual branches more in terms of deposits (and other volume magnitudes) than in terms of branch profit and loss accounts. Finally, present regulations enable a bank to exercise lending activity in a geographic area of wider extension the larger the volume of its deposits. This increases the benefits which can be obtained from deposit growth (and would lead even a profit-maximising bank towards higher interest rates on deposits and a larger deposit volume).

7. The analysis may seem to neglect the role of the monetary base in constraining the potential volume of *aggregate* bank deposits through the reserve requirements. In fact, we fully acknowledge the role of the monetary base as a determinant of bank deposits, with a few qualifications that provide further insights into the outstanding growth process of bank deposits in Italy. It must first be observed that the trend growth rate of the monetary base has been higher than in most countries, mainly due to the huge budget deficits noted above and to a high degree of monetisation of the deficits. It has then also to be noticed that a system of expansion-oriented banking firms operating under deposit rate flexibility may increase to some extent the value of both the multiplier and the monetary base. The former effect depends on the great ability that banks have to drain monetary base from the public into their reserves through use of deposit rate policy. The same behaviour may shift the public's portfolio preferences from government securities to bank deposits and thus require a greater creation of monetary base for a given budget deficit. Attempts by the monetary authorities to increase the non-monetary financing of deposits through the offer of higher interest rates on government securities may also be defeated if banks respond by increasing their deposit rates. See F. Cotula and P. de' Stefani (1979) p. 411.

8. Namely, the behaviour of public finance and particularly the size and composition of public sector deficit; a rent control system discouraging investments in houses; the slow pace of legislative and institutional changes that would allow the emergence of new types of financial intermediaries and of securities with some protection from inflation; the legal provisions and political pressures to reduce labour mobility and thus decrease profitability of firms and increase the risk on their liabilities; the backward state of

corporate laws; the inadequate supervision on the stock exchanges; the tax treatment of financial instruments penalising direct issues by firms; the fact that until recently the state refrained from supplying short-term securities to the market.

9. For a detailed analysis of this structure, the reader is referred to the chapter devoted to Italy in Inter-Bank Research Organisation (1978).

0. Other controls, placed mainly on the institutions operating in the short term (banks), are designed by the law in view of attaining the objective of stability. The most important among them are: reserve requirements, rigid controls on foreign exchange operations, and various restrictions on credit activity, among which the most important is that which requires banks to apply for preventive authorisation when extending to a single customer credit for an amount greater than the value of bank capital.

1. The ceiling, when it was introduced in July 1973, extended to an eight-month period. It has since been renewed many times and it has been in force until now with the exclusion of the short period from March 1975 to October 1976. The portfolio requirement, introduced in June 1973 for the period of six months, has then been regularly extended each six months.

12. In its present version, the ceiling applies to the total volume of credit extended by each bank to its customers with individual credit lines of over Lire 100 million.

13. This is presently 6.5 per cent of the increase in deposits. It has been higher in the past, attaining its maximum value (42 per cent) in the second half of 1976.

14. For a more detailed analysis of the ways in which banks have been indirectly pushed to buy government securities, the reader is referred to Banca Commerciale Italiana (1978).

15. See on this point M. Monti and B. Siracusano (1979).

16. A detailed exposition of the theory is in M. Friedman (1969). An example of the application of the theory to the evaluation of the efficiency of the banking system is B. Griffiths (1972).

17. These criticisms of the theory of the optimum quantity of money are discussed in the studies on 'money and development', among which E. S. Shaw (1973, especially chapters 2 and 3) and P. McKinnon (1973). These studies refer mainly to underdeveloped countries, whose economies are quite different from the Italian economy. We think that they may be of some interest for the high emphasis they place on the banking system. This is considered in the studies on money and development by far the most important channel for the financing of economic activity.

18. The optimality condition is taken from E. S. Shaw (1973) p. 66, where it is formulated in the following way: 'Interest allowances should exhaust earnings of the monetary system after provision of all costs. The costs include factor payments and a competitive return on net worth. They should include as well premia for insurance of money holders against default by private money issues.'

19. For a detailed analysis of the inefficiencies of the type here outlined following from the overexpansion of bank intermediation, the reader is referred to F. Cingano (1978).

20. It is worth noting in this connection that a large fraction of the funds which

are diverted to special credit institutions are not allocated according to market principles but take the form of subsidised loans which benefit from grants in aid by the state and the regions according to a complex network of incentives.
21. On the negative effects on the stability of the banking system deriving from the growth of the market of commercial paper, see J. P. Judd (1979). Of particular interest is the following sentence (p. 39): ' . . . the switch to commercial paper by many prime-rated bank loan customers reinforces the postwar trend toward greater bank exposure to financial-market risk caused by the decline in capital cushions and holdings of low-risk financial investment'.
22. A few banks seem to be already spontaneously leaning towards the behaviour we consider desirable. Statements to this effect are in F. Cingano (1978) and may partly be traced back to a previous tradition, see R. Mattioli (1967).
23. M. Monti (1977). A discussion of the problem of excess bank intermediation and some remarks on these proposed measures is contained in the Banca d'Italia's (1979) latest annual report.

REFERENCES

Banca Commerciale Italiana (1978) *Monetary Trends* (June).
Banca d'Italia (1979) *Relazione del Governatore sull 'anno 1978* (Rome: May).
Baumol, W. (1967) *Business Behaviour, Value, and Growth* (New York: Harcourt, Brace, and World).
Carli, G. (ed.) (1978) *La struttura del sistema creditizio italiano* (Bologna: Il Mulino).
Carli, G., M. Monti and T. Padoa-Schioppa (1977) 'Development and Stability of Financial Structures – Some General Remarks Using the Italian Case', in J. E. Wadsworth, J. S. G. Wilson and H. Fournier (eds), *The Development of Financial Institutions in Europe, 1956–1976* (Leyden: Sijthoff).
Caron, M. (1978) 'Il finanziamento degli investimenti per settori economici nel periodo 1970–77', *Banca d'Italia: Bollettino.*
Cesarini, F. (1976) *Struttura finanziaria, sistema creditizio e allocazione delle risorse in Italia* (Bologna: Il Mulino)
Cingano, F. (1978) 'La banca: mestiere e professione', *Bancaria* (March).
Cotula, F. and P. de' Stefani (1979) *La politica monetaria in Italia. Istituti e strumenti* (Bologna: Il Mulino).
Friedman, M. (1969) 'The Optimum Quantity of Money', in *The Optimum Quantity of Money and Other Essays* (Chicago: Aldine).
Griffiths, B. (1972) 'The Welfare Cost of the UK Clearing Banks Cartel', *Journal of Money, Credit and Banking* (May).
Hodgman, D. P. (1974) *National Monetary Policies and International Monetary Cooperation* (Boston: Little Brown and co.).
Inter-Bank Research Organisation (1978) *The Regulation of Banks in the Member States of the EEC* (Netherlands: Sijthoff and Noordhoff).
Judd, J. P. (1979) 'Competition Between the Commercial Paper Market and Commercial Banks', *Federal Reserve Bank of St Francisco Economic Review* (Winter).

Mattioli, R. (1967) *Relazione del Consiglio di amministrazione della Banca Commerciale Italiana sull'esercizio 1965* (Milan: Capriolo Massimino).

McKinnon, R. (1973) *Money and Capital in Economic Development* (Washington: Brookings Institution).

Monti, M. (1971) 'A Theoretical Model of Bank Behaviour and Its Implications for Monetary Policy', *L'Industria*, no. 2.

Monti, M. (1977) *Intervento al Convegno sul tema Risparmio e credito, oggi* (Rome: Federazione Nazionale dei Cavalieri del Lavoro).

Monti, M. and T. Padoa-Schioppa (1979) 'Structural Changes and Cyclical Behaviour of the Italian Banking System', in A. S. Courakis (ed.), *Inflation, Depression and Economic Policy in the West* (London–Oxford: Mansell Publishing–Alexandrine Press).

Monti, M. and B. Siracusano (1979) 'The Public Sector's Financial Intermediation, the Composition of Credit and the Allocation of Resources', *Review of the Economic Conditions in Italy*, no. 2.

OECD (1973) *Monetary Policy in Italy* (Paris: May).

Shaw, E. S (1973) *Financial Deepening in Economic Development* (New York: Oxford University Press).

Vicarelli, F. (1979) *Capitale industriale e capitale finanziario: Il caso italiano* (Bologna: Il Mulino).

Comment on Monti and Porta

PAUL DE GRAUWE

Let me first stress the qualities of this chapter. It has the right combination of economic analysis and institutional description. I also found it to be refreshing. When reading it I was *struck* by the following In most countries, regulators believe that the existing system of regulations is the only one that can operate in the country in question Any change would lead to unspeakable financial disasters. For example there is a strong belief in many countries that a removal of the restrictions on deposit rates would lead to a collapse of the banking system. The Italian chapter was refreshing because it illustrated that the absence of deposit rate ceilings has as yet not led to a collapse. Of course other regulatory devices are used in Italy (absence of regulation in Italy would have been surprising). And as Monti and Porta indicate these too have undesirable side-effects. What the Italian experience shows is that deposit rate ceilings are not inevitable devices if one wants to maintain a stable banking system.

The main story set out by Monti and Porta can be summarised as follows. The authors start from a number of empirical observations These are, first, that Italians have a strong liquidity preference and large financial surpluses. Second, these surpluses are channelled mainly through the banking system, which is unregulated on the liability side and is therefore able to pay high interest rates. Third, controls exist on the asset side. These controls take the form of credit ceilings and subsidies (for example, the state carries the risk). The net effect of these regulatory devices is to increase the size of bank intermediation above what it would have been without the existing regulatory structure.

This is a rather interesting story. However, the reader may want to be more convinced and have more evidence concerning some of the empirical observations made by Monti and Porta.

For example, the authors point out that the nominal interest rates on demand deposits have been high in Italy. The question, however is whether these are high in relation to the inflation rates observed in Italy. I would venture that in the last few years the real interest rates on demand deposits in Italy have been comparable to the ones obtained in countries where no interest is paid on demand deposits and where the inflation rates have been relatively low. This is illustrated in Table 6.4. Despite the fact that nominal interest rates on demand deposits were zero, the real interest rate on demand deposits in low inflation countries has not been significantly different (Germany, Belgium, Netherlands). In all fairness, it should be added that the point Monti and Porta are making is that the interest rate on demand deposits in Italy is high in comparison with other Italian financial assets (for example, bonds). It would have been interesting to have some more empirical evidence on this point than what is provided by the authors.

TABLE 6.4   Interest rates on demand deposits and inflation rates, 1974 –8

Year	Italy		Germany	Belgium	Netherlands
	Interest rate	Inflation rate (CPI)	Inflation rate	Inflation rate	Inflation rate
1974	10.0	19.0	7.0	12.7	9.5
1976	11.0	16.8	4.5	9.2	8.8
1978	10.25	12.0	2.6	4.5	4.1

SOURCE   *International Financial Statistics.*

In the remainder of this comment I would like to concentrate on a theoretical issue raised by the authors. The main conclusion is that the Italian regulatory system has contributed to a level of bank intermediation which is higher than in other countries and which the authors tend to qualify as excessive. A first point I would like to make is that it is not clear *a priori* that a combination of credit ceilings and subsidised loans contributes to an expansion of bank intermediation. Both regulatory devices tend to work in opposite directions. This is illustrated in Figures 6.3 and 6.4.

The L_D and L_S lines represent the bank loan demand and supply curves; r_L is the loan rate; D_D is the deposit demand curve. The vertical difference between the L_S and L_D lines represents the bank's intermediation margin, which is assumed to be exogenous. In Figure 6.3, the effect

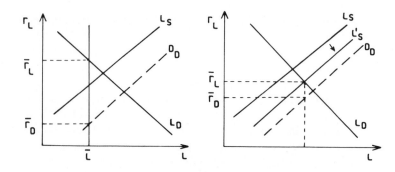

FIGURE 6.3   Credit ceiling   FIGURE 6.4   Loan subsidy

of a credit ceiling is represented. As is well known, if the credit ceiling is effective, it leads to an increase in the intermediation margin (that is, the difference between the loan rate r_L and the deposit rate r_D). At the same time, the amount of bank loans and deposits is reduced. Thus, if effective, credit ceilings generally lead to a reduction of the size of banking intermediation.

Figure 6.4 represents the same loan market assuming that bank loans are subsidised. This subsidy can take different forms. One can subsidise loan demand (in that case the L_D curve would shift upwards) or one can subsidise the supply, for example when the state carries the credit risk. In that case, the L_S line shifts to the right. The latter is shown in Figure 6.4, where the subsidy scheme shifts the L_S line to the new level L'_S. The net effect is to reduce the margin between deposit and loan rate, and to increase the size of banking intermediation.

One can conclude that if, as a result of the regulatory system, the size of the banking intermediation in Italy is too high, this must be due to the fact that the effects of the subsidy scheme dominate the effects of the credit ceilings.

7. Government Intervention in the French Financial System[1]

FLORIN AFTALION

1. INTRODUCTION

The main reason for the existence of financial systems is intermediation between savers and investors. Financial intermediaries channel funds from economic units which are ready to lend to other units which would like to borrow. Assessments about how well intermediation is achieved are made in general on the basis of *allocation efficiency* (how well the system matches lenders and borrowers; there should be nobody ready to lend at rates below the market rate or ready to borrow at rates above the market rate) and *cost efficiency* (which is the amount of funds diverted from lenders and borrowers for the functioning of the system).

Financial intermediaries can be either markets where primary and secondary securities are exchanged or firms which make loans either against deposits or against long-term securities. Banks keep their liabilities in the form of demand or time deposits. Traditionally, they have the important role of providing the economy with means of payment. Because of this money creation function, they are submitted in all countries to various controls on the part of central authorities. Controls are also exerted in order to limit risk-taking and ensure the soundness of the financial system.

Most of the literature devoted to either studying the efficiency of banking systems or analysing the impact of controls assumes competition between profit-maximising banks. It also assumes that central authorities intervene by setting general rules of conduct and by having a central bank operate on money markets and foreign exchange markets.

In France, as well as in other European countries, central authority

157

intervention is much more complex than this. It is aimed at providing certain sectors of the economy or segments of the population with loans at below what would otherwise be the market rate. It uses not only a comprehensive set of bank regulations but also special non-profit-maximising institutions to channel funds to privileged individuals or firms. Funds provided to these institutions are not always earmarked for special uses. An institution such as *Caisse des Dépôts et Consignations* (see section 2.6) uses excess funds to intervene in financial markets. Its purchases on the money market are not less than those of the central bank. Therefore, the functioning of the French financial system and the problems related to monetary control cannot be understood without taking its specific structure or rules and institutions into account.

Our purpose in this study is to give a general overview of the French financial system with an emphasis on government intervention. At this stage we will not attempt to analyse the ultimate effects of this intervention. We will merely assess how different institutions channel funds to certain well determined economic sectors and what means of control are used by government. Thus we hope to lay the ground for further work, which should inquire into the true reasons of government intervention as well as into its ultimate impact on the economy.

The structure of the remainder of this chapter will be as follows. Section 2 gives a brief description of the instruments, institutions and regulations used to channel loans at below market rates for housing, agriculture, exports, industrial development and local entities. The *Caisse des Dépôts et Consignations*, the institution used for the latter category, constitutes a special case, and will be described as such. Section 3 asks some of the questions raised by the existence of a system of credit allocation such as the one described here.

2. THE INSTITUTIONAL FRAMEWORK

2.1 General outlook

There are five sectors of the French economy which receive special loans at below market rates. These are housing, agriculture, exports, industrial development and local entities.

Credit selectivity is achieved not only by regulating commercial banks, but also by utilising specially-designed and government-controlled institutions. These deal directly with the public and discount bank loans made under well-defined conditions. They are financed by

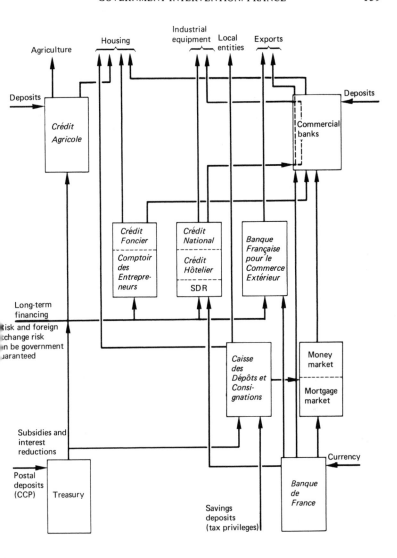

FIGURE 7.1 Flows of funds in the French financial system

demand deposits (*Crédit Agricole*) or saving deposits (*Caisse des Dépôts et Consignations*), by long-term loans (usually government guaranteed) or Treasury subsidies for interest 'improvements'. Commercial banks can seek refinancing on the money market where the *Banque de France* intervenes for monetary policy purposes together with the *Caisse des*

Dépôts et Consignations, which is a permanent purchaser of commercial or financial paper. Commercial banks can also discount loans made under certain conditions (exports and industrial development) at very low rates directly at *Banque de France*.

The main institutions involved in the French financial system and the related flows of funds are schematised in Figure 7.1. The remainder of this part of the chapter will describe these institutions and give some details concerning specific special loans.

All figures quoted below are from the 1977 *Rapport du Consei National du Crédit* (an official agency in charge with regulating the banking system) or from the various annual reports.

Notice that in recent years, credit expansion was submitted to growth control.[2] One of the means government has used to expand certain types of loans has been to exonerate them from growth control. This feature will be mentioned when it occurs.

2.2 Credits for housing

Credits for housing are channelled through three different institutions, two of which, *Crédit Foncier de France* and the *Comptoir des Entrepreneurs*, devote their activities entirely to this sector. They will be briefly described here. The third institution, the *Caisse des Dépôts et Consignations*, has a more complex role and will be discussed at a later point (section 2.6). A list of the abbreviations used is given in Appendix 7.1.

The first intermediary, the French Institute for Real Estate Credit (*Crédit Foncier de France* – CFF), is a publicly-owned stock company. However, it is controlled by the government which, among other privileges, appoints the *Gouverneur* and the two *Sous-Gouverneurs*, who in effect manage the *Crédit Foncier de France*; it also regulates the CFF's activities. These are mainly long-term loans for housing either granted directly to borrowers or rediscounted to commercial banks. Most of these loans carry a below market interest rate, and will be discussed below. The CFF is also charged with administering the secondary market for mortgage loans.

A second intervening institution is the Entrepreneurs' Financing Office (*Comptoir des Entrepreneurs* – CDE), also a publicly-owned but government-controlled stock company. Its function is to finance housing in the initial construction period during which mortgages cannot be obtained.

In 1977, the main types of loans channelled through these two institutions were the following:

(i) Special immediate loans (*Prêts spéciaux immédiats* – PSI). These loans can be granted in two cases. To individuals if their revenues are below certain limits and they want to acquire homes corresponding to certain norms. To firms building houses under these norms (rent charged is then controlled) and renting them to the same categories of revenues as above.

In 1977 (after 24 March), interest charged for PSI was 7.40 per cent for the first ten years and 10 per cent afterwards. There was no control imposed on their expansion.

(ii) Agreed real estate loans (*Prêts immobiliers conventionnés* – PIC). These loans can be granted on less stringent conditions than the PSIs (no revenue ceiling), not only by CFF and CDE but also by all the institutions specialised in housing financing (including commercial banks).

Interest charged in 1977 (after 21 June) was 9–9.25 per cent during the first years to 12–12.50 per cent in the last years. Specialised institutions were allowed to partially refinance these loans at CFF (depending on the type of housing financed) at rates varying from 7 to 10.50 per cent. A small proportion of these credits was submitted to expansion control.

As can be seen from Table 7.1, CFF and CDE issue a minor amount of ordinary loans at market rates. For all the special loans granted at below market rates, government intervention is necessary. It is achieved by guaranteeing CFF and CDE bond issues and also by providing these institutions with subsidies to make up for losses. In fact, these subsidies are indirect. They are channelled through the *Caisse de Consolidation et de Mobilisation des Crédits à Moyen terme* (CACOM), which is part of the *Caisse des Dépôts et Consignations* system. CACOM makes long-term loans to CFF at the rate necessary to ensure that PSIs and PICs can be made without loss.

At the end of 1977, CFF – CDE had approximately 73.18 billion FF of credits for housing outstanding (of these, 19.12 billion had been rediscounted to *Banque de France* or sold on the mortgage market). 6.40 billion FF were loans at the market rate and the remaining 55.78 billion FF were special loans.

(iii) Housing loans linked to special savings forms (*Epargne-logement*). The latter is a savings instrument which allows the saver at a later point in time to benefit of a reduced rate loan. The amount which can be borrowed and the interest rate charged depends on the interest payments (rate and total amount) which were received during the saving period. Government subsidises these instruments (in general, the subsidy is proportional to the interest accumulated during the saving period – notice that the corresponding rate is very low: 2.5 to 3.5 per cent in 1977). The total amount of subsidies for 1977 was 0.92 billion FF. The savings-linked loans can be obtained from any commercial bank or from the savings institutions. The government's subsidy is channelled through the CFF to all the banks.

The structure of the housing loans is illustrated in Table 7.1, which shows the various loans for housing extended in 1977 and the amounts outstanding at the end of that year. On top of the categories already examined, lines 7 to 10 refer to loans granted by an institution of the CDC group (see section 2.6). Given that these are financed at very low cost, even for categories 8 to 10 which receive no government support, the interest rate charged is at below the free market rate. Line 6

TABLE 7.1   Loans to housing *(in billion FF)*

Type of credits	Increase in 1977	End of 1977
1 Special CFF–CDE loans	6.54	66.78
2 Ordinary CFF–CDE loans	1.26	6.40
3 Savings-linked housing loans	6.22	22.32
4 Real estate loans (*prêts conventionnés*)	4.59	17.84
5 Supported CNCA loans	1.26	15.43
6 Supported government loans	(0.74)	18.81
7 CPHLM loans	16.49	106.12
8 Other CDC loans	3.40	36.79
9 Personal loans for housing issued by savings institutions	7.44	22.45
10 Loans complementary to savings-linked housing loans	1.71	5.95
11 Loans admitted on the mortgage market	10.55	83.84
12 Discountable medium-term loans	(0.93)	17.17
13 Medium- and long-term non-discountable loans	4.47	62.86
14 Short-term loans to real estate firms	1.68	24.26
Total	63.94	507.02

ipported government loans, represents a stock which is being mortised; no such loans are issued anymore. Finally, loans granted by ommercial banks which can be sold on the mortgage market carry a :latively low interest rate. The reason for this is not only that they have certain degree of liquidity. Since CDC is a very important investor on iis market (see section 2.6) and its funds are obtained at a regulated low ite, its intervention will maintain the mortgage rate at an artificially low :vel.

From the preceding discussion it can be seen that government can influence the interest rates of loans for housing in different ways:

(i) Direct subsidisation and interest rate regulation for categories 1, 3, 4, 6, 7. We have been unable to compute the total amount of government intervention in 1977. However, for 1975 the *Rapport Barre* shows a total of 9.91 billion FF.

(ii) Allowing for financing of institutions at low rates. This is possible either through regulation of deposit rates, tax privileges (or interest paid for type A passbook at savings banks or on profits for *Crédit Agricole*) or government guarantee on bond issues or through a combination of these, as is done for categories 1, 3, 4, 5, 7, 8, 9 and 10.

(iii) Permitting rediscounting at *Banque de France* at a fixed and low rate, as for category 12.

Thus out of 507.02 billion francs of loans for housing outstanding at he end of 1977, only 93.52 billion FF (18.4 per cent) can be considered .o carry a free market rate. Out of 63.94 billion FF of new loans issued in 1977, loans at the market rate represent only 7.41 billion or 11.6 per cent, .n even smaller proportion.

Among subsidised and special loans, those granted by CPHLM category 7 in Table 7.1) carried the lowest interest rates. This was 3.60 ber cent for the ordinary loans of this institution.

2.3 Loans to agriculture

Financial government intervention in the agricultural sector takes place through a specialised institution: the Mutual Agricultural Credit Institute (*Crédit Agricole Mutuel*). On the local level, it is composed of approximately 9500 local co-operative banks, ninety regional banks and a central unit, the National Agricultural Credit Institute (*Caisse*

Nationale du Crédit Agricole – CNCA). The latter is a public cred institute controlled jointly by the Minister of Agriculture and th Minister of Finance.

Local banks receive demand deposits and short-term savings an issue medium-term debt instruments (bonds). They make short-ter loans. Excess funds are centralised at the CNCA, which invests them o the money market and apportions interests received between loca banks. Long-term savings (*Epargne logement*, time passbooks, bond are collected by CNCA, which makes advances to regional banks fo medium- and long-term loans.

Crédit Agricole Mutuel assets consist of three types of loans as well a of investments on the money market and the mortgage market. Notic that in 1977 and before, *Crédit Agricole Mutuel's* profits were no submitted to taxation. They will be taxed at 33 per cent in 1981 wit progressive rates in 1979 and 1980.

(i) *Short-term loans.* Up to two-year loans are granted by local bank two- to seven-year maturity loans can be refinanced at CNCA There are no government subsidies for these loans, but a ceiling o interest rates charged is imposed by the controlling authority (10. per cent in 1977). In fact, this ceiling is never operational sinc there is always a lower one imposed by CNCA itself (8.75 per cen until October 1977, 8.50 per cent for the rest of 1977) which is ver stable. Actual rates are often even lower than the ceiling, th difference varying for different local banks. There were 28.4 billio FF short-term loans outstanding at the end of 1977. This categor is submitted to growth control.

(ii) *Medium- and long-term 'improved' loans* are loans with maturitie varying from two to twenty years, financed with long-ter resources of the CNCA. For different categories there are differen interest rates, from 4 to 6 per cent in 1977, which are fixed b government. Government also agrees on a formula for computin the cost of financing these loans (a mix of bonds and long-ter savings). The difference between interest received and interest paid multiplied by the amount of loans granted gives the amoun of subsidies that the government will give to CNCA; or if thes subsidies are fixed by the budget, the total amount of supported loans will be determined. In 1977, the increase in supported loan was 12.62 billion FF and at the end of that year the total amoun outstanding was approximately 100 billion FF. Also for 1977 total subsidies received by CNCA was 4.6 billion FF. Notice that according to *Rapport du Conseil National du Crédit 1977*, 15.43

billion FF of supported medium- and long-term CNCA loans were in fact for housing.

iii) *Medium- and long-term ordinary loans*, finally, are submitted to growth control except for credits to housing. The interest rate charged on them in 1977 was 7 per cent. Their total amount outstanding at the end of 1977 was approximately 50 billion FF.

.4 Loans for exports

ince the end of the First World War, France has had a chronic problem ith recurring balance of payments deficits. Starting in 1946, the overnment has tried to remedy this situation by providing loans to xporting firms at below market rates. The task of administering and in ome cases financing these loans has been entrusted to the *Banque rançaise pour le Commerce Extérieur*.

The French Export Bank (*Banque Française pour le Commerce xtérieur* – BFCE) is a private company whose shareholders are the *anque de France*, the *Caisse des Dépôts et Consignations*, the *Crédit ational*, the *Caisse Nationale du Crédit Agricole* and the nationalised anks. The members of the board (*Conseil d'administration*), the hairman and the general director are appointed by the Minister of e Economy. BFCE has a dual activity: it functions as a commercial ank with a strong foreign department and is also in charge of adminis- ring and in certain cases financing the different forms of export edits.

There are different types of loans (see Table 7.2) related to exports ccording to their maturity:

(i) *Short-term loans* (for less than eighteen months) can be granted either to finance sales on credit to foreign buyers (mobilisation credits for foreign claims) or to finance construction of heavy equipment intended to be exported before a special procedure designed for this type of operation can be applied (prefinancing credits).

Mobilisation credits for claims originated on foreign countries are granted by commercial banks at an interest derived from a base rate (TBB)[3] increased with a spread. This rate is lower by one percentage point than the lowest short term domestic rate (*taux de l'escompte des créances commerciales*). These loans can be re- discounted at the *Banque de France*. Their growth is only partially submitted to control (*encadrement du crédit*).

Prefinancing credits are short-term loans that firms can obtain

TABLE 7.2   Credits for exports *(in billion FF)*

Type of credits	Growth in 1977	End of 1977
Mobilisation credits for claims originated on foreign countries[a]	5.37	28.84
Prefinancing credits[a]	1.40	21.44
Mobilisable medium-term credits	14.89	49.81
Non-mobilisable medium- and long-term credits	5.50	20.24
Total	27.16	120.33

[a] Of which:

Short-term credits discounted at *Banque de France*	3.59	5.13
Medium-term credits discounted at *Banque de France*	8.03	34.09

under certain conditions in advance of a medium-term loan. These loans are granted by commercial banks at especially low rate they are discounted at BFCE which, in turn, refinances itself on the money market. The government subsidises the difference between the market rate and the discount rate. The growth of these credit is only partially submitted to controls.

(ii) *Medium-term loans* (less than seven years) for sales to countrie outside the European Community are granted at six different rate depending on the country and the length of the credit (≤ years In 1977, these rates varied between 7.25 and 8 per cent. Such low rates are possible because part of these loans can be rediscounte at the *Banque de France* at 4.5 per cent (the effective cost of the rediscountable portion to banks was 5.55 per cent in 1977). The non-rediscountable portion has to be financed at the mone market's going rate. Given that this rate is highly volatile, the discountable proportion is continually modified so as to enabl banks to charge the fixed special rate. The role of the BFCE is to verify that all the *Banque de France* procedures are correctl followed and, when medium-term credits are granted to exportin firms, to give insurance that they will be repaid. Growth of medium-term loans is only partially submitted to credit contro

(iii) *Long-term loans* (over seven years). These loans are granted b commercial banks and rediscounted at BFCE. They carry lower than market rates (however, less favourable than medium-term loans). The BCFE is allowed to issue long-term loans with government guarantee in order to finance long-term lending. The difference between the rate charged for discounting long-term loans and the true cost is financed by the government. These long-term loans are not subjected to quantitative controls.

2.5 Loans for industrial development

After the Second World War, large sectors of the French industry had been destroyed or had become obsolete. The government wanted to help industrial reconstruction by providing medium-term improved loans and facilitating long-term loans. Since it was thought that the banking system was unable to fulfil this task, a special channel was to be used. It consists mainly in the National Credit Institute (and also in the Credit Institute for the Hotel Industry and the Regional Development Institutes).

Crédit National, the National Credit Institute, is a publicly-owned stock company. Being an institute with a special juridical statutory form, it is in fact managed by government appointees. It is mainly financed by long-term loans. They are not government guaranteed but the Treasury pays one point of interest charges. When loans are issued abroad, government guarantees against foreign exchange risk.

These resources are used for making long-term loans. Most of these are ordinary loans (in 1977 at 11 per cent): 57.2 per cent of new loans made in 1977 by *Crédit National*. The remaining 42.8 per cent were special loans granted for instance to firms with export activities for major projects approved by the authorities or for small businesses. The rates on these special loans were between 8.5 and 9.5 per cent. Notice that most special loans were instituted in recent years; therefore, their contribution in total long-term loans outstanding is less than their proportion of new 1977 loans. *Crédit National* also grants loans at its own risks, but by using Treasury resources. Long-term loans are not submitted to credit controls.

Concerning medium-term loans, *Crédit National* acts as an intermediary between commercial banks and *Banque de France*. It checks if medium-term loan applications correspond to *Banque de France* criteria. If they do, it is advisable to discount them after they have been granted by a commercial bank. After discounting them, it immediately rediscounts them at *Banque de France*.

The interest rate on discountable three- to five-year medium-term loans (*crédits à moyen terme mobilisables*) is the TBB rate – that is, the

banks' base rate – increased by 1.55 per cent (of which 0.25 per cent goe
to *Crédit National* for discounting). Medium-term loans are submittee
to credit controls.

At the end of 1977, the total amount of discountable medium-term
loans granted by commercial banks was 39.81 billion FF, of which only
a minor fraction had effectively been discounted at *Banque de France*
Table 7.3 shows how non-discountable medium- and long-term loan:
had been distributed by various institutions.

TABLE 7.3   Non-discountable medium- and long-term loans for industrial
development *(in billion FF)*

Type of credits	Increase in 1977	Outstanding end of 1977
National Credit Institute:		
Crédit National	3.96	30.60
CDC	1.57	8.18
Treasury	—	36.71
Other (*Crédit Hôtelier*, regional development institutes)	5.39	28.74
Total	10.92	104.23

2.6 Caisse des dépôts et consignations (CDC)

Among the French government-controlled financial institutions, the
Caisse des Dépôts et Consignations plays a special role. Under a Charter
which has remained unchanged since its creation in 1816, it collect:
funds from various sources and manages them independently in a spirit
of 'public interest'.

Although it receives deposits from *notaires* and from social security
its main source of funds are savings banks (*caisses d'épargne*). At the end
of 1977, they represented 82 per cent of total liabilities of 428.7 billion
FF, of which 296.91 billion FF were from type A savings passbooks,
28.11 billion FF from type B savings passbooks and 26.22 billion FF
from books and other schemes of savings for housing purposes
(discussed in section 2.2).

Interest payments were limited in 1977 to 6.5 per cent on all savings
passbooks (the same limit was imposed on similar bank instruments),
but type A passbooks' interest were tax exempt (but each deposit was

imited to 32,500 FF per person before 14 November and to 38,000 FF after this date).

Loans to the housing industries were granted either by the savings banks or by the central authority of CDC under procedures discussed in section 2.2. Table 7.1 shows the total of these different loans as well as those extended by *Caisse de Prêts aux organismes HLM* (CPHLM), a special institution being part of the CDC group. It receives funds from the savings banks, on which it has to pay interest of 7.60 per cent; it also receives long-term loans from various institutions and government subsidies (4.07 billion FF in 1977) as well as government funds for interest reductions (1.50 billion FF in 1977).[4] Interest rates on these loans varied from 3.60 per cent upwards.

At the end of 1977, the total CPHLM amount of loans outstanding was 106.12 billion FF (an increase of 16.49 billion FF). Total loans to the housing industry issued by CDC, savings banks or CPHLM at the end of 1977 amounted to 180.55 billion FF.

Loans at under the market interest rates (8 to 9.75 per cent in 1977) to local authorities and public entities are also extended by CDC through a specialised institution: *Caisse d'Aide à l'Equipement des Collectivités Locales* (CAECL). The total amount of such loans outstanding at the end of 1977 was 114.0 billion FF.

It must also be noted that CDC also extends various direct loans and that it is a very important institutional investor. At the end of 1977, it held 11.30 billion FF worth of mortgage market securities, 71.30 billion FF worth of marketable securities (mainly long-term bonds) and 63.77 billion FF worth of money market securities.

Table 7.4 shows a breakdown of all the loans outstanding at the end of 1977 at commercial banks and at special institutions. Notice that only a few loans were extended at market rates, together with 93.52 billion FF of loans for housing (see section 2.2). The corresponding subtotal is 586.07 billion FF or 39.4 per cent of a total of 1488.91 billion FF.

The interest rates on special loans were as low as 3.6 per cent for forty-year maturities, most of the CPHLM loans (see section 2.6), while the market rate in 1977 ranged from 10.30 per cent upwards (mobilisation credits for commercial claims in the fourth quarter). Interest rates on long-term loans for housing ranged from 12 per cent (for mortgage loans) to 18 per cent.[5]

Although we could not find the exact figures, we can estimate that the direct budgetary government contribution was in the 15 to 20 billion FF range (or approximately 3.5 to 4 per cent of the budget).

TABLE 7.4   Summary of different loans outstanding at the end of 1977
(in billion FF)

Type of credits	Outstanding end of 1977
Loans for housing (including short-term loans to *sociétés immobilières*)	507.02
Loans for agriculture (including 11.98 to local entities)	150.78
Loans for industrial development (granted by CN, SDR, *Crédit Hôtelier*)	104.23
Loans to local entities	114.00
Loans for exports	120.33
Short-term loans to business[a]	289.29
Short-term loans to households[a]	34.72
Other medium- and long-term loans to business[a]	168.54
Total	1488.91

[a] Loans at free market rates.

3. CONCLUDING REMARKS

In the preceding pages we have described the means by which the French government channels funds to privileged sectors of the economy. We have shown that the scope of this form of intervention is very important, probably unusually so for a developed country.

Since government has set up special financial institutions and regulates commercial banks in order to provide certain sectors with loans at 'below market' rates, it forces the economy to be inefficient. Concerning the distortions introduced by government action, three types of questions should be asked to which unfortunately no answer can be provided at this stage:

(i) What are the immediate results obtained in the privileged sectors? By how much have these sectors grown as a result of intervention as compared to a free market situation? We are not equipped to seek answers to such questions and surprisingly we have not found any government (or other) estimates of what these answers could be.

(ii) What is the cost of intervention? Here we would like to know, for instance, the impact of intervention on availability and rates of ordinary loans. Unfortunately, we can offer no satisfactory answer to this question either. Our estimates indicate that credit subsidies have amounted in 1977 to approximately 15 to 20 billion FF. It is impossible to assess a social cost to funds obtained by discounting credits for exports at very low rates at the central bank. More generally, the total welfare loss due to economic misallocation should be estimated.

(iii) How does the French financial system function and what are the problems related to money supply control? Concerning this question, we have developed a model (not presented here) which catches some of the important traits of the French financial system. Our results show that money supply control can be more difficult than in the case of a 'free market' banking system. In particular, control through the imposition of credit limitation of the type used in France can be ineffective.

APPENDIX 7.1   LIST OF ABBREVIATIONS

BFCE	*Banque Française pour le Commerce Extérieur* (French Export Bank)
CACOM	*Caisse de Consolidation et de Mobilisation des Crédits à Moyen Terme* (Institute for Consolidation and Mobilisation for Medium Term Credits)
CAECL	*Caisse d'Aide à l'Equipement des Collectivités Locales* (Institute for Equipment Aid to Local Authorities)
CDC	*Caisse des Dépôts et Consignations* (Deposits and Consignment Institute)
CDE	*Comptoir des Entrepreneurs* (Entrepreneurs' Financing Office)
CFF	*Crédit Foncier de France* (Real Estate Credit Institute of France)
CNCA	*Caisse Nationale du Crédit Agricole* (National Institute for Agricultural Credit)
CPHLM	*Caisse de Prêts aux Organismes HLM* (Credit Institute for Special Housing Offices)
FF	French franc
PIC	*Prêts immobiliers conventionnés* (Agreed real estate loans)
PSI	*Prêts spéciaux immédiats* (Special immediate loans)
SDR	*Sociétés de Développement Régional* (Regional Development Institutions)
TBB	*Taux de base bancaire* (Prime rate at commercial banks)

NOTES

1. This research has been financed by a grant from the Fondation pour la Nouvelle Economic Politique, 107 Av. Henri Martin, Paris 16è, France.

2. Limiting the rate of growth of credits outstanding.
3. TBB = *taux de base bancaire* – equivalent to the US prime rate.
4. *Caisse de Prêts aux Organismes d'Habitations à Loyer Modéré* (1977).
5. *Banque de France* (1977).

REFERENCES

Aftalion, F. (1979) 'Le contrôle monétaire en présence d'institutions financières non bancaires', *Cahier de recherche CERESSEC*.

Banque de France (1977) *Compte-rendu.*

Caisse des Dépôts (1977) *Rapport au Parlement.*

Caisse de Prêts aux Organismes d'Habitations à Loyer Modéré (CPHLM) (1977) *Rapport annuel.*

Conseil National du Crédit (1977) *Rapport annuel et annexes.*

Rapport du groupe de réflexion présidé par R. Barre (1976) 'Le Financement du Logement', *La Documentation Française.*

Rapport du groupe de réflexion présidé par J. Mayoux (1979) 'Le développement des initiatives financières locales et régionales', *La Documentation Française*

S.N. (1973) 'La Caisse des Dépôts et Consignations, notes et études documentaires', *La Documentation Française* (January and June).

S.N. (1975) 'Le Crédit Foncier de France, notes et études documentaires', *La Documentation Française* (December).

Comment on Aftalion

ALAIN SIAENS

The importance of subsidised financial institutions in France, as analysed by Florin Aftalion, raises interesting questions.

(i) The French financial system lacks allocative efficiency, according to Aftalion's own definition: there should be nobody ready to lend at rates below the market rate or ready to borrow at rates above. Obviously, many privileged categories borrow below the market rate and below the rate they would be prepared to borrow at: housing for about 88.4 per cent of its total in 1977, agriculture, exporters, local authorities and public entities, industrial investors, even hotels (we are pleased to learn that we are subsidised by French taxpayers when staying in French hotels). All in all, two-thirds of total borrowing is subsidised by government's resources channelled through special institutions. Debtors include some of the most vocal and influential groups in our society: farmers, homeowners, non-financial corporations. The categories left over having to pay the market rate are limited indeed.

(ii) Doesn't the system look as if the cost of capital is an ugly one? Are interest rates as an economic variable less understood by and not familiar to Latin countries, owing to historical developments described by the sociologist Weber or even by Peyrefitte in his *Le mal français*? As a matter of fact, during the last fifty years, French interest rates, in real terms, whatever they may pertain to, were negative on average, even before taxes paid by savers.

Savers who lend are in no way helped but instead penalised by inflation: they pay taxes on their financial capital itself, and 100 per cent taxes on the real income derived from it.

The cost of subsidising the majority of the borrowers is supported by citizens in general, by savers essentially, not even by the few borrowers at the market rate. Artificially lowering interest rates becomes illogical in a world characterised by inflation and by an inadequate fiscal system. An inflationary bias is built in.

(iii) Even if one does not discuss the objective of helping and discriminating, lowering the specific costs of borrowed capital is not necessarily the optimal way to achieve such a goal. How much did the privileged borrowers grow as a result of such interventions as compared to a free market allocative mechanism? Aftalion rightly finds it surprising that no government estimate gives us in any way an idea of the effects or the opportunity cost of such methods. They are deeply rooted as if positive results go without saying.

(iv) The efficiency of liquidity creation and control. The model shows why the money supply is less well controlled when so many financial institutions obtain new resources through special discounting mechanisms etc. This seems to imply that their normal sources of funds are losing importance or that at the uses side the funds are more solicited.

Furthermore, as Aftalion describes the institutions, most long-term subsidised loans are exempt of quantitative controls, as in the case of financing industrial development, housing and exports; medium- and long-term ordinary loans to agriculture are indirectly determined by the budget. If monetary policy is conducted in terms of credit, monetary aggregates such as M2 or M3 are uncontrollable so far as corresponding assets are long-term subsidised loans. Now, for monetary policy, is it not irrelevant that M2 counterparts are short- or long-term loans?

Once again such financial accommodations hinder monetary policy and encourage inflationary biases.

8. Monetary Policy and the Loan Rate in the Netherlands[1]

ROBERTO E. WESSELS

1. INTRODUCTION

The conventional wisdom approach to controlling the growth of money is that the central bank can, if it wishes, control the money supply process by discretionary control over the amount of liabilities it issues.

Direct control over the growth of central bank liabilities – in monetarist parlance: the monetary base or high-powered money – gives the monetary authorities proximate control over the expansion of commercial bank assets; in general, control over the growth of monetary assets in the economy. Through the expansion of its liabilities, the central bank provides the reserve base which, for self-imposed or statutory reasons, the commercial banking sector employs to sustain the growth of monetary assets such as demand deposits; control over the reserve base therefore implies control over the growth of monetary assets, as banks cannot expand their liabilities unless the supply of reserve assets is proportionally increased. Moreover, as in a fractional reserve system, commercial banks issue a multiple of the reserve base in the form of monetary assets, variations in the monetary base which, as we have seen, are supposedly controlled directly by the central bank, will have powerful effects upon the money supply process.

What is basically untenable about this approach is the implied assumption that the central bank should, in its endeavour to control money supply, disregard the eventuality that a liquidity squeeze – arising from a strictly observed limit on the growth of the monetary base – could lead to a breakdown of the banking system and from there to a protracted economic crisis.

This assumption is in very serious conflict with one of the central bank's main functions: being the lender of last resort. The central bank is not only responsible for its performance in the control of the money supply, it also must ensure the continuity of the financial system. And, as must be quite obvious, being the lender of last resort and pursuing control over the monetary base are responsibilities that cannot be discharged independently. Thus the central bank will often be forced to retrench on previously set monetary base targets in the face of unacceptable risk situations brought about by a policy of inflexible monetary restraint.

This does not mean, however, that the central bank can never refuse to accommodate an individual bank, only that if it does so, it must be convinced that the means sought after are readily available, for example, in the form of excess reserves with other banks, at a price, elsewhere.

In the aggregate, however, if there is a net liquidity deficiency in the banking sector, meaning that banks can no longer meet their reserve requirements, the central bank must act, either by lowering (temporarily) reserve requirements, or by making reserves available either through the discount window or by means of advance facilities.

The methods by which the central bank deals with these problems are therefore of considerable relevance to the analysis of the control of money supply. Pioneering work in this field has been done by F. Aftalion and L. J. White.[2] In this chapter, we attempt to expand their contribution by considering some new approaches to the problem.

In the chapter, two different modes of making advances available to the commercial banking system are considered. The first is by means of a perfectly interest-elastic supply of advances at the current discount rate. The second method considered is a quota system, limiting the recourse to advance facilities and penalising offenders by means of (variable) surcharges over the discount rate.

The implications of these arrangements for the working of monetary policy instruments are considered using the neo-classical model of bank behaviour as an analytical framework, and the Dutch institutional arrangements serving as background decor.

2. THE NEO-CLASSICAL MODEL OF BANK BEHAVIOUR

The literature of the neo-classical theory of firm behaviour, as applied to banks, has been developed by M. A. Klein, M. Monti, J. J. Pringle, P. D. van Loo and S. H. Wood.[3]

n their models, banks are assumed to maximise a criterion function,
erally a definition of profits, under a balance sheet restriction. The
imum value of the criterion function, which determines the com-
ition of the banks' assets and liabilities, occurs where the marginal
rn on all categories of assets and the marginal costs of all sources of
ds are equal.

Marginal costs and marginal returns depend on the structure of the
ility and asset markets. Notably, in competitive markets, individual
ks face infinitely interest-elastic supply or demand schedules; that is,
rkets with exogenously given rates to individual buyers and sellers.
Financial markets, however, are primeval examples of markets where
perfect competition is the rule rather than the exception. Thus, supply
demand schedules will generally be increasing, respectively decreas-
functions of the rate of interest. If, however, we assume that in the
nomy there is some asset which is in perfectly elastic supply to the
ks, the rate of return on this asset is the 'peg' on which all other rates
hung because, as we have seen, at the optimum, the bank will equate
marginal returns and marginal costs.[4] As the peg-rate is constant, all
er rates will be equated to it. The peg-rate, if it exists, is therefore a
cial variable; it is changes in this rate that leads to – *ceteris*
ibus – changes of the optimal allocation of assets and liabilities of the
ks' portfolios.

In Aftalion and White's model, the central bank's discount rate is the
g-rate of the economy by virtue of two assumptions.[5] First, the central
k is assumed to be willing to provide unlimited amounts of advances
fixed rate. Second, their results implicitly assume that advances from
central bank are always some positive magnitude. Thus, even when
demand deposit market is competitive, implying that the supply of
nand deposits is perfectly elastic to the individual bank, positive
tral bank advances peg the demand deposit rate at its opportunity
t: the discount rate. There is, of course, no basis for this line of
ught. Either the peg-rate is above the discount rate and the banks
d no demand deposits, which is an unlikely state of affairs, or it is
ow the discount rate in which case one wonders why the banks
row from the central bank at all.[6]

Dropping the restriction that advances must always be positive leads
to the conclusion that the rate, on which profit-maximising banks will
se their loan rates in a system of perfectly interest-elastic supply of
erves, is not necessarily always equal to the discount rate. However, in
s system the peg-rate will certainly never be higher than the discount
e. This finding provides an important rationale for the custom,

adopted in many European countries, to peg loan rates to the discount rate.[7] The practice of pegging loan rates to the discount rate originally evolved from the willingness of the central bank to provide advances at fixed rate. By maintaining the loan rate slightly above the discount rate, bank was certain that it would never incur marginal losses if it was forced to rediscount notes or bills at the central bank. Moreover, the supply of loans was, no doubt, more atomistic than it is nowadays, allowing little leeway for the exercise of monopoly power (and higher rates). Though concentration in the banking industry has increased dramatically, the custom of pegging the loan rate to the discount rate has nonetheless been maintained. A formal, theoretical justification of this practice is difficult to give. This does not mean, however, that we are therefore dealing with an irrational phenomenon.

This type of loan-pricing policy corresponds to two different market models of market behaviour. First, if the discount rate is effective (that is the banks are in the 'Bank'), pegging the loan rate to the discount rate implies that the banks act as though the loan rate was determined competitively. Second, whenever the real peg-rate is lower than the discount rate, that is whenever advances from the central bank are zero the banks act as monopolists by charging their customers a loan rate which is higher than the opportunity cost of their funds. Thus, loan rates are set somewhere between the competitive price and the short-run monopoly price, which is precisely what oligopoly theory, recognising the interdependence of competition among the few, would predict.

The arrangement of keeping the loan rate pegged to the discount rate offers a number of attractive features to the commercial banks. First collusion is passive. The banks do not need to take any initiatives to either raise or lower loan rates; they simply *all* follow the central bank's lead. This is done quite easily by explicitly tying loan rates to the discount rate, for example a typical loan rate would be discount rate plus 2 per cent. The second advantage is that changes in the loan rate are communicated very cheaply to loan customers by the newsmedia announcing a change in the central bank's discount rate. The third advantage is a psychological one. Loan rate increases are seen to be manifestly caused by the central bank's policy and not by the banks' inherent greed for profits. The banks, therefore, do not need to justify increases to their customers because they have been willed by the central bank. One last factor must be mentioned. Though it probably falls outside the domain of economic analysis, it is nonetheless very relevant to our description of the working of the financial system. It is what P. L. Joskow calls the ethos of the market.[8] Co-operative ethos or a

eluctance to engage in hard-nosed competition often occurs in es-
ablished industries where firms are bound by common customs and
raditions, and which notably tend to frown upon all-out competitive
behaviour, preferrring the signalling of policy intentions through
nformal channels. The banking community fits this description ex-
remely well, and the influence of the market ethos on the decision-
making process is probably considerable. This point is well worth
bearing in mind when we discuss the introduction of the general
urcharge in section 4.

In the next section, we describe the working of a model with a pegged
loan rate and derive some results for comparative static changes in
nstruments of monetary policy.

3. THE BASIC MODEL

Following Aftalion and White, we assume to be dealing with an economy
comprising three sectors: a central bank, a group of commercial banks
and the public.[9]

The central bank's balance sheet can be expressed as:

$$S + A = R + C \qquad (1)$$

where S = treasury obligations held by the central bank
$\quad A$ = advances by the central bank to the commercial
$\qquad$ banks ('refinancing')
$\quad R$ = reserves held by the commercial bank against deposits
$\quad C$ = currency held by the public

Advances are provided by the central bank at a fixed rate r_A, thus the
amount of advances borrowed by the banks is an endogenous variable of
the model. We assume that the stock of treasury obligations, S, is an
exogenous variable; that is, the central bank is not committed to
pursuing interest rate policies through sales and purchases of government securities.

The activities of the commercial banks are reflected by their balance
sheet which is equal to

$$L + R = D + A \qquad (2)$$

where L = loans to the public
$\quad D$ = demand deposits

The reserve requirements imposed on the commercial banks is of the form

$$R \geq kD \qquad (3)$$

which satisfies $0 < k < 1$. We assume that (3) is always an equality; that is, that banks never hold excess reserves.

Following the discussion of the pegging of the loan rate, the commercial banks set their loan rate r_L equal to the discount rate r_A. In practice, the banks charge their customers a surcharge over the discount rate. As the individual surcharges very seldomly change we can, for practical purposes, take the average surcharge as a constant, denoted here by γ.

Thus the loan rate function can be expressed as:

$$r_L = \gamma + r_A \qquad (4)$$

Given the price of loans, the public determines the amount of loans by means of the following demand function

$$L = L(r_L, X); \qquad L_{r_L} < 0 \text{ and } L_x > 0 \qquad (5)$$

where X is a vector of exogenous variables affecting the demand for loans.

The public's demand for currency, C, is assumed to be proportional to demand deposits, D, and depends on r_D, the interest rate paid on demand deposits. Hence we have

$$C = e(r_D).D; \qquad e_{r_D} < 0 \qquad (6)$$

The model shown in equations (1) to (6) is not complete; the rate of interest paid on demand deposits must yet be determined. Assuming that banks work to profit-maximising goals, we consider two cases: either the demand deposit markets are *competitive*, in which case r_D is *given* to the individual bank, or competition is limited or *imperfect* and r_D is determined by *price-setting practices*. In order to keep the analysis simple we shall, in the latter case, rely on a monopoly model and disregard the complications of price-setting behaviour in an oligopolistic market environment.

When the demand deposit markets are *competitive*, and demand deposits are in elastic supply to individual banks, the working of the model is quite straightforward. Given the rate on advances r_A, the loan rate r_L determines the amount of loans L. Next, substituting (6) and (3) into (1) and consolidating the resulting expression with (2) yields the equilibrium amount of demand deposits, for given rate r_D.

$$D = \frac{L+S}{1+e} \qquad (7)$$

Equation (7), in turn, determines the amount of currency with the public C, and the commercial bank reserves, R. The amount of advances are determined by means of the balance sheet constraint (1). Taking the case now that the demand deposit market is *monopolistic*, the demand deposit rate, r_D, can be derived from the first-order conditions for the maximisation of the following profit function

$$\Pi = r_L L - r_A A - r_D D \qquad (8)$$

which, after substitution of the appropriate restrictions, viz. equations (1) and (2), becomes

$$\Pi = r_L L - r_A (1-\theta)L + r_A \theta S - r_D \frac{L+S}{1+e} \qquad (9)$$

where $\theta = \dfrac{1-k}{1+e}$

Setting the derivatives of Π with respect to the demand deposit rate r_D equal to zero, we obtain

$$r_D = (1-k)r_A + \frac{1+e}{e_{r_D}} \qquad (10)$$

Once this rate has been determined, the working of the model proceeds analogously to the model with a competitively determined rate r_D.

What do these models imply for the conduct of monetary policy? The answer to this question will be couched in terms of the effects that monetary policy instruments have on the stock of money. The latter variable is generally defined as being equal to:

$$M = C + D \qquad (11)$$

Substituting (6) and (7) into (11), we can also express equation (11) a

$$M = S + L[r_L(r_A), X]$$ (12

We will employ equation (12) to analyse the effects of monetary polic
instruments on the stock of money by considering three instrument
open market operations, changes in reserve requirements and discoun
rate changes. First, let us consider the case where the rate on deman
deposits is taken as *given*; that is, the competitive demand deposit marke
model. The impact of changes in the instruments of monetary policy o
the stock of money is equal to (assuming the instruments to b
independent):

$$\frac{\partial M}{\partial S} = 1; \qquad \frac{\partial M}{\partial k} = 0; \qquad \frac{\partial M}{\partial r_A} = L_{r_L} < 0$$

Recalling the discussion on the way the model works, these results ar
not surprising. Open market operations affect money only on a one-to
one basis because loan demand – the other source of changes in th
money stock – is not affected. Note that this implies that open marke
operations alter the composition of the public's assets without affectin
their relative prices. However, if wealth is included as an argument of th
loan demand function, open market operations will obviously have
larger impact (than 1) on the stock of money.[10]

Changes in reserve requirements do not affect the stock of money. In
competitive market, demand deposits are in perfectly elastic supply t
the individual bank. Thus the *individual bank* reacts to an increase i
reserve requirements by taking in more deposits. Of course, when w
aggregate to all banks this process cannot be carried through withou
limit; at a certain point the banks will be forced into the 'Bank'. Howeve
as the central bank's supply schedule of advances is infinitely elastic
banks can offset additional reserve requirements by borrowing mor
from the central bank. We thus have the case in which the discount rate i
the peg-rate by virtue of the banks being forced to borrow from th
central bank and because the central bank is willing to provide advance
at a constant rate.

We are thus left to draw the conclusion that changes in the discoun
rate are the only instrument the central bank has with which it ca
attempt to control the stock of money. If, however, $|L_{r_L}|$ is small, o
believed to be so, then the central bank must be willing at times t
increase the discount rate dramatically in order for it to be effective, a

ction which could have considerable side effects; for example, an influx
f short-term foreign capital which would then have offsetting effects on
ne central bank's restrictive policy. This is probably the reason why
estrictive monetary policy in countries with fixed discount rates is so
ften imposed in the form of loan ceilings, and not indirectly through
igher interest rates. The difference between the two systems, however, is
osmetic rather than substantial.

Let us now consider the case where the demand deposit rate is
eterminded by the price-setting behaviour of a monopolist, cf. equation
10). The previous results on the working of monetary policy still apply,
ven though in this case open market operations will affect the demand
eposit rate. The point to note here is that the loan rate is not a function
f the demand deposit rate, thus neither open market operations nor
eserve requirement changes have any *secondary effects* on other
ariables affecting the determination of the money stock, that is, the
mount of loans outstanding.

As long as the commercial banks' loan rate pricing policies remain
nchanged (that is, loan rates are kept pegged to the central bank's
liscount rate and the central bank is willing to provide advances at that
ate), the only instrument the central bank can wield is the discount rate.
he question of how demand deposits are priced, that is the structure of
he demand deposit markets, is an irrelevant one for the conduct of
nonetary policy.

In order to increase the effectiveness of its monetary policy instru-
nents, the Dutch central bank has since 1973 dramatically changed the
ules by which banks can avail themselves of advances. The next section
s devoted to incorporating these changes into the model and to
nalysing the working of monetary policy under the new conditions.

4. AN ALTERNATIVE SCHEME FOR CENTRAL BANK ADVANCES

A recent development in the Dutch money market has been the
ntroduction of a quota system for the recourse that commercial banks
nay have to the central bank's advance facilities. A detailed description is
;iven by P. C. Timmerman.[11]

The quota system establishes formal limits to the amount of funds
which the commercial banks may borrow at the current discount rate.
The quota limit is fixed as a percentage of a lagged average of liabilities
ubject to reserve requirements. If, for whatever reason, the quota is

exceeded, the central bank imposes a penalty rate on offenders which takes the form of a (variable) surcharge over the discount rate. For reasons that can easily be determined, this change of the central bank policy eliminated the main premise of the argument for pegging the loan rate to the discount rate; whenever the advances quota is exceeded, the banks' marginal costs increase while their marginal revenue remain constant.

Faced with this situation, the commercial banks collectively announced the imposition of a so-called *general surcharge* on existing loan rate Since its introduction in 1973, the surcharge has been set at levels varying between 0 and 3 per cent. Although the decision to change the surcharge level is formally taken by each bank individually, a collusively reached agreement appears to exist between banks: not only do the banks publish the same change in their surcharge rate, but they do so practically simultaneously, the notices often appearing side-by-side in the press. The collective introduction of a general surcharge (on loan rates) indicate that the commercial banks now act as price setters in the loan market adjusting the surcharge in order to fix the loan rate at levels considered to be more appropriate to their desired rates of profit.

In order to analyse the influence of these changes, the basic model given in section 3, must be modified in two respects. First, we must add term representing the general surcharge to the loan rate schedule Second, the central bank's rate for advances now obeys two different regimes, depending on whether or not the quota for advances is exceeded.

Symbolically, the model can be expressed as follows. Let us denote the function of the total cost of borrowing from the central bank by $p(A)$ then

$$p(A) \begin{cases} = r_A A & \text{if} \quad A \leqq \overset{\thicksim}{A} \\ = r_A \overset{\thicksim}{A} + \int\limits_{\overset{\thicksim}{A}}^{A} g(\alpha)d\alpha & \text{if} \quad A > \overset{\thicksim}{A} \end{cases} \tag{13}$$

where $\overset{\thicksim}{A}$ represents the quota ceiling. We assume that $p_A > 0$ holds.

Denoting the general surcharge by r_S, the banks' loan-rate function is now equal to

$$r_L = \gamma + r_A + r_S \tag{14}$$

where r_S can be derived from first-order conditions for profit maximisation.

Assuming that the banks choose to optimise r_L and r_D, letting A be implicitly determined by the balance sheet constraints, the effect of the policy change on the optimal values of r_L and r_D can be analysed by considering two cases. The first in which we assume that profit-maximising levels of r_D and r_L imply $A \leq \tilde{A}$; the second, in which the opposite is true. That is to say, by considering solutions for r_D and r_L which we assume satisfy the restriction $A \leq \tilde{A}$ in the first case, and $A > \tilde{A}$ in the second case.

Case I: quota is not exceeded $(A \leq \tilde{A})$

The banks' profits are given by:

$$\Pi = r_L L - r_A A - r_D D$$

From first-order conditions we can derive

$$r_D = (1 - k)r_A + \frac{1 + e}{er_D}$$

$$r_L = -\frac{L}{L_{r_L}} + r_A + \frac{1}{e_{r_D}}$$

$$r_S = -\frac{L}{L_{r_L}} + \frac{1}{e_{r_D}} - \gamma$$

Thus, in this case, the surcharge level is set as the difference between the banks' marginal loan revenue and marginal demand deposit cost and the fixed surcharge γ, that is, the general surcharge is used to adjust marginal revenue to its monopoly optimum.

Case II: quota is exceeded $(A > \tilde{A})$

The banks' profit function is now given by

$$\Pi = r_L L - r_A \tilde{A} - \int_{\tilde{A}}^{A} g(\alpha)d\alpha - r_D D$$

From first-order conditions we can derive

$$r_D = (1 - k)g(A) + \frac{1 + e}{e_{r_D}}$$

$$r_L = -\frac{L}{L_{r_L}} + g(A) + \frac{1}{e_{r_D}}$$

$$r_S = -\frac{L}{L_{r_L}} + \frac{1}{e_{r_D}} - \gamma + g(A) - r_A$$

The difference of the level of the general surcharge between Case I and Case II is the term $g(A) - r_A$, which represents the difference between the effective marginal advance rate and the discount rate. Thus, when the quota is exceeded, the banks will try to pass the increased cost of borrowing from the central bank to their customers.

What inferences can we draw from this model for the working of monetary policy? Recalling that the main objective of monetary policy is to control the supply of money, and that we have defined money as equal to

$$M = C + D = S + L(r_L, X)$$

and that, moreover, the loan rate is now a function

$$r_L = r_L(r_A, r_S)$$

it is then obvious that the effects that monetary policy instruments have on the stock of money will depend on the way the general surcharge is affected by changes in the central bank's instruments.

The direction in which the money stock changes, following changes in an instrument of monetary policy, can be easily derived by totally differentiating r_D and r_S with respect to the three instruments. Using second-order conditions, the results shown in Table 8.1 apply. The implied impact multipliers for the stock of money are given in Table 8.2. The results presented in Table 8.2 are quite remarkable. First, it is obvious that monetary policy achieves totally different results depending on whether the banks are within the quota or not. Second, it is no longer the case that increases in the discount rate will always lead, via increases in the loan rate, to a decrease in the demand for money. It is quite conceivable that the opposite be true: that is, when the general surcharge is lowered more than the discount rate is increased, the total effect on money demand will be positive. Finally, changes in the central bank's holdings of Treasury obligations, S, are shown to have multiplier effect when $A > \tilde{A}$.

To see how the multiplier effect works, let us consider the case where

TABLE 8.1   Partial derivatives of r_D and r_S

Case I $(A \leqq \hat{A})$	Case II $(A > \hat{A})$
$\dfrac{\partial r_D}{\partial r_A} > 0$	$\dfrac{\partial r_D}{\partial r_A} < 0$
$\dfrac{\partial r_D}{\partial k} < 0$	$\dfrac{\partial r_D}{\partial k} > 0$
$\dfrac{\partial r_D}{\partial S} > 0$	$\dfrac{\partial r_D}{\partial S} < 0$
$\dfrac{\partial r_S}{\partial r_A} > 0$	$\dfrac{\partial r_S}{\partial r_A} < 0$
$\dfrac{\partial r_S}{\partial k} = 0$	$\dfrac{\partial r_S}{\partial k} > 0$
$\dfrac{\partial r_S}{\partial S} = 0$	$\dfrac{\partial r_S}{\partial S} < 0$

TABLE 8.2   Impact multipliers for the money stock

Case I $(A \leqq \hat{A})$	Case II $(A > \hat{A})$
$\dfrac{\partial M}{\partial r_A} = \left(1 + \dfrac{\overset{+}{\partial} r_S}{\partial r_A}\right) \bar{L}_{r_L} < 0$	$\dfrac{\partial M}{\partial r_A} = \left(1 + \dfrac{\overset{+}{\partial} r_S}{\partial r_A}\right) \bar{L}_{r_L} \overset{<}{_>} 0$
$\dfrac{\partial M}{\partial k} = 0$	$\dfrac{\partial M}{\partial k} = \dfrac{\overset{+}{\partial} r_S}{\partial k} \bar{L}_{r_L} < 0$
$\dfrac{\partial M}{\partial S} = 1$	$\dfrac{\partial M}{\partial S} = 1 + \dfrac{\overset{-}{\partial} r_S}{\partial S} \bar{L}_{r_L} > 0$

the central bank *increases* its holdings of government obligations S. The primary effect is an increase of the central bank's liquid debt (C and R). Secondary effects occur due to the subsequent easing of money market conditions which lower the cost of demand deposits, allowing the commercial banks to substitute demand deposits for advances. The *decrease* of the amount of advances borrowed under the quota scheme then *lowers* the marginal cost of making loans, allowing the banks to lower the level of the general surcharge.

By imposing a quota on the amount of advances which may be borrowed at the fixed discount rate, the Dutch central bank has managed to increase the potential effectiveness of its open market operations. However, whenever advances are brought back to levels *below* the quota, multiplier effects will cease to be present and the central bank will again have to rely on the discount rate as its sole instrument of monetary policy.

5. SUMMARY AND CONCLUSIONS

Discretionary control of the growth of the monetary base is often advocated as being the correct approach to money supply control problems; if the central bank is prepared to abide firmly by its decision on how much base money it will allow into the system in order to achieve its money supply target and lets the market decide what the appropriate rate of interest must be, it will be in effective control of the money supply.

This approach is deficient insofar as it disregards the social costs of enforcing a strict rationing of central bank liabilities upon the economy. If, as is quite likely, these costs are high, and the central bank does not wish to incur them, or simply cannot because it must continue to function as the lender of last resort, it will have to consider other means of attempting to control monetary aggregates.

Our conclusion from the institutional and analytical arguments put forward is that, ultimately, all the instruments of monetary policy considered in this chapter must rely on the cost of central bank advances permeating into the cost of credit and thence into the money supply process. Though increases in reserve ratios or open market operations can be shown, on paper, to influence the cost of bank credit and thus the money supply, the lender of last resort function effectively precludes that the central bank can passively watch whenever banks are not able to meet prescribed liquidity levels; it must, in effect, provide the liquidity, albeit at a price, and hope that in time higher interest rates will dampen loan demand. The banks will then reduce their liabilities, thus decreasing the amount of monetary assets in the economy or at least the rate of their growth.

The effectiveness of monetary policy therefore depends on the extent to which the demand for loans responds to changes in the loan rate, a matter on which there is still considerable dispute. To quote from a recent article by the President of the Dutch central bank, 'it is not certain to what extent the demand for credit will respond to an increase in nterest rates. In a situation with market inflation and attendant nflationary expectations, its effectiveness becomes an open question.'[12]

The lack of consensus in an area of such obvious policy relevance is, of course, a challenge to the profession. We should, however, not be too sanguine about the adequacy of the analytical framework presented here. Much work remains to be done, for example, making allowances for the openness of the economy, before meaningful hypotheses can be put to empirical verification.

NOTES

1. Comments of J. Vuchelen on an earlier draft are gratefully acknowledged. Cheerful and untiring secretarial support was provided by Saskia ten Asbroek and José Hooijmans. Finally, sharing a work-habitat with Tom Wansbeek has contributed much to the final product without, however, implying any responsibility whatever for remaining errors.
2. F. Aftalion and L. J. White (1977).
3. M. A. Klein (1971); M. Monti (1972); J. J. Pringle (1973); P. D. van Loo (1979); J. H. Wood (1975).
4. J. J. Pringle (1973) p. 992.
5. F. Aftalion and L. J. White (1977).
6. If the discount rate level is below the peg-rate, this would imply that the discount rate does not represent an effective opportunity to borrow, advances being allocated by means other than price.
7. See the surveys by D. R. Hodgman (1974) and J. Vuchelen (1978).
8. P. L. Joskow (1975).
9. F. Aftalion and L. J. White (1977).
10. J. Vuchelen (1978) p. 345.
11. P. C. Timmerman (1977).
12. J. Zijlstra (1979) p. 17.

REFERENCES

Aftalion, F. and L. J. White (1977) 'A Study of a Monetary System with a Pegged Discount Rate under Different Market Structures', *Journal of Banking and Finance*, pp. 349–71.

Aftalion, F. and L. J. White (1978) 'A Study of a Monetary System with a Pegged Discount Rate under Different Market Structures: a reply to J. Vuchelen', *Journal of Banking and Finance*, pp. 351–4.

Hodgman, D. R. (1974) *National Monetary Policies and International Monetary Cooperation* (Boston: Little Brown).

Joskow, P. L. (1975) 'Firm Decision-making Processes and Oligopoly Theory'. *American Economic Review* (Papers and Proceedings) pp. 270–9.

Klein, M. A. (1971) 'A Theory of the Banking Firm', *Journal of Money, Banking and Credit*, pp. 205–18.

Monti, M. (1972) 'Deposit, Credit and Interest Rate Determination unde Alternative Bank Objective Functions' in K. Shell and G. P. Szegö (eds *Mathematical Methods in Investment and Finance* (Amsterdam: Nortl Holland).

Pringle, J. J. (1973) 'A Theory of the Banking Firm', *Journal of Money, Credit an Banking*, pp. 990–6.

Timmerman, P. C. (1977) *The Intervention Policy of the Netherlands Bank in th Money Market* (Amsterdam: De Nederlandsche Bank, Reprint 33).

Van Loo, P. D. (1979) 'On the micro-economic foundations of bank behaviou in macro-economic models', Mimeographed (Rotterdam: Erasmu University, Report 7901/M).

Vuchelen, J. (1978) 'A Study of a Monetary System with a Pegged Discount Rat under Different Market Structures: Comments on the article by F. Aftalio and L. White', *Journal of Banking and Finance*, pp. 339–50.

Wood, J. H. (1975) *Commercial Bank Loan and Investment Behaviour* (New York John Wiley).

Zijlstra, J. (1979) 'Monetary Theory and Monetary Policy: A Central Banker' View', *De Economist*, pp. 3–20.

Comment on Wessels

JOZEF VUCHELEN

The chapter by Roberto Wessels is concerned with the determination of loan rates under different institutional systems regulating borrowing of commercial banks from the central bank.

In the first part of the chapter, the pegging of the loan rate to the discount rate is discussed and explained by a kind of risk aversion behaviour of commercial banks: marginal losses will be avoided if banks are forced to borrow from the central bank.

The author does mention loan pricing cartels, suggesting a monopolistic loan market; but a strict pegging of the loan rate to the discount rate is only optimal in a competitive loan market since, in a monopolistic loan market, the loan rate would not be strictly pegged to the discount rate: the monopolistic profit margin is not a constant, except in rather special cases.

One can ask why banks form a cartel to fix the loan rate at a level that could also result out of simple price competition. The author offers three explanations, consisting of some attractive features of linking the loan rate to the discount rate: the initiative for loan rate adjustments is with the central bank (in other words, commercial banks consider the central bank as the price leader in the loan market); there is a reduction of information costs; finally, the blame for higher loan rates is transferred to the central bank. These explanations take the behaviour of commercial banks as a starting point. Other explanations, maybe as acceptable, can be found in the behaviour of the central bank. I will mention two explanations.

(i) The central bank could think that price competition would result in disorderly conditions on the capital market and therefore favours and stimulates a link loan-discount rate.

(ii) The central bank could favour the link in the belief that an interest rate monetary policy will be more effective. This is true as long as we accept the absence of uncertainty. If this is not the case, it has to be taken into account that a rigid link loan-discount rate will lead to variations in the non-price terms of loan contracts. Information about these non-price terms is more difficult to obtain so that discount rate changes will not predict perfectly changes in the total cost of loans.

In the third place, the Aftalion–White model, summarised in section 2, is broadened so as to take an endogenous borrowing cost into account. The model is solved for the monopolistic loan–monopolistic deposit market case. Since this part of the chapter is the most interesting one, I would like to comment in some detail.

It is argued that the quota penalty rate system for borrowing from the central bank eliminated the main argument for pegging the loan rate to the discount rate. The implied causality runs from the introduction of the new system to a change in the loan rate setting function. One can ask if this was the only reason for the change. If the answer is affirmative, it would be interesting to know the reasons for the introduction of the new borrowing cost system. Was the objective not to break the peg loan discount rate? If the answer on the first question was negative, the central bank could have introduced the new borrowing cost system in order to obtain a better control on discounting of the commercial banks without having to alter systematically the discount rate. Does this imply that there is a non-monetary cost associated with discount rate changes?

I do not have enough knowledge of the monetary system in the Netherlands to give answers to these questions. What I can do is to analyse the quite similar Belgian experience. Up to April 1969, borrowing from the Belgian central bank was limited by an internal and external ceiling.

In reality, these ceilings were never effective, so that it could be assumed that borrowing from the central bank was freely available. In May 1969, the discount facilities of a commercial bank became a function of its deposits. By changing the borrowing quota (that is, the relation with deposits), the central bank could now reduce borrowing of commercial banks when the ceiling was (or became) effective without having to alter the discount rate. In July 1974, the central bank introduced a system comparable to the one discussed by R. Wessels.

Commercial banks in Belgium, however, broke the peg of the loan rate to the discount rate about one year before the penalty rate system was added to the quota borrowing line. From this experience it may be asked if the disappearance of a rigid link between the loan and discount rate in the Netherlands in 1973 was only due to the introduction of the quota system.

At least six reasons can be found why the link loan discount rate broke up in Belgium in 1973:

(i) Market interest rates and the discount rate no longer moved parallel in 1973: the rise in market rates was much larger than in the discount rate.
(ii) Not all loan rates are based on the same discount rate. In 1973, some discount rates increased more than others so that the relative cost of loans, based on a constant link loan-discount rates, would have changed significantly.
(iii) The relative importance of discountable paper declined rapidly since 1965. Up to 1965, discountable loans amounted to about 60 per cent of total loans; in 1970, this had dropped to 50 per cent, in 1973 to 40 per cent.
(iv) The discount ceiling had dropped from 16 per cent in 1969 to 4 per cent in 1974.
(v) The marginal cost of deposits increased rapidly in 1973, due to increasing interest rates and an increase in the relative importance of large deposits with an interest rate based on short-term international money market rates.
(vi) The National Bank favoured the disappearance of the link in order to limit the psychological effects of discount rate changes.

It would be interesting to know to what extent the same conditions applied in the Netherlands. Was the introduction of the new borrowing cost system not an opportunity for the commercial banks to change their loan rate setting function?

Commenting further on some other points, as far as I know, the discount cost is somewhat more complex than written in expression (13). The rate paid on borrowing from the central bank does not increase in a continuous way with the level of borrowing. More exactly, the discount rate on borrowing is a stepfunction. I do agree that the formulation of expression (13) is an approximation, but it has to be taken into account that borrowing cost will be overestimated at some points and underestimated at other points. This could be important when the model is estimated.

Concerning the surcharge, it has to be noted that it consists of two parts: a monopoly profit margin and the effect of the penalty rate system. It is not clear to me why the introduction of the quota penalty rate system changed the competitive nature of the loan market from a perfect competitive to a monopolistic one. More precisely, why do banks only exploit their monopoly power under a penalty borrowing cost system?

Further, Wessels writes that 'whenever advances are brought back to levels below the quota, . . . the central bank will again have to rely on the discount rate as its sole instrument of monetary policy, . . . '. If this is accepted, it implies that when the quota is not effective, commercial banks determine their loan rate as if they operated in a perfect competitive market, since in a monopolistic loan market the reserve coefficient affects the money stock. Does this imply that when the quota is effective in one month and not in the following month, the loan rate will be determined first in a monopolistic and then in a competitive way?

Finally, in the multiplier analysis, changes in the penalty rate function $(g(\alpha))$ are not analysed. It would be interesting to search for the effects of changes in this relation. This function $(g(\alpha))$ can be considered as a fourth and fifth instrument of monetary policy (the slope and its origin $\tilde{A}$). A study can also be made of the relative effectiveness of discount rate changes and changes in the penalty rate function. Are they really complementary instruments as one would conclude from a first analysis? Maybe such a study can also be helpful in understanding why the system was introduced.

Concluding, I would like to say that the extension of the Aftalion–White model to the case of a quota penalty rate borrowing system is very relevant for different European countries. This study was a first attempt with very interesting results. I hope some empirical results will be presented in the near future.

9. Monetary Restraint Through Credit Control in the United Kingdom – the Lessons of Recent Practice

ROY A. BATCHELOR and BRIAN GRIFFITHS

1. INTRODUCTION

This chapter presents a play within a play. Its core is an analysis of the distortions caused by the recent system of direct controls on bank liability expansion in the United Kingdom, the supplementary special deposit scheme, vulgarly termed the 'corset'. Around this analysis we want to develop a broader thesis: that the existence of such controls should be viewed not as a response to new or transitory pressures, but as the inevitable result of the defective intellectual framework within which the authorities have tried to square their monetary, fiscal and debt management policies for the past thirty years.

This is an important connection to make, for two reasons. First, it suggests that the money supply process in the United Kingdom is not just ungainly by comparison with some textbook ideal – what system is not? – but that its operation necessarily imposes costly and inequitable distortions on bank credit markets. The recent application of a corset on bank liability expansion produces the particular set of distortions discussed below. Earlier attempts to influence the scale and priorities of bank lending, and to manipulate interest relativities, produced others.

Second, there is little hope of a more efficient system evolving naturally out of present policies. Indeed, the innovations and insti-tutional changes which the authorities have nerved themselves to introduce have in practice not only exaggerated the existing welfare costs of monetary control but also given the authorities further financial incentive to preserve the *status quo*.

This has happened partly because the authorities have been happy to introduce the trappings of an ideal control system only where there was no obvious conflict with other political objectives or perceived institutional constraints. A vivid example of the problems to which such half-hearted attitudes to reform may lead is the way the policy of announcing monetary targets has reacted with the corset controls. The information content of targets is of social value insofar as it promotes rational, stabilising behaviour by businesses in the real economy and a matching smooth flow of finance from a decentralised competitive banking system. As we shall see, the coexistence in the United Kingdom of monetary targets with a highly oligopolistic banking system, subject to intermittent direct controls, has generated as much instability as the controls themselves. Moreover, attempts by the banking system to anticipate and evade the corset controls have diminished the usefulness for business planning of the monetary targets themselves, since the balance sheet adjustments involved have made the targeted variable, broad money (sterling M3), a poor index of monetary growth.

The most insidious feature of current monetary policy is not, however, this well-meaning attempt to apply selected pieces of the first-best monetary policy to an environment from which market imperfections have not been eliminated. It is rather that the authorities have taken other actions which turn existing market imperfections to their own financial advantage. Again, the corset provides a good illustration. The structure of controls effectively subsidises public debt, a point elaborated upon below. A similar criticism can be levelled at the authorities' recent move to a minimum price tender in the market for new government stock. Despite appearances, this does not really move the market closer to a competitive tender system, but does ensure that any speculative profits between announcement and sale accrue to the government rather than the market.

The authorities currently have both the system of monetary control and the present technique of bank regulation under review. We have made the case elsewhere for a radical shift to a base control system, and are satisfied that the appropriate institutional reforms would be feasible.[1] The morals we would like to draw from the present study are, first, that less radical non-market-based control systems inevitably involve some kind of distortionary direct controls on bank operations; and, second, that the authorities should not be seduced by the financial

enefits to their debt management programme which can be squeezed
ut of such compromise systems. The costs to the private economy in
erms of instability and market distortions appear much greater.

. MONETARY POLICY INNOVATIONS 1971-9

During the 1950s and 1960s, the monetary authorities in the United
Kingdom had at their disposal three types of instruments with which to
ontrol bank behaviour: Bank Rate, which governed the general level of
domestic interest rates; ratio requirements on the structure of bank
portfolios; and direct controls on the scale and direction of bank
ending.

Interest rate policy was, however, aimed at the promotion of real
economic growth. This policy initially involved cheap money policies to
stimulate investment, but latterly involved artificially raising short-term
interest rates to offset in the capital account the constraints on growth,
imposed by persistent deficits in the current account of the balance of
payments. By convention, banks did come to observe minimum cash
and liquid assets ratios, but these ratios were never varied in an
aggressive fashion. Nor could the supply of liquid assets be effectively
estricted. The authorities' overriding concern to stabilise gilt prices
meant that banks holding apparently less liquid public debt could at any
ime swap them for cash at known, non-penal prices.

The most significant event in bank portfolio regulation was the
introduction in 1958 of calls for 'special deposits' at the Bank of
England. These deposits did yield the going Treasury bill rate, but did
not qualify as liquid assets and were in the first instance explicitly called
o reduce the banks' capacity to expand loans and advances. As time
wore on, however, variations in the rate of call of special deposits fell
below the rate needed to restrain advances by the amount the authorities
intended, and the function of special deposits became essentially
symbolic – an indicator of the authorities' stance.

Desired changes in advances were consequently brought about
entirely through direct controls over bank-lending practices. Direct
controls have been with the United Kingdom banking system almost
continuously since it emerged from the 1930s depression. During the
1939–45 war, banks were asked to restrict advances, except those made
for defence purposes, and to avoid any credit expansion which might
contribute to a general rise in prices.

In the postwar years, controls were invoked to insulate the domestic

economy from any general inflationary or deflationary side-effects of th
narrowly-focused interest rate policy. Latterly, the controls were als
used to reinforce that policy, by specifying investment and export
related priorities for bank lending. These dirigistic measures eventuall
reached such a pitch that in the decade 1961–71 ceilings or directives o
bank asset management were inoperative in only two years.[2]

Since 1971, three important changes have been made to this system o
control. First, the 'Competition and Credit Control' experiment attem
pted to wrench the emphasis of policy away from direct controls toward
market-based techniques, based on interest rate variations. The secon
major innovation was the introduction in 1973 of a novel form of direc
control, the 'corset', on bank liability expansion. This effectivel
signalled the failure of the first experiment, but retained much of it
terminology. The third innovation, largely independent of the others
was the institution of a series of pre-announced targets for monetar
growth. Before looking more closely at the interactions of these thre
policies, it may be helpful to sketch their main features.

2.1 Competition and credit control

Under this title the Bank of England floated, in May 1971, a nev
framework for monetary control which would permit a complet
reassignment of its traditional policy instruments. More weight was t
be placed on interest rate variations, reinforced if necessary by th
rationing of bank liquidity, and less weight was to be placed on direc
controls, as means to monetary restraint.[3]

Two motives lay behind this reform. First, interest rates appeared t
have lost their comparative advantage in tackling real rather tha
monetary problems. Domestic investment was not highly sensitive to th
cost of capital; and the emergence of persistent current accoun
surpluses in the years following the sterling devaluation of 1967 mad
temporary interest rate inducements to capital inflows redundant. O
the other hand, there was econometric evidence of a stable, interest
sensitive demand for money which could be exploited by tailorin
interest rate variations to the desired rate of monetary expansion
Second, institutional changes in financial markets made glaringl
obvious the inefficiencies and inequities caused by prolonged restric
tions on bank lending and arbitrary liquid asset requirements. Dis
intermediation occurred. The financing needs of banks' corporate
clients were increasingly met, not through the conventional banking
network, but through fringe institutions or direct intercompany

ransactions. Banks also found their asset structure was so inflexible as to prevent their competing against unregulated, often foreign-based, institutions in the rapidly expanding parallel markets in interbank and local authority debt, and Eurocurrency deposits.

The proposed reform was based on a restructuring of bank balance sheets and, although the substantive parts of the reform have collapsed, its terminology is still in use. The balance sheet layout is given as Table 1.1. The objective was to control banks' eligible liabilities (L1–A1), a monetary aggregate which includes not only current and deposit accounts, but also net liabilities acquired by banks through the issue of certificates of deposit and the attraction of interbank and non-sterling deposits. The demand for such liabilities was to be controlled by variations in the levels of interest rates; and interest rates were in turn to be determined not by an announced Bank Rate, but by bill market operations. Bank Rate was consequently replaced by a Minimum Lending Rate, which indicated the terms on which discount houses could seek last resort assistance from the Bank of England; and this Minimum Lending Rate was pegged at $\frac{1}{2}$ per cent above the market-determined Treasury bill rate (rounded to the nearest $\frac{1}{4}$ per cent). The supply of eligible liabilities was to be controlled, if necessary, by variations in the supply of a newly defined class of reserve assets (A2) and by a return to the aggressive use of calls for special deposits (A3). Banks were required to hold a stock of reserve assets amounting to not less than 12.5 per cent of their eligible liabilities; and the possibility of banks switching costlessly between reserve assets and marketable government stock was reduced by the Bank of England's refusal to guarantee cash for such stock on demand.

The attempted reassignment of monetary policy instruments failed spectacularly. Between December 1971 and December 1973, eligible liabilities – and the overlapping broad money stock, sterling M3 – grew at a rate of almost 30 per cent per annum, despite a rise in Minimum Lending Rate from 5 to 13 per cent and a 20 per cent per annum contraction in the stock of outstanding Treasury bills, the dominant public sector reserve asset.

This monetary explosion cannot be entirely explained by the expected process of 'reintermediation', nor by the coincidental property market boom. The new control system was defective. At a technical level, the fact that two-thirds of banks' reserve assets consisted of discount market liabilities (A2.2.1) rather than liabilities of the monetary authorities clearly meant that reserve asset pressure could not be effectively applied, in spite of the authorities' attempts to control the sources of call money

TABLE 9.1 Control of the United Kingdom banking system: balance sheet terminology

Liabilities	Assets
L1. *Eligible liabilities*	A1. *Negative eligible liabilities*
L1.1 Non-interest bearing sterling current accounts[a]	
L1.2 Interest-bearing	
L1.2.1 Sterling deposit accounts	
L1.2.2 Interbank deposits	A1.2.2 Interbank deposits
L1.2.3 Sterling certificates of deposit	A1.2.3 Sterling certificates of deposit
L1.3 Non-sterling liabilities[b]	A1.3 Non-sterling assets[b]
	A1.4 Transit item adjustment[c]
	A2. *Reserve assets*
	A2.1 Public sector debt
	A2.1.1 Deposits at Bank of England
	A2.1.2 Treasury bills
	A2.1.3 Government stocks with less than one year to maturity[d]
	A2.2 Private sector debt
	A2.2.1 Call money deposits with discount houses[e]
	A2.2.2 High-grade commercial bills
	A3. *Special deposits*[f]
	A4. *Loans and advances*
	A4.1 Marketable
	A4.1.1 Public sector
	A4.1.2 Other
	A4.2 Non-marketable
	A4.2.1 Discount houses
	A4.2.2 Other

L5. *Other Liabilities*	A5. *Other assets*
L5.1 Notes issued	A5.1 Notes held
L5.2 Capital	A5.2 Assets leased
L5.3 Suspense accounts and other funds	A5.3 Suspense accounts and other funds

Memorandum: bills accepted

. Of a maturity below two years.
. Including such deposits with or loans to branches overseas and in the Republic of Ireland.
. By convention, 60 per cent of items in course of transmission are deducted from liabilities to avoid double-counting.
. Including nationalised industry stocks guaranteed by the government.
. Also certain other named money brokers.
. Including, after December 1973, supplementary special deposits.

by obliging the discount houses to hold at least half of their assets in the form of fairly liquid public debt. This was not the problem in 1971–3, however. Banks' holdings of call money with the discount market grew at only 10 per cent per annum as against the 25 per cent per annum growth in other types of reserve asset. In our view, the real problem was more fundamental.[4] Having designed a control system appropriate for a competitive money supply process, the authorities found themselves unable or unwilling to bring about competitive conditions in gilt-edged and bank credit markets.

The implications of this intellectual schizophrenia for current policy issues are explored in the final section of this chapter. Here we simply note that in 1971–3, it set in train two cumulative processes of monetary expansion. First, although interest rates did rise, to protect the interests of house mortgage holders the authorities resisted movements toward the very high nominal interest rates which would have been necessary to choke off the demand for bank lending. This increased expectations of inflation so that the real cost of borrowing from banks fell further, loans expanded and inflation expectations were revised even further upwards. By the end of 1973, *ex post* real rates of interest were negative. Second, the clearing banks maintained their practices of offering no interest to current account holders, and of moving base rates for lending in concert and at infrequent intervals. As interest rates rose, these imperfections meant that the banks could bid quite high rates to attract non-current account liabilities, such as certificates of deposit, without reducing

profits unduly, but at the same time offer loans on terms which lagge
behind the general level of interest rates. This narrowing of differentia
between deposit and loan rates, together with rising inflatio
expectations, induced many companies to accumulate precautionar
bank deposits on the basis of loans from the banking system itself.

2.2 The corset

In an effort to interrupt these cycles in bank credit expansion, th
authorities had recourse in December 1973 to a new set of direct contro
over banks in the United Kingdom.[5] This signalled the abandonment c
their attempted reassignment of monetary policy instruments. Althoug
the controls were intended to be temporary and have twice bee
suspended, they have been subsequently reactivated and in the yea
1974–9 have been more often on than off.

The form of the new scheme is novel in that the controls are applie
not to bank lending, as in the 1960s, but directly to the growth in certai
bank liabilities. The scheme rests on three elements: the choice of a bas
period from which the subsequent growth in banks' interest-bearin
eligible liabilities is measured, a ceiling or series of ceilings on tha
growth, and a scale of penalties exacted from banks exceeding th
maximum permitted growth.

The base periods chosen for the first and subsequent applications c
the corset are shown in Table 9.2, along with figures for the maximu
growth beyond that base permitted in each month the corset operatec
The limit set in December 1973, for example, was an 8 per cent growt
between the average level of interest-bearing eligible liabilities held b
banks on the makeup days of the three months October–Decembe
1973 and the average level held in the three months April–June 1974. I
April 1974, the ceiling on growth was eased to a rate of 1.5 per cent of th
base stock per month, but the controls were removed only in Februar
1975. In November 1976, this 'corset' on the expansion of bank
interest-bearing eligible liabilities was reactivated with a constraint of
per cent growth between the period August–October 1976 an
February–April 1977, rising to 4 per cent in June 1977. Again th
scheme was rolled forward, in May 1977, this time at a rate of 0.5 pe
cent of the base stock per month in the period June–August 1977. Mos
recently, the corset was activated in June 1978. This time the base ha
been backdated even further, to the period October 1977–March 1978
and the controls maintained for much longer. The original ceiling of
per cent above the base for the months August–October 1978, rising t

TABLE 9.2   The corset ceilings, 1973–9

	First activation		Second activation		Third activation	
	Month	IBELS ceiling	Month	IBELS ceiling	Month	IBELS ceiling
					1977	
					Oct ⎫	
					Nov ⎪	
					Dec ⎪	
					1978 ⎬	100
					Jan ⎪	
			1976		Feb ⎭	
	1973		Aug ⎫		Mar	
	Oct ⎫		Sep ⎬	100	Apr	
mposed	Nov ⎬	100	Oct ⎭		May	
	Dec ⎭		Nov		Jun	
	1974		Dec		Jul	
	Jan		1977		Aug ⎫	
	Feb		Jan		Sep ⎬	104
	Mar		Feb ⎫		Oct ⎭	
	Apr ⎫		Mar ⎬	103	Nov	105
	May ⎬	108	Apr ⎭		Dec	106
	Jun ⎭		May	103.5	1979	
	Jul	109.5	Jun	104.0	Jan	107
	Aug	111.0	Jul	104.5	Feb	108
	Sep	112.5	Aug	105.0	Mar	109
	Oct	114.0			Apr	110
	Nov	115.5			May ⎱	113
	Dec	117.0			Jun ⎰	
	1975				Jul ⎫	
	Jan	118.5			Aug ⎬	116
	Feb	120.0			Sep ⎭	
					Oct ⎫	
					Nov ⎬	119
					Dec ⎭	

0 per cent by April 1979, was rolled forward to 16 per cent for the period July–September 1979 and subsequently – in the first budget of the new Conservative government in June 1979 – to 19 per cent for the period October–December 1979.[6]

Banks exceeding these limits are required to lodge with the Bank of England non-interest bearing supplementary special deposits at a rate determined by the extent of their transgression. The scales of penalties applied are set out in Table 9.3. These have been slightly less savage in the 1976–7 and 1978–9 activations than in the original scheme. Banks

TABLE 9.3   The corset penalties, 1973–9

Percentage of base by which actual IBELS exceed ceiling	Special supplementary deposits: percentage of excess IBELS	
	First activation	Second and third activations
0–1	5	5
1–3	25	5
3–5	50	25
Over 5	50	50

may now exceed the corset ceiling by up to 3 per cent before the cost rise from 5 per cent of the excess to a prohibitive 25 per cent.

2.3 Monetary targets

The imposition of any quantitative restraints on bank liability expansion requires that the authorities have some implicit objective for the growth of the money stock in total. The first ceiling for the growth interest-bearing eligible liabilities was certainly chosen with an eye to the implications which this would have for the growth of the broad mone stock, once that growth was added to the expected growth in curren accounts and government-backed cash. At that time, however, the projected monetary growth was kept as an internal objective. Tw events subsequently pushed the authorities towards announcing the target in advance.

First, the current account balance of payments slipped massively into deficit in the years 1974–6, necessitating a loan from the Internationa Monetary Fund in December 1976. As a precondition of the loan, the Fund insisted that the authorities aimed in the financial year 1977/8 at specific reduction in public sector borrowing and in the rate of domesti credit expansion. A less specific guideline for the growth of sterling M was also laid down. These conditions reflected the IMF's monetar approach to the balance of payments, the belief that the balance of payments mirrored excess domestic money creation and so could b controlled by money stock control. This was particularly persuasive i the United Kingdom context, since the surplus years 1970–1 were year of monetary restraint while the deficit years were, as we have seen, year of substantial monetary growth.

Second, the Labour Cabinet – or at least the Chancellor of the

Exchequer – underwent an intellectual conversion to the idea of pre-announced monetary growth targets. They were less concerned with the balance of payments implications of the numbers chosen than with the possibility that such targets could stabilise the inflation expectations of businesses and unions. If such targets were believed, wage bargaining would be made much simpler and formal incomes policies abolished; and a staged reduction in the target could be used to reduce the general level of inflation. A series of target ranges for the broad money stock sterling M3 was announced in the period 1977–9.

The targets announced by the Treasury have not always been strictly observed, and this naturally diminishes their effectiveness in improving labour market efficiency and reducing inflation. Table 9.4 summarises the record. In particular, we should note that although the original target for 1976–7 was comfortably met, the actual growth rate of sterling M3 was rather above the maximum of 13 per cent per annum in the second half of 1976; and we should note that the 1977–8 target was overshot by a large margin, with the growth rate of sterling M3 exceeding 13 per cent from September 1977 onwards. In spite of this erratic performance, the targets have been taken more and more seriously by the monetary authorities and by money market participants, and the whole procedure was formalised in the budget of April 1978. Henceforth a range is to be set for the twelve-monthly

TABLE 9.4   Monetary targets in the United Kingdom, 1976–9

Announcement	Financial year covered	Domestic credit expansion		Sterling M3	
		Target[a]	Outcome	Target[b]	Outcome
July 1976	1976/7			12	7.2
December 1976	1976/7	9000	4900	9–13	7.2
	1977/8	7700	3800		
March 1977	1977/8			9–13	15.3
April 1978	1978/9	6000	7400	8–12	10.9
November 1978	1978/9[c]			8–12	13.4
June 1979	1979/80[d]			7–11	11.5[e]
November 1979	1979/80[e]			7–11	17.2

[a] £ billions (i.e. thousand millions).
[b] Annualised percentage changes.
[c] October to October.
[d] June to June.
[e] Annualised, June 1979–October 1980.

growth of sterling M3, with the range coming under review every six months.

3. WELFARE EFFECTS OF THE CORSET

The supplementary special deposit scheme represents a novel method of credit control.[7] Its impact on financial markets is less obviously distortionary than the earlier regime of direct rationing of bank advances. The operation of the scheme does, however, impose real costs on society, and we move now to a consideration of how these costs arise.

A bank may take three attitudes to the imposition of a ceiling on the growth of its interest-bearing eligible liabilities. It may ignore the ceiling; it may observe the ceiling; or it may try to evade the ceiling. The nature of the welfare cost of corset controls depends on which of these happens. In the first case, the corset can be translated into a simple tax on bank lending. In the second, the corset can be translated into a subsidy on public debt; and some disintermediation occurs. In the third, which involves anticipatory reshuffling of bank portfolios, the main cost lies in fluctuations in interest differentials.

3.1 The cost of violation

In certain circumstances it may prove profitable for a bank to violate the first, and even the second, tranche of penalties. The bank must be able to command a spread, between the rate it pays on new deposits and the rate it receives from the corresponding loans and reserve asset holdings, sufficient to offset the loss of interest entailed in making supplementary special deposits. Breaking through the corset ceiling in fact remains profitable so long as

$$RLA - RIBEL > \frac{k}{1-k}(RIBEL - RRA) + \frac{SSDR}{1-k}RRA$$

where $k = RAR + SDR + SSDR$, and RLA, $RIBEL$ and RRA are rates of interest on bank loans and advances, banks' interest-bearing eligible liabilities and banks' reserve assets respectively; and RAR, SDR and $SSDR$ are the prescribed reserve asset, special deposit and supplementary special deposit ratios respectively. Table 9.5 sets out the minimum margins between returns on bank deposits and reserve assets compatible with given bank lending margins, at various levels of interest rates and corset penalties. If this margin is negative, banks will certainly

TABLE 9.5   Conditions for profitable violation of corset ceiling[a]

	Minimum margin between bank deposit rates and reserve asset rates ($RIBEL - RRA$)					
	First tranche, $SSDR = 0.05$			Second tranche, $SSDR = 0.25$		
Margin between bank lending and deposit rates ($RLA - RIBEL$)	$RRA =$			$RRA =$		
	5	10	15	5	10	15
1	2.66	1.46	0.26	-1.63	-4.73	-7.83
2	6.54	5.34	4.14	-0.16	-3.26	-6.36
3	10.42	9.22	8.02	1.31	-1.79	-4.89
4	14.30	13.10	11.90	2.78	-0.32	-3.42
5	18.18	16.98	15.78	4.25	1.15	-1.95

Calculations assume a 12.5 per cent reserve asset ratio and a 3 per cent special deposit ratio, so that in the first tranche $k = 0.205$, and in the second 0.405.

fail to attract marginal deposits since the funds would be better employed invested in reserve assets. Table 9.5 shows that it is almost always worth incurring the first tranche of corset penalties, but almost never the second – and, by implication, never ever the third. Only if the general level of interest rates is very low (say, $RRA = 5$) and the margin between lending and deposit rates very high (say $RLA - RIBEL$ between 3 and 5 percent) is a substantial violation of the corset profitable.

Actual violations of the corset suggest that banks are learning to face the corset penalties in a rational way. Whereas in the first application of the corset, the bulk of violations fell, carelessly, into the third tranche of penalties, in the most recent application the majority of institutions which have overstepped their deposit limits have done so only marginally. Some have fallen into the second tranche of penalties, but very few indeed have fallen into the third.

For all banks which venture beyond the corset ceiling on the growth in their interest-bearing eligible liabilities, the penalties act as a simple tax on marginal business at a rate which, as Table 9.6 shows, progresses with the general level of interest rates. With reserve asset yields around 10 per cent, it amounts to a tax of just under 2.5 per cent (2.66 − 0.18). How this is distributed between borrowers and lenders depends on the scope for reducing the interest paid on deposits. If this is already close to the yield on reserve assets, the tax will be wholly shifted on to borrowers. In practice, many banks are passing the tax forward by requesting

TABLE 9.6   Costs of violating corset in first tranche[a]

General level of interest rates (RRA)	Minimum margin between bank lending and bank deposit rates (RLA – RIBEL)	
	Without corset	With corset
5	0.18	1.46
10	0.18	2.66
15	0.18	3.86

[a] Assuming again 12.5 per cent reserve asset ratio and 3 per cent special deposit ratio, and assuming the margin of deposit rates over reserve asset rates to be 1 per cent.

corporate customers to transfer funds into non-interest-bearing 'compensating accounts' in return for agreeing overdraft facilities or credit lines.

3.2 The costs of observance

The corset was specifically designed to prevent banks from bidding for new interest-bearing eligible liabilities. The reduced demand for these liabilities reduces their yield relative to that of comparable public sector investments such as Treasury bills and local authority debt. Whereas under the competition and credit control scheme it could be argued that bank behaviour and restrictions on the issue of public sector reserve assets distorted interest differentials in favour of private sector debt, it can be argued that the corset control produces a distortion in the opposite direction. It operates as a concealed subsidy to the public sector.

Apart from this gross shift in interest rate relativities, the corset produces two further side-effects, one of which actually promotes the aims of competition and credit control while the other is totally destructive of these aims. First, banks have an increased inducement to compete for current account deposits. They have not actually resorted to paying interest on these accounts but have reduced bank charges to corporate customers who switch from deposit to current accounts and so help reduce the banks' interest-bearing eligible liabilities. Second, the higher cost of bank loans gives borrowers and lenders an inducement to by-pass the banking system altogether and deal directly with each other. The corset encourages exactly the same kind of disintermediation as occurred as a result of controls on bank advances in the 1960s.[8] Banks have connived after this by encouraging clients to issue bills. The banks then accept (countersign) these bills and arrange for their purchase. The amount of these bills does not appear in the banks' balance sheets, but banks profit from the commission on such deals. The scale of this acceptance business has risen dramatically during each application of the corset. During 1974, it increased in value by nearly 50 per cent, while advances increased by just 20 per cent; between November 1976 and August 1977 these two growth rates were rather closer, at 12 per cent annum and 9 per cent per annum respectively. Between June 1978 and June 1979, however, acceptances grew at the staggering annualised rate of 75 per cent, while advances increased at only 16 per cent.

Growth in acceptance business on this scale renders the chosen monetary target useless as an indicator of the growth of credit in the financial system. Sterling M3 grew 11.5 per cent between June 1978 and June 1979; sterling M3 plus acceptances grew by 14.5 per cent. The corset is, indeed, well-named. It conceals monetary growth without actually preventing it.

3.3 The costs of anticipation

The existence of monetary targets has made it possible for the banking system to anticipate the imposition of corset controls. Since the corset is framed in terms of a ceiling on growth beyond the level of interest-bearing eligible liabilities obtaining in some base period, it is in the banks' interests to accumulate such liabilities, so as to provide a base high enough to accommodate its lending plans during the period in which the corset is expected to operate. This has very clearly occurred prior to the second and third applications of the corset. Figure 9.1 analyses the reactions of interest-bearing eligible liabilities to actual and targeted monetary growth in 1977–8. The target was overshot in the autumn of 1977, and – after about three months' delay to confirm that this overshooting was a permanent feature – the stock of interest-bearing eligible liabilities held by banks grew very rapidly, at a rate of about 20 per cent per annum. This was far in excess of the growth in the broad money stock. An identical pattern of accumulation following an overshooting of the monetary target was observed just before the earlier 1976–7 corset was introduced.[9]

The monetary authorities have recognised this problem. A glance back to Table 9.2 shows that they have backdated the base of the corset further and further with each successive application. They have not, however, succeeded in eliminating all of the anticipatory build-up from the base figures for interest-bearing eligible liabilities. To this extent the

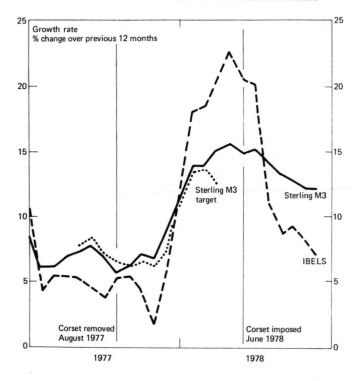

FIGURE 9.1   Money growth, bank liabilities and the corset

SOURCE   Bank of England, *Quarterly Bulletin.*

corset has not bitten as effectively as intended, since the ceilings set lay for a time well beyond the banking system's expected area of operations. There is some evidence, for example, that the 1976–7 corset was *never* a binding constraint on bank activities – witness the relatively flat profile of bank acceptances noted above – while the most recent corset, imposed in June 1978, has been binding only since May 1979.

This anticipatory behaviour, if successful, means that the corset does not act as a tax on banks. It does not, however, mean that there will be no welfare costs. The costs in the case of an anticipated corset consist not in any tax burdens but in the stability of interest rate relativities which are opened and reversed before and after the corset is imposed.

In order to accumulate interest-bearing eligible liabilities, a bank must acquire supporting reserve assets. Typically, these will not be

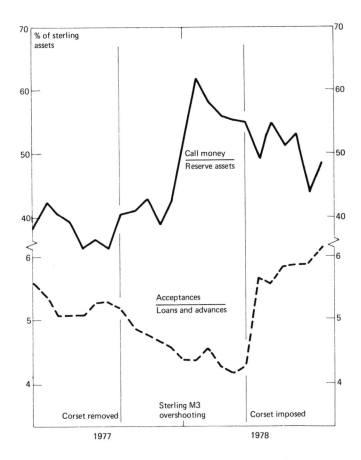

FIGURE 9.2   Reactions to the corset: bank assets and acceptances

SOURCE   Bank of England, *Quarterly Bulletin.*

readily provided by the monetary authorities, so that the main constituent of reserve asset growth will be call money with the discount houses. Call money can be created by banks in two ways. One simply involves switching claims on the discount market out of bank bills and into call money deposits. Such a procedure has the incidental advantage of directly increasing interest-bearing eligible liabilities, since discount market holdings of bank bills would normally count as a negative interbank liability. Alternatively, banks can generate new call money deposits by borrowing interbank funds or selling marketable, mainly public sector, assets. This can also create new interest-bearing eligible liabilities directly if the discount houses are persuaded to balance the call money by holding new bank issues of sterling certificates of deposit. Figures 9.2 and 9.3 follow this process through the run-up to the current corset. Figure 9.2 illustrates the rapid rise in the call money proportion of reserve assets; and Figure 9.3 illustrates the discount houses' accumulation of sterling certificates of deposit. Again, similar patterns can be traced in 1976.

After the corset is imposed, these transactions are unwound, as the charts very clearly illustrate. What has happened in the period surrounding the correctly anticipated introduction of a corset is that the relative demands for a number of financial assets has swung first one

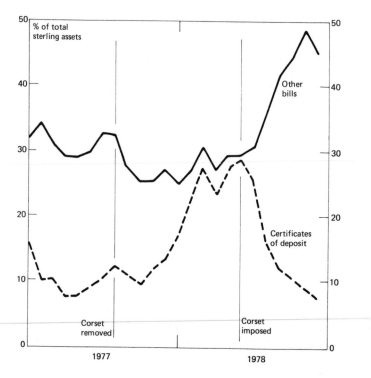

FIGURE 9.3   Reactions to the corset: discount house assets

SOURCE   Bank of England, *Quarterly Bulletin.*

way and then the other. As a result, relative yields on these assets also fluctuate. This will cause resource misallocation and may, by creating uncertainty, reduce the total scale of non-bank indebtdeness. Table 9.7 shows how anticipatory behaviour in the period August 1977–June 1978 reduced the yield on bank bills relative to certificates of deposit, through the first mechanism described above, and increased the rate offered on certificates of deposit relative to the yield on Treasury bills (which were, in any case, scarce) through the second mechanism. The margins involved may seem small. Such is the size and efficiency of these markets, however, that artificially created margins measurable only in sixteenths would be sufficient to direct large quantities of non-bank funds from their most effective uses.

TABLE 9.7   Anticipations of corset controls and relative yields

Yield gap between sterling certificates of deposit[a] and	Period		
	Corset on Jan.–Jul. 1977	New corset anticipated Aug. 1977– May 1978	Corset on June. 1978– Mar. 1979
Eligible bank bills	$-\frac{1}{8}$	$+\frac{1}{8}$	$-\frac{1}{8}$
Treasury bills	$+\frac{1}{8}$	$+\frac{1}{2}$	$+\frac{3}{8}$

[a] All instruments have three-month maturity, and all yields are averages of weekly observations of true yields.
SOURCE   LDA (Corporate Finance) Ltd.

4. THE CONTROLS FIX

The manipulation of ceilings on bank liabilities, then, produces inefficiencies in money markets. Its destabilising influence on interest rate relativities makes the corset, if anything, more undesirable than the equally inefficient ceilings on bank lending which were maintained in the 1950s and 1960s. The monetary authorities in the United Kingdom appear, however, to have an incurable addiction to direct controls. At present, there are rumours of moves to impose ceilings on acceptance business. This would certainly prevent the corset being evaded but might well divorce the commercial bill market from the banking system entirely, as threatened to happen in the late 1960s. Equally nostalgic are reports that the Bank of England has informally requested the clearing banks to restrain their lending. We end, therefore, by suggesting an explanation, and a cure, for the authorities' attachment to such controls.

The persistence of controls is not accidental. It can be attributed to two groups of factors. One of these was earlier identified as the fundamental cause of the breakdown of the competition and credit control experiment; namely the reluctance of the government to iron out imperfections in the bank credit and gilt-edged markets. The other, lesser, consideration is that the controls themselves and some of these market imperfections have recently become sources of profit to the public sector.

The problem of inducing effective competition in the United Kingdom banking system looks formidable. The industry has a long history of cartelisation and has even now a well-developed mechanism for internal consultation. Yet if monetary policy is not to be turned into a game between the authorities and the banks, with the customers as losers, some reform is essential. In many markets, the problem has solved itself through the entry of other institutions and foreign banks. In others, the problem could be much reduced by the authorities changing the rules of the game or playing more aggressively within the current rules.

Under the basic framework of competition and credit control, bank liquidity is constrained by the availability of a broad class of reserve assets. The supply of those assets cannot be readily controlled. If the basic framework is to be retained, it is essential that the authorities be prepared to use ratio controls aggressively by calling for and releasing special deposits in response to predictable fluctuations in the relationship between the total money stock and the reserve asset base.

However, the fact that the authorities have operated an imperfect market in government debt has meant that, even during the competition and credit control experiment, special deposits could not be used in their designated role as a restraint on growth in bank liabilities. They have instead been used largely to compensate for any destablising effects on the money stock which might have resulted from excess supplies or demands in the gilts market. After competition and credit control was introduced, the authorities quickly abandoned their intention of controlling the money stock by fixing an interest rate which would generate, through the demand for money function, the desired figure. As we have seen, the nominal interest rates necessary were considered unacceptably high; the official explanation was that the demand for money function had become too unstable after 1971 or had simply broken down. Instead, the authorities considered operating on the supply side counterparts of broad money stock growth: the public sector borrowing requirement, reductions in private sector holdings of public debt, bank lending to the private sector, and net flows abroad from the private sector. Of these, only the debt sales could be readily managed, so this provided the focus for control. Unfortunately, the method of marketing gilt-edged debt was not reformed. The authorities did not issue the amount of stock necessary to mop up excess money and let the price of the stock be market-determined. They instead pursued the traditional practice of guessing at the price which would sell the necessary amount of stock, placing a large amount of stock on the market, and letting actual sales take their course at that fixed price. Knowledge of the demand function for gilt-edged stock is, if anything, less well-founded and certainly less well researched than the demand for money. In the light of this, the authorities often practised interest rate 'overkill'. They set prices which would certainly sell at least the amount of stock necessary to achieve some target reduction in the money stock. On average, then, sales were excessive and bank liquidity was squeezed unnecessarily severely.

It is clear that the authorities have used *ad hoc* releases of special deposits to offset the destabilising effects of gilts sales on monetary growth. The inverse correlation between monthly gilts sales and changes in the stock of special deposits is very high: -0.31 in the period 1975–9. Equally striking is the fact that the timing of major gilts sales was not well-judged. The contemporaneous correlation between money growth and gilts sales is only -0.22, but between money growth and gilts sales three months later, it is -0.57. The upshot of these observations is that special deposits cannot make their necessary contribution to the workings of the competition and credit control framework so long as the government insists on fixing the price of gilt-edged stock and on using gilts sales to offset excessive monetary growth. Since this second notion seems dubious, and since even the present system of marketing gilts does not provide stability in their prices, it seems sensible to operate a genuine market in gilts, issue them in small, regular doses, and allow special deposits to contribute – as originally intended – towards the reserve asset control system. In other words, any workable version of the competition and credit control framework entails a thoroughgoing reform of the market in gilt-edged stock.

All this amounts to little more than patching up of an essentially unsound framework. The fundamental difficulty lies in the uncontrollability of the quantity of reserve assets currently supplied to the banking system and in their artificial nature. Deposit expansion could, however, be exercised through a group of assets which are direct liabilities of the monetary authorities and for which the bank and non-bank public have a naturally continuous, stable demand – namely those comprising the monetary base. The base consists of coin issued by the Treasury, notes and deposit issued by the Treasury, and notes and deposits issued by the Bank of England. It covers the only ultimately acceptable forms in which interbank transactions, and transactions between banks and their creditors, can be settled. Some movement towards a base control system represents an attractive alternative to the patching up of the competition and control framework.

The reforms actually undertaken in bank regulation and in the regulation of the gilts market have not so far moved in this direction. They have moved in a much more sinister way. The corset, as we have seen, subsidised the sale of public sector debt. Early in 1980, the authorities closed a loophole in the gilts marketing system which made it possible for purchasers to make a capital gain between the announcement of the price at which the new stock would be marketed and the day trading in the stock began. The capital gain now accrues to the government. What seems to be happening is that the authorities are not taking steps to remove the imperfections they create in financial markets. They are merely ensuring that wherever such imperfections occur, excess profits are siphoned into public funds. We fear that these subsidies may make the authorities less inclined to undertake the radical reforms of the monetary control system which would best serve the interests of the economy at large.

NOTES

1. B. Griffiths (October 1979).
2. A useful account of the exercise of instruments of monetary policy in the 1960s is by J. H. B. Tew (1978).
3. The reform was initiated by the Bank of England, 'Competition and Credit Control' discussion paper issued on 14 May 1971; this paper and subsequent extensions of the scheme are reprinted in *Bank of England Quarterly Bulletins* (1971).
4. For an alternative, contemporary, view of the breakup of the competition and credit control experiment, see C. A. E. Goodhart (1975).
5. Described in *Bank of England Quarterly Bulletin* (1974).
6. As this chapter was being prepared for publication, this ceiling was further extended to cover the period to June 1980, the maximum permitted growth being 1 per cent per month above the average stock of interest-bearing eligible liabilities held on the makeup days of November and December 1979, and January 1980. Since June 1980 the corset has been suspended.
7. An excellent description of the mechanics of control through the sup-

plementary special deposit scheme is provided by G. Pepper and R. Thomas (1979).

8. The removal in October 1979 of all exchange controls on the outward movement of capital has introduced further possibilities of disintermediation. Since the supplementary special deposit scheme applies only to banks' sterling operations in the United Kingdom, additional demands for credit can be met through overseas offices. The extent to which this Eurosterling loophole will be exploited is hard to predict. For banks, it is a simpler operation than the negotiation of acceptance credits; but the Bank of England has informally requested banks to observe the spirit of the corset controls by not referring borrowers to their foreign branches.

9. G. Pepper and R. Thomas (1979) argue that the buildup in interest-bearing eligible liabilities does not reflect anticipatory behaviour, but rather the authorities' attempts to apply reserve asset pressure as a first line of defence against excessive monetary growth. In the face of a restricted supply of public sector reserve assets, the banks will accumulate other kinds of reserve assets, particularly call money with the discount houses, and as a counterpart to these transactions, interest-bearing eligible liabilities will coincidentally rise. We are inclined to believe the authorities' assertion that they have never applied severe reserve asset pressure except by accident. As pointed out on p. 199 above, it was certainly not their first response to the monetary explosion of 1973 which ushered in the corset controls.

REFERENCES

Goodhart, C. A. E. (1975) 'Problems of Monetary Management: the UK Experience', *Reserve Bank of Australia, Papers in Monetary Economics.*

Griffiths, B. (1979) 'The Reform of Monetary Control in the United Kingdom', Centre for Banking and International Finance, The City University, *Annual Monetary Review* (October).

Pepper, G. and R. Thomas (1979) 'The Interaction between the Corset and Reserve Asset Control' (Oxford: paper presented to the Money Study Group Conference, Brasenose College, September).

Bank of England (1971) 'Competition and Credit Control', *Quarterly Bulletin* (June, September and December).

Bank of England (1974) 'Credit Control: A Supplementary Scheme', *Quarterly Bulletin* (March).

Tew, J. H. B. (1978) 'Monetary Policy', in F. T. Blackaby (ed.), *British Economic Policy 1960–1974* (Cambridge University Press, for the National Institute of Economic and Social Research).

Comment on Batchelor and Griffiths

FRANK BOLL

In their stimulating and combative chapter, R. Batchelor and B. Griffiths evaluate the way monetary policy has lately been conducted in the United Kingdom. In particular, they consider the so-called corset, instituted since 1973, under which transgressions of imposed ceilings on certain bank liabilities have to give rise to the lodging of non-interest-bearing deposits with the Bank of England. The main points they make in this respect are (i) that the corset reflects the defective intellectual framework within which monetary policy has been conducted, (ii) that its operation imposes costly and inequitable distortions on bank credit markets, and (iii) that the corset's welfare costs appear much greater than its financial benefits as regards debt management.

All in all, my thinking, both as an economist and as a citizen concerned with the interests of the community at large, is in unison with these points of view because, on the whole, most of the value judgments underlying the concept of economic efficiency also tend to be mine. Having said this, let me nonetheless assume the role of the devil's advocate.

First of all, the pervading spirit of the chapter smacks of the currently fashionable opinion that what governments do in the economic sphere is either silly or to their own advantage. (In the context of the chapter under review, one may think here of direct controls which have been with the UK banking system since the 1930s.) That seems a little bit too simple. Such an attitude follows directly from considering solely the criterion of economic efficiency in evaluating interventions. For instance, efficiency presupposes a given distribution of power, wealth and income. Any change in these by way of interferences – for example impeding market clearing mechanisms or explicit and implicit taxes and subsidies – may then be construed as inefficient. That is, however, no

218

wholly to the point. Canalisation of such changes is the nitty gritty of policy. Indeed, governments' main task is to uphold the overall features characterising the political system they represent, among others by channelling broadly felt desiderata in a way compatible with that task. (Of course, in the discussion of such desiderata or odiosa, governments themselves should actively take part.) For example, private home-owning gives people a stake in the political stability of their country and has many other integrative benefits as well. So, why not subsidise mortgage holders? Because that is not Pareto-optimal as opposed to giving an equivalent grant in terms of money? Not necessarily, because in various respects individuals should not always be the only judges of the social interests. Indeed, there exists also the public goods aspects of interventions.

This discussion concerning efficiency at once leads me, as self-appointed devil's advocate, to point (ii) above, namely that direct controls like the corset impose costly and inequitable distortions. That distortions are costly (in terms of the economic inefficiencies they create) is by definition correct. However, one fails to see the meaning of 'inequitable distortions'.

Finally, as regards point (iii), no argumentation whatsoever is provided for saying that the corset's welfare costs appear much greater than the benefits in terms of the lower servicing costs of the debt. Is that necessarily so? The corset's welfare costs amount to an implicit tax on some today. Lower servicing costs mean *ceteris paribus* lower explicit taxes for some tomorrow. Now, what would be the balance of such costs if the implicit taxes of today fell mainly on the very people whose explicit taxes of tomorrow would thereby be lowered – which is far from unlikely?

10. Banking Policy and Commercial Bank Behaviour in Greece[1]

ANTHONY S. COURAKIS

1. INTRODUCTION

Although control of commercial banks is a feature to be found in all developed or developing economies, little attempt has to date been made to examine the implications of the variety of policy instruments employed for this purpose, on the behaviour of such institutions and hence on the extent to which stated objectives are achieved. Indeed, controls are often introduced, abolished or intensified on little more than an *assertion* of ability to identify the direction of impact of the measure in question, despite the fact that no clear perception, less so any precise quantitative appraisal, of the effect of the prior structure of controls exists.

The problem is particularly acute when one examines complex structures of controls like those maintained by the monetary authorities in Greece.[2] Yet examine them we must, particularly if as a recent document of the Bank of Greece states:

> For the near future, major modifications in institutional arrangements concerning money and credit are contemplated with the aim of discontinuing the present detailed system of selective credit controls and differentiated interest rates.[3]

With this objective in mind, therefore, this chapter comprises an attempt to:

(i) describe the principal features of the structure of banking controls deployed by the Greek monetary authorities;

(ii) secure some insight on the impact of controls and on commercial
bank behaviour in Greece.

With regard to some of its aspects, this study *must* be regarded as
exploratory rather than exhaustive, a perspective in accord with the
motivation to campaign for consistency in the analysis of behaviour of
Greek banks and in policy implementation even at the cost of what,
from a different standpoint, I view as desirable: increased complexity. In
his sense, the study is 'a first attempt', and further exploration is already
n progress.[4] But while stressing caution, I ought also to remind
he reader of the proverb that *even a trip of one thousand miles must start
with a first step.*

2. AN OUTLINE OF CONTROLS BEARING ON THE ASSET AND LIABILITY STRUCTURE OF COMMERCIAL BANKS

Not unlike many other countries, central bank policy in Greece assumes,
in addition to responsibility for monetary management, the burden of
influencing the allocation of credit to the various sectors of the
economy.[5] To these ends, a complex system of quantitative controls has
been developed over the last twenty years that, to the outsider at least,
may appear to resemble a peculiar concoction of elements of French
credit policy combined with Anglo-Saxon reserve ratios and Italian style
government debt ratios as well as administered rates on deposits and
credits.

For classificatory purposes – and leaving aside various restrictions on
he amount and/or the percentage increase of credit granted to any one
customer[6] – one may[7] distinguish four kinds of controls bearing on the
activities of commercial banks in Greece:

(i) required 'reserve' ratios on bank liabilities;
(ii) reserve and rebate ratios on bank credits;
(iii) credit ratios against liabilities;
(iv) ceilings on interest rates paid and levied by banks.

i) Required reserve ratios on bank liabilities

There are two categories of such requirements. In particular, since 1972,
banks are compelled to hold specified proportions of the various
categories of their deposits in an interest-bearing account with the Bank

of Greece. These proportions, to be referred to in what follows as *cash ratios on liabilities*, have varied over time[8] and as between different types of deposit,[9] but now stand uniformly at 7 per cent of *all private deposits* (including foreign currency deposits). Simultaneously, however, banks are compelled to observe a *securities ratio* relating to investments in Treasury bills, government bonds and bonds of public enterprises. As in the case of cash ratios on liabilities, the authorities have in the past applied different ratios to different types of deposit,[10] though here again the requirement now stands at the same percentage for all private deposits, including foreign currency deposits.

(ii) Reserve/rebate ratios on bank credits

As regards credits, commercial banks are subject to compulsory *non-interest-bearing* deposits of specified percentages on certain categories of their lending, while enjoying rebates against other categories.[11] Such reserve/rebate ratios have also varied considerably (in terms of level and incidence) since their introduction in 1966; but a pattern of penalties on short-term credit, particularly to 'the domestic and import trade', and of subsidies on 'credit to exporters and tobacco dealers' and long-term credit for capital formation (excluding housing loans) is clearly discernible throughout the period.

(iii) Credit ratios against liabilities

Besides the above, however, such institutions are, since 1957, required to extend a fixed percentage (currently, and for many years, standing at 15 per cent for 'large banks'[12] and 10 per cent for 'small banks') of their *total deposits in drachmas* to medium- and long-term loans for financing 'productive' investment, and since 1966 a different percentage (6 per cent for 'large banks' and 4 per cent for 'small banks') of *the increase* in such deposits – relative to the end of 1965 – is earmarked for credit to handicrafts. A bank which fails to meet these requirements must place a sum equal to the difference in an *interest-bearing* account with the Bank of Greece or, in the case of the former – on the approval of the authorities – in Treasury bills.[13]

Viewed from the standpoint of asset ratios on commercial bank liabilities, these requirements, in effect, comprise two further categories of compulsory ratios – to be referred to in what follows as the '15 per cent ratio' and the '6 per cent ratio' respectively – in the sense that banks are obliged to hold these percentages of the corresponding eligible liabilities in specific categories of assets, namely the above-mentioned loans and deposits with the Bank of Greece (or Treasury bills). Alternatively, these requirements, from a viewpoint that derives from the union of (i) and (ii) above, can be treated as equivalent to a 15 per cent (5 per cent for 'small banks') and a 6 per cent (4 per cent for 'small banks') compulsory interest-bearing deposit with the Bank of Greece ratio on the corresponding liabilities, combined with a 100 per cent equal interest charged rebate (over and above the reserve or rebate to which the loan may be subject in accordance with the reserve/rebate arrangements on credits described above) per drachma of loans granted within these two categories of credit, so long as the total credit granted for each of the two categories does not exceed the amount corresponding to the percentages stated above.[14]

(iv) Controls on interest rates

What makes the Greek structure of control more intriguing is the fact that, in addition to the above, all interest rates on deposits and credits are subject to specific and periodically revised ceilings, set by the Currency Committee. As in the case of reserve ratios on credits, the structure of ceiling rates posited[15] favours activities such as exports and long-term capital investment, and penalises borrowing by commercial concerns and for imports. Ceilings on deposit rates, on the other hand, are based on length of notice required for withdrawal, while the Committee also sets, and from time to time varies, the rate at which commercial banks can borrow from the Central Bank.

3. ON THE RATIONALE, IMPLICATIONS AND COMPLICATIONS OF THE PRESENT STRUCTURE OF CONTROLS

While, as I have already mentioned, none of the elements of control bearing on commercial banks is unique to Greece, the particular combination employed is rather unusual.

As regards monetary policy, the constraints imposed on bank portfolio choices bear on the equilibrium volume of deposits in various ways. From a behavioural standpoint, all compulsory ratios, to the extent that they reduce the expected return from bank assets, reduce the equilibrium volume of bank deposits. Leaving aside for the moment ceilings on deposit rates, a compulsory cash ratio on deposits, one that is binding, comprises a tax on deposits or equivalently a tax on the acquisition of other assets available to the particular institution considered. If no interest is paid on compulsory reserves, it constitutes an interest-free loan to the government (that is, to the issuer of the liability in the form of which the compulsory reserves are expressed). If interest is paid on such compulsory reserves, then the tax is obviously smaller but, as in the previous case, equal to the difference between the rate paid and that at which such assets would be voluntarily held in the volume prescribed by the reserve ratio. From this standpoint, a compulsory cash ratio affects the volume of deposits (and loans) in exactly the same manner as a securities ratio of the same percentage, and in securities yielding the same return (and being subject to the same variation in return) as that paid on compulsory cash reserves. Furthermore, a similar function is performed by the 15 and 6 per cent described above, to the extent that these are binding and hence induce a less preferred asset portfolio composition than that which will prevail in their absence.

Ceilings on interest rates also bear on the size of bank assets and liabilities. On the other hand, it is only when such ceilings apply, and thus banks are prevented from reaching the equilibrium volume of deposits defined (whether with or without compulsory ratios) by their (utility or profit) maximising actions, that their responses may be said to be such as to '. . . fit the elementary textbook exposition of the [deposit] multiplier process',[16] the widows' cruse.[17] But even in this case, 'the ratio' relevant to deposit creation is equal to what was termed above the 'cash ratio on liabilities' if and only if we are entitled to assume that banks can acquire from the public such assets, as they are compelled to hold in accordance with the 'securities ratio' and the 15 and 6 per cent ratios. Conversely, if banks can only acquire such securities from the government (or central bank) and the latter accumulates the proceeds, the deposit multiplier of a particular *initial* increase in cash holdings (and deposits) is no greater than that implied by the inverse of the sum of the cash and securities ratios (independently of what the public's cash deposits ratio may be).[18] And if, in addition, banks cannot grant 15 or 6 per cent loans at the margin with a yield higher than (or equal to) the rate paid on their compulsory reserves with the Bank of Greece in accordance with these regulations, the multiplier at the margin is defined by the sum of the three ratios (that is, including the 15 and 6 per cent ratios, besides the cash and securities ratios). Combined with the realities of the securities market in Greece[19] and the fact that for much of the period under review, 1969i–1977iv, none of these banks advanced loans of the kind defined by the 15 and 6 per cent requirements in the amount prescribed. Indeed, during this period, none of the banks *ever* granted loans to handicrafts of the prescribed amount, and only the National Bank of Greece ever reached the 15 per cent allotment of 'long-term loans for productive investment'.[20] Such reasoning brings to the surface some intriguing evidence regarding monetary policy in Greece, when we observe – as we do in Appendix 10.3 – that effective reserve ratios of 100 per cent and more have sometimes applied at the margin on certain kinds of deposit.

Obviously the above has direct implications for total credit granted to the private sector also. But credit policy, as I have already noted, aims to influence the distribution of funds to the various sectors of the economy, and it is to this end that reserve/rebate ratios and ceilings on rates charged by banks are determined. In this context, probing for consistency, it will seem reasonable to assume that the precise choice of maxima loan rates, set by the Currency Committee, rests on the belief that the authorities are able to predict the demand for the various categories of loans supplied at different rates of interest, and that they have a clear view of what the total volume and composition of loans granted at any point in time ought to be if intertemporal social welfare objectives are to be fulfilled. Formally, this implies a choice of rates by the Currency Committee that equates demand on the part of the borrower with the amount considered optimal by the authorities for the corresponding loan categories. This is not, however, sufficient to ensure that loans granted are, in volume, in accord with social objectives, since at these rates the commercial banks' supply of loans of the various categories may not be equal to what the authorities consider optimal. For supply to equal desired demand – targeted quantities – the authorities differentiate between rates paid by the borrower and implicit returns to the banks through the structure of reserve and rebate ratios described earlier.

The latter appears a rather standard tax/subsidy arrangement. But *as the ceilings on interest rates indicate, the particular loan volumes desired are not only pursued through the differential tax/subsidy scheme, that reserve/rebate ratios imply.* Rather, these ratios are set at such levels as to ensure equalisation of apparent yields[21] on these credits, generally at a rate marginally higher than that on Treasury bills, which perhaps in the authorities' perception of the scheme of things serves to define the opportunity cost of loans for these banks.

As I have argued elsewhere,[22] the combination of ceilings on interest rates, charged by banks to the public, and reserve/rebate ratios – for which, incidentally, no official or unofficial explanation, rationale or justification, is anywhere else to be found – permits a solution in which the attainment of the desired distribution of loans can be achieved without net injections (or withdrawals) accruing to the banks of the kind that attainment of the same loan volumes through reserve/rebate ratios *alone* would in general imply. At the same time, and whether or not the latter is what motivated the introduction and maintenance of loan rate ceilings cum reserve/rebate ratios arrangement, it must be stressed that *the structure of reserve ratios that ensures equality between socially desired loan volumes and privately supplied quantities of such instruments cannot be computed without prior explicit definition of the behavioural functions of these intermediaries.* Correspondingly, the rate equalisation' scheme does not necessarily ensure the indifference of commercial banks regarding the structure of their loan portfolios, nor their tacit acceptance of whatever composition of loans the authorities consider fitting unless – besides attributing to the authorities' prior knowledge of the demand functions of the public for the various loan categories – banks are oblivious to risks and other characteristics which, in addition to expected returns, pertain to the various assets comprised in their portfolios.

4. ASPECTS OF COMMERCIAL BANK BEHAVIOUR[23]

Consider the following simplified balance sheet of a commercial bank.

Assets	*Liabilities*
Cash	Sight deposits
Deposits with the central bank	Savings deposits
	Time deposits
Treasury bills	Capital and reserves
Bonds	Other
Loans	
Other	

Granted regulatory constraints and market characteristics, the various items on the assets and liabilities sides may, in general, be defined to comprise three categories of quantities:

(i) assets and/or liabilities with regard to which the intermediary acts as a price taker and a quantity setter;

(ii) assets and/or liabilities with regard to which it acts as a price and quantity taker;

(iii) assets and/or liabilities with regard to which it acts as a price setter and a quantity taker.

The actions of the intermediary relate to a choice of such quantities and prices as are under its control, so as to maximise its welfare. The latter is a convenient way of stating the issue, since any action may – as Aristotle told us long ago – be represented as one of choice between alternative states. Yet it tells us nothing (that is its virtue, one might add) about how welfare is to be understood in any precise context. On this, previous research on bank behaviour comprises two basic strands. The first and analytically more simple approach is to assume that welfare can be proxied by profit and, drawing on the conventional theory of the firm, to proceed in explaining bank portfolios as the outcome of choices pursued in monopolistic asset and liability markets.[24] The second proceeds along the lines of portfolio selection models to accord more emphasis to the risk elements in the situation, be it in the form of stochastic quantities or stochastic prices (returns).[25]

In vacuum, both approaches may seem plausible. Yet on reflection we will notice that the former kind of model, limited as it is to one characteristic and thus capable *in general* of accounting for holdings of only one asset (or liability) of category (i) above, flies in the face of the fact that intermediaries do choose to hold more than one asset with regard to which they act as price takers and as quantity setters. To be sure, this does not preclude the applicability of such a model in the context of the specific constraints bearing on the activities of commercial banks in Greece. But it does encourage the question of whether an alternative model that affords recognition to other characteristics of experience that, besides expected returns, impinge on these intermediaries' choices – a model, that is, which challenges one of the basic assumptions on which present policy appears to rest – can be dismissed as an inappropriate description of the behaviour of these economic units. This is particularly so when attention is paid to the fact that commercial banks in Greece have consistently 'failed to respond to the incentives' provided by the system in a way that accords with the authorities' objectives, a phenomenon that has provoked comments to the effect that their behaviour does not conform to any maximising principles. Accordingly, in what follows, expected utility maximisation is tendered as an alternative framework capable of interpreting behaviour in Greece. The specific model adopted is, I wish to note, highly restrictive; only a beginning[26] towards an assessment of responses, in the setting described in section 2 above, from a different viewpoint to that which profit maximisation renders.

4.1 Expected utility maximisation and commercial bank behaviour[27]

Suppose that bank preference can be described by a utility function of the form:

$$U(W) = b - ce^{-\alpha(W)} \tag{1}$$

where the marginal utility of terminal wealth, W, is always positive, that is $U'(W) > 0$, but decreasing as terminal wealth increases, that is $U''(W) < 0$, while absolute risk aversion is invariant to changes in terminal wealth.

Suppose that the portfolio comprises n types of assets (liabilities being treated as negative assets) and let V be an $n \times 1$ vector of quantities of these assets. Let m be an $n \times 1$ vector of stochastic returns per unit of such assets in the period to which the maximising decisions of the bank in question relate. Then:

$$W = (i + m)'V \tag{2}$$

where i is an $n \times 1$ unit vector.

Now V, as we have seen above, comprises three categories of assets. But suppose, as is arguably relevant to the Greek case, that maximisation of $U(W)$ is confined to quantity-setting decisions, yields being dictated by the monetary authority.[28] In that case, V should be partitioned in V_z, a $z \times 1$ vector of choice set items, and V_q a $q \times 1$ vector of exogenously determined items, while accordingly m_z and m_q are vectors of returns on such assets. The intermediary chooses V_z so as to maximise $E[U(W)]$ which, on the assumption that stochastic returns on the various components of the portfolio are normally distributed, relates to maximising

$$E[U(W)] = E(W) - \tfrac{1}{2}\alpha E\{[W - E(W)]^2\} \tag{3}$$

equal to

$$E[U(W)] = Y'_z V_z + Y_q V_q - \tfrac{1}{2}\alpha E[(e_z V_z + e_q V_q)^2] \tag{4}$$

where $Y_j = 1 + \hat{m}_j$, $m_j = E(m_j)$, $e_j = (1 + m_j) - Y_j$.

Maximising (4) subject to the budget constraint

$$i'V = i'_z V_z + i'_q V_q = 0 \qquad (5)$$

where, in accordance with bank balance sheet conventions, capital and reserves are included in V as a liability[29], yields, after manipulation, the solution

$$V_z = \frac{1}{\alpha} G Y_z - H V_q \qquad (6)$$

where

$$
\left.
\begin{aligned}
G &= S_{zz}^{-1} - \frac{S_{zz}^{-1} i_z i_z S_{zz}^{-1}}{i'_z S_{zz}^{-1} i_z} & S_{zz} &= E(e_z e'_z) \\[2mm]
H &= G S_{zq} + B i_q & S_{zq} &= E(e_z e'_q) \\[2mm]
B &= \frac{S_{zz}^{-1} i_z}{i'_z S_{zz}^{-1} i_z}
\end{aligned}
\right\} \qquad (7)
$$

while inspection reveals that:

(i) G is symmetric;
(ii) all row sums and column sums of G are zero;
(iii) all diagonal elements of G are positive;
(iv) the elements of B sum to unity;
(v) all column sums of H are equal to unity.

Behaviourally, therefore, and by no means surprisingly, choice of such quantities as are within the sphere of the bank's quantity-setting decisions, depends on the vector of expected returns on such quantities, the vector of quantities of exogenous items, including the bank's net worth, and on the variance covariance matrices of returns between choice set items, and between choice set and exogenous items.

4.2 Defining a choice set and reflecting on features of the balance sheet of commercial banks in Greece

Tables 10.1 and 10.2 present a summary statement of the balance sheet position of the aggregate of commercial banks in December 1975.

Of the various assets and liabilities, deposits of whatever type may be treated as not subject to banks' quantity-setting decisions.[30]

TABLE 10.1   An overview of the asset and liability structure of Greek commer cial banks in December 1975

	Code	As a propor- tion of total assets[a]
Assets		100.00
Cash	V_{C1}	1.44
Non-interest-bearing deposits with B of G – free	V_{C2}	1.09
Non-interest-bearing deposits with B of G – compulsory	V_{C3}	0.43
Interest-bearing deposits with B of G – compulsory	V_{C4}	2.81
Foreign exchange	V_{FE}	3.20
Treasury bills – free	V_{T1}	2.22
Treasury bills – compulsory	V_{T2}	16.39
Loans 8 % res. rat. category within credit ratios	V_{L1}	0.63
Loans 8 % res. rat. category outside credit ratios	V_{L2}	21.08
Loans 25 % res. rat. category within credit ratios	V_{L3}	0.12
Loans 25 % res. rat. category outside credit ratios	V_{L4}	7.20
Loans 5 % rebate category within credit ratios	V_{L5}	5.16
Loans 5 % rebate category outside credit ratios	V_{L6}	2.89
Loans 23 % rebate category within credit ratios	V_{L7}	3.31
Loans 23 % rebate category outside credit ratios	V_{L8}	12.06
Bonds – free	V_{B1}	2.85
Bonds – compulsory	V_{B2}	3.19
Bank premises	V_{BP}	2.27
Other assets	V_{OT}	11.66
Liabilities		100.0
Sight deposits – private	V_{D1}	7.25
Sight deposits – public	V_{D2}	1.57
Savings deposits – no notice	V_{D3}	37.85
Savings deposits – at notice	V_{D4}	4.00
Time deposits – private, more than 3 months	V_{D5}	16.02
Time deposits – public	V_{D6}	0.54
Deposits of special credit institutions	V_{D7}	1.33
Restricted deposits	V_{D8}	1.36
Deposits in foreign exchange	V_{D9}	10.80
Various obligations in foreign exchange	V_{OF}	0.67
Bank of Greece advances	V_A	3.68
Capital and reserves	V_K	4.09
Other	V_{OH}	10.84

[a] There is a discrepancy with regard to some of these items between the amounts appearing in the statistics published by the Bank of Greece (B of G) and the statistics held internally in the bank.

TABLE 10.2   Reserve ratios, credit ratios and the composition of loan portfolios[a]

Credit ratio category	Reserve ratio category (in percentage of total assets)				Total in percentage of corresponding requirement[b]
	8%	25%	−5%	−23%	
5% ratio category	(V_{L1a}) 0.593	(V_{L3a}) 0.121	(V_{L5a}) 5.159	(V_{L7a}) 2.04	69.1
6% ratio category	(V_{L1b}) 0.032	(V_{L3b}) 0.003	(V_{L5b}) 0.003	(V_{L7b}) 1.27	38.4

[a] Symbols in brackets denote the code of the corresponding category.
[b] That is, the ratio: actual amount of total loans granted in each credit ratio category to the amount implicit by the outstanding volume of corresponding eligible liabilities in the 15 per cent (5 per cent for small banks) and 6 per cent (4 per cent for small banks) ratios respectively.

Correspondingly, reserves against liabilities must also be treated as non-choice set items.[31] On the other hand, 'free' deposits with the Bank of Greece can be regarded as choice set items, while the same is true of 'free' Treasury bills and 'free' bonds if we assume the absence of supply constraints regarding availability of such assets. In the case of the various loan categories, however, and reserves against such loans, the issue is more complex.

To examine the latter issue, let us focus on the twelve loan categories defined in Tables 10.1 and 10.2. The simple returns *on own funds* employed corresponding to these categories in December 1975 are shown in Table 10.3. As is apparent, the returns per drachma of loans granted within the 15 and 6 per cent regulations are such as to suggest that banks are unlikely to wish to remain below these percentages. Thus if the 15 and 6 per cent floors are not met, it may (even in the context of a risk model) seem 'safe' to assume that this is due to insufficient demand for such loans (at the going rate) on the part of the borrower, rather than unwillingness on the part of the banks to supply such funds.

The latter, we may note, has important implications for our understanding of Greek experience. In particular, as Halikias has noted, for many years commercial '. . . banks did not expand their activity on long term financing of private business investment to the extent that they were urged to by the authorities',[33] a fact which he correctly suggests is '. . . doubtful whether [it] should be attributed chiefly to reluctance on the part of the banks to undertake greater risks'.[34] Yet, by my reasoning,

TABLE 10.3   Rates of return on own funds employed[a] *(December 1975)*

Reserve ratio category	8%	25%	−5%	−23%
Rate charged to the borrower	12.500	14.500	11.000	9.000
Outside the 15% and 6% credit ratios	11.574	11.600	11.579	11.688
Within the 15% and 6% credit ratios	93.750	38.000	More than 100%	More than 100%

a. The rates of return shown in this table are calculated as explained in note 32.

it has not been the case that '. . . under the structure of interest rates in force throughout the period, *short term lending was more profitable than long term lending*'.[35] On the contrary, the evidence presented above, and that resulting from Tables 10.1 to 10.3, reveals that when the overlapping nature of credit ratios and reserve/rebate ratios on loans is systematically taken into account, long-term lending (within the 15 per cent ratio limits appears to have been – and continues to be – considerably more profitable than short-term lending. Consequently, insufficient credit for long-term capital investment and other ventures qualifying for the credit ratios described above is – one feels tempted to surmise when looking at commercial banks as a whole – due to deficient demand for such credit at the rates set (for borrowers) by the authorities.

Since the rates set by the Currency Committee, however, are *maximum* rates, the hypothesis of deficient demand at such rates begs the question of why banks do not lower their rates on such loans given, for example, that a two point reduction in lending rates will still – except insofar as considerably greater risks of default are perceived as attaching to such loans – ensure for the banks a considerably higher return on own funds than that secured from all other components of their portfolio. Abstracting from differences as between banks – see Appendices 10.4 to 10.8 – two possibilities exist in this context. The first is that the demand for such loans over the relevant region is deemed by banks to be inelastic, so that rational decisions command that they do not lower their rates. Conversely, if demand for such loans is not inelastic, or if rate discrimination is feasible, then it must also follow that banks can increase their profits by reducing actual rates charged to levels below the maxima set by the Currency Committee, and that their failure to do so[36] stems either from ignorance of the precise nature of the penalties and inducements implicit in existing arrangements, or because they interpret the rates set by the authorities for such loans as norms to be adhered to without further ado, or because such norms *induce* (or manifest) a kinked oligopoly situation.

Notice that in both these cases a different choice of rates by the Currency Committee, a lower set of ceiling rates pertaining to such loans, could – in principle at least – ensure a closer attainment of the loan volumes implicit in credit ratios as desirable. As shown in Appendices 10.6 to 10.8, however, it is also the case that the performance of the various banks in relation to the 15 and 6 per cent regulations has varied markedly as between banks. Thus, whereas the National Bank of Greece has since 1972 recorded medium- and long-term loans for fixed investment in excess of 15 per cent of eligible liabilities and, indeed, has since 1969 maintained total loans and investments of the kinds posited in the provisions of the NE 1509/14.9.68 in excess of this percentage,[37] the other large banks – and so also, for the 5 per cent applicable to them, the small banks – have consistently failed to do so. Besides emphasising the differences between banks and lending further stress on the possibilities mentioned at the end of the last paragraph, this feature also raises important questions about the distributional effects of existing policies and the role or importance attached to the behaviour of the National Bank of Greece in policy design. It is conceivable, for example, that the responses of this bank – which, as Appendix 10.4 reveals, accounts for more than 50 per cent of total deposit and loan business in Greece – loom so large in the Currency Committee's calculations that the structure of rates set by this body are geared towards this bank rather than the collectivity of banks. In this respect, the Currency Committee may act as the mouthpiece of 'the price leader' National Bank, while loan market imperfections, including perhaps the authorities' own criteria for loan category eligibility, sustain the unused margins recorded for other banks.

Insofar as the latter comprises a plausible scenario, it may also be argued that the bias against other banks is partially offset by the tendency to allow banks to invest part of their obligatory 15 or 5 per cent of eligible liabilities in Treasury bills. But at any rate, the suggestion hazarded in the previous paragraph also raises the question of whether a similar case can be made regarding the implementation of the 6 per cent regulation. In contrast to the 15 per cent regulation, however, we here find, as I mentioned earlier – see also Appendix 10.8 – that neither the National Bank of Greece nor any of the other banks have, at any time during the period under review, granted loans to handicrafts (of the kind eligible for rebates within the provisions of this regulation) anywhere near the amounts that – abstracting from loan quality – would in the light of the corresponding inducements be thought desirable.

All this does, of course, suggest that to simply regard all loans of the categories described in the credit ratios as independent of these intermediaries' quantity (or price) setting decisions may be simplistic. Certainly the behaviour of the National Bank of Greece cannot be easily squeezed into such a mould. Since, however, from an analytical standpoint it can be shown that ambiguities as to whether a particular balance sheet item is or is not a choice set item are best dealt with by treating the asset in question as a nonchoice set item, for no misspecification is thereby generated nor loss of generality results at the empirical level,[38] it was deemed expedient to treat all loans in the credit ratios categories as components of V_q.

By contrast, all other loans were defined as choice set items. Such treatment implies that, to the extent that the supply of credit to any particular loan category falls short of the level desired by the authorities, we have *deficient supply* at the rates received by the banks – a phenomenon that calls for upward revision of the ceiling on the rate charged on the particular loan category considered or, equivalently, reduction in the reserve ratio – rather than *deficient demand*, as the rationale of the rate equalisation scheme will lead us to believe (leading to the recommendation that attainment of the desired loan volume requires downward revision of the ceiling rate charged on borrowers). This contrast need not, of course, dull our willingness to regard other loans as choice set items *a priori*. On the other hand, it should be borne in mind that such components of the portfolio are in general not amenable to variation with the same degree of ease as, say, Treasury bills, a fact that may mar the time series estimates that rely on functions which do not embody distributed lags.[39]

Of the remaining items, holdings of foreign exchange and various obligations in foreign exchange carry a somewhat ambiguous status, since in their case the relative exercise of initiative by the commercial banks and control of the monetary authorities is not clearly or continuously ascertainable. In view of this and our earlier remarks regarding the correct procedure in resolving ambiguities of this kind, it was thought safer to treat them as components of V_q. The same was assumed to hold for all remaining balance sheet items with the exception of Bank of Greece advances which, given the – despite noises of concern – accommodating policy of the Bank of Greece, were defined as choice set items.

Granted such reasoning, then, in conjunction with our earlier notation, we have

$$
\begin{aligned}
V_z &= [\,V_{C1}\ V_{C2}\ V_{T1}\ V_{L2}\ V_{L4}\ V_{L6}\ V_{L8}\ V_{B1}\ -V_A\,] \\
V_q &= [\,V_{C3}\ V_{C4}\ V_{T2}\ V_{L1a}\ V_{L1b}\ V_{L3a}\ V_{L3b} \\
&\quad\quad V_{L5a}\ V_{L5b}\ V_{L7a}\ V_{L7b}\ V_{B2}\ V_{BP}\ V_{OT}\ V_{FE} \\
&\quad\quad -V_{D1}\ -V_{D2}\ -V_{D3}\ -V_{D4}\ -V_{D5}\ -V_{D6}\ -V_{D7} \\
&\quad\quad -V_{D8}\ -V_{D9}\ -V_{OF}\ -V_K\ -V_{OH}\,]
\end{aligned}
\tag{8}
$$

Some of these items, however, may be aggregated together without too much loss of generality. This can be said to be true, on the choice-set side, for cash and free deposits with the Bank of Greece.[40] Similarly with regard to non-choice set items, it was deemed expedient to follow the practice adopted in other studies[41] and aggregate the last two items on the assets side with the corresponding on the liabilities side. What of loans within the 15 and 6 per cent regulations and deposits, however, and what of the *compulsory* holdings of deposits with the Bank of Greece, Treasury bills and bonds?

With regard to these, various possibilities exist. Should we, for example, aggregate private deposits of a particular (say 'sight') category with public deposits of the same category? Should we aggregate savings 'at notice' with savings 'at no notice' or with 'time' deposits? And so on. How are we to decide? One is tempted to say that these are empirical questions. And so they are, to some extent, implying, for non-choice set items at least, that we ought to examine the validity of hypotheses such as that demand for choice set items is independent of the distribution of, say, sight deposits as between private and public; that is, that the coefficients of response of choice set items to changes in either of these components of the portfolio are the same (the Homogeneity of Response tests as we may, for simplicity, call them). Yet, granted this, there is a prior question to be raised when examining commercial bank behaviour under reserve ratio controls. This key question is *whether compulsory reserves of any given type* (in this case non-interest-bearing, interest-bearing, and so on) *should be treated as distinct components of the portfolio to be incorporated in our analysis* – as indeed they are presented in Table 10.1 – *in oblivion of the deposit or loan category from which they derive, or whether they should be distributed among and aggregated with the deposit and loan categories that comprise their source?*

The rationale for the first approach[42] is simply that since yields and other characteristics pertaining to deposits (or loans) are different to those pertaining to each category of reserves required against these deposits (or loans), it is invalid to aggregate any particular category of loan or deposit with the compulsory reserves to which it gives rise. Yet this reasoning is false,[43] since these assets and liabilities – sight deposits let us say, and the reserves held against them – do not comprise alternatives for any market participant; certainly not for the banks themselves. To put it differently, the treatment of deposits and compulsory reserves as distinct violates the *perfect complementarity* condition that characterises their relationship. Recognition of this fact compels that compulsory holdings of any asset be aggregated with the corresponding liability or asset to which they are uniquely linked. The compulsory reserves are equivalent to a unit tax on loans or deposits and thus comprise a 'proper bundle' with the loans and deposits to which they correspond. The difference in apparent rates of return or other characteristics is a red herring, no less, since the rates of return on loans and costs of deposits *cannot* be defined independently of the reserve ratios – that is to say of the compulsory reserve holdings – themselves.

This reasoning, furthermore, reveals that with regard to the subsidiary aggregation questions raised above, the categories of loans and deposits should be *no less* than those explicit in the structure of penalties or inducements maintained by the authorities, unless we are prepared to argue that the structure of controls is a matter of indifference to the banks.

Accordingly, V_z and V_q become

$$\left.\begin{aligned}
V_z &= \left[V_{C12}\ V_{T1}\ \overline{V}_{L2}\ \overline{V}_{L4}\ \overline{V}_{L6}\ \overline{V}_{L8}\ V_{B1} - V_A \right] \\
V_q &= \left[V_{L1a}\ V_{L1b}\ V_{L3a}\ V_{L3b} - \overline{V}_{D1} - \overline{V}_{D2} - \overline{V}_{D3} - \overline{V}_{D4} \right. \\
&\quad \left. - \overline{V}_{D5} - \overline{V}_{D6} - \overline{V}_{D7} - \overline{V}_{D8} - \overline{V}_{D9} - \overline{V}_{OF}\ V_{OTH} \right]
\end{aligned}\right\} (9)$$

where

$$\left.\begin{aligned}
V_{C12} = V_{C1} + V_{C2}, \quad V_{OTH} = V_{BP} + V_{OT} - V_K - V_{OH},
\end{aligned}\right.$$

and

$$\left.\begin{aligned}
\overline{V}_{Li} &= V_{Li}(1 + \lambda_i) & i &= 2, 4, 6, 8 \\
\overline{V}_{Lj} &= \lambda_j V_{Lj} & j &= 1, 3, 5, 7 \text{ for } a \text{ and } b \\
\overline{V}_{Dk} &= V_{Dk}(1 - p_k^\pi - p_k^\sigma - p_k^\tau) + p^\beta V_{Dk_{1965}} \\
& & k &= 1, 2, \ldots 8
\end{aligned}\right\} (10)$$

with λ_i and λ_j being the reserve ratios on loans, p_k^π, p_k^σ being respectively the cash ratios and security ratios on liabilities, p_k^τ the sum of the credit ratios on each type of deposit,[44] p^β is the 6 per cent incremental reserve ratio and $V_{Dk_{1965}}$ is the volume of deposits outstanding in December 1965.

It should be noted that V_{C12} is not unambiguously defined. In particular, although the current accounts of commercial banks with the Bank of Greece are, when in surplus, non-interest-bearing, the same does not apply when negative amounts (overdrafts) are recorded. In the latter case, the levy of penalty rates suggests a similarity to advances, though the rates charged have, in this case, depended during the period under review on the length of the outstanding overdraft and/or the amount drawn.[45] Such considerations have prompted the estimation of the two different sets of relationships shown below and should be borne in mind in the discussion following.

4.3 Expected yields and actual rates

The construction of anticipated returns for various choice set items is the one aspect of our structure still untouched. In this context the usual practice is to treat actual rates as the basis for construction of the proxies for expected returns, that is to say that actual rates comprise the universe of information on which expected yields on the various choice set items are computed by the decision-taking unit in question.[46] A limiting case, which granted the nature of choice set items of Greek commercial banks is not obviously unreasonable in the present context, is to assume that current rates comprise the relevant proxy for expected rates. Thus

$$\hat{m}'_z = [r_C \; r_T \; r_{L2} \; r_{L4} \; r_{L6} \; r_{L8} \; r_B \; r_A] \tag{11}$$

where

r_C = zero

r_T = the rate on six-month Treasury bills

r_{Li} = the loan rates defined in the second row of Table 10.3

r_B = the bond rate as defined by the running yield on
development bonds

r_A = the rate charged by the Bank of Greece on discounts
and advances

all defined on an annual basis.

5. A TALE OF A GREEK COMMERCIAL BANK

The data sample on which this study draws relates to the largest Greek commercial bank, the National Bank of Greece, during the period 1969 first quarter to 1977 fourth quarter. During the sample period, this bank accounted for 54 per cent of the total deposit taking business and 60 per cent of the total loan volume of commercial banks.[47] Given its relative size, it cannot readily be treated as a typical (representative) bank, and the comparisons made in Appendices 10.4 to 10.8 of this chapter also point in this direction. Consequently, any inferences to be drawn for the aggregate of 'large' banks from the results shown below can only be speculative, the difficulty being compounded for 'small' banks as a result of the differences in controls pertaining to them. Even so, however, the exercise of focusing on this bank is not only worthwhile as an example of the analysis that we may choose to undertake in due course, for other banks, but also particularly revealing in the context of the widely held belief that banking policy in Greece amounts to policy *vis-à-vis* the National Bank of Greece.

5.1 Specification

Given our choice of bank and time period, it looks almost like an easy ride to estimating the model previously described. Alas, our troubles are far from over. For the particular definitions of the various aggregates that I have argued for above, they can only be carried over directly to a time series context if and only if the definitions of the various groups of assets are time invariant. In practice, however, the monetary authorities have not only varied the reserve ratios and interest rates pertaining to the various loan categories, but have also periodically altered the composition of these categories by shifting particular types of loans from one interest rate or reserve ratio category to another. To construct continuous series, therefore, we must define a set of loan aggregates of order no less than $\rho + \zeta$, where ρ are the loan categories defined above, and ζ are the number of sub-aggregates subject to alterations in treatment relative to other members of their original reserve groups.[48]

Consistent application of this principle, even for the short span of years of the sample period, would probably have produced a considerable increase in the eight loan categories defined for December 1975. Yet this principle could only be followed to a limited extent, in view of the fact that for some of the category changes that have taken place during this time interval no information was forthcoming, despite repeated requests for explanation from various bodies responsible for these statistics. For the present, therefore, it was deemed pertinent to (i) correct the more blatant errors in the loan statistics[49] and (ii) identify the remaining categories between which such shifts had taken place and proceed, with due regard to their corresponding reserve ratios, to define new aggregates over such categories, leaving as one of Milton's unresolved questions, the issue of the extent to which gross errors have been committed by the Currency Committee (and other bodies responsible for money and credit matters in Greece) in the enforcement of reserve ratios and in policy design in general.

Approaching the issue in two stages, the loan categories shown in Table 10.4 were first constructed for the period 1969ɪ to 1977ɪᴠ, with appropriate sub-divisions of the first row as between the 15 and 6 per cent credit ratios.

TABLE 10.4   Considered loan categories, 1969ɪ to 1977ɪᴠ

Primary reserve ratio	Low reserve ratio	High reserve ratio	Low rebate	Medium rebate	High rebate	Other reserves	Aliakmon and Edoc Eter
Credit ratios	V_{L1}	V_{L3}	V_{L5}	V_{L7A}	V_{L7B}	V_{L9}	V_{L11}
Outside credit ratios	V_{L2}	V_{L4}	V_{L6}	V_{L8A}	V_{L8B}	V_{L10}	V_{L12}

Of these, the first three columns correspond exactly to the analogous categories of Tables 10.2 and 10.3. On the other hand, column four of Table 10.2 is now decomposed into two columns in order to take account of the differences in the reserve ratios applying to its constituent groups in earlier years. Furthermore, two new categories are created, of which 'other ratios' relate to a loan category subject to zero reserve/rebate ratio for the years 1969ɪ to 1973ɪᴠ and low reserve ratio thereafter, while 'Aliakmon and Edoc Eter' denotes loans to these companies that – although subject throughout this period to the low rebate ratios – were initially outside the credit ratio arrangement, but have qualified for such privileged treatment since 1972ɪɪɪ.

Granted this, then, in the light of our discussion so far the following set of relationships can be defined:

$$\dot{V}_z = \frac{1}{\alpha} G \dot{Y}_z - H \dot{V}_q \tag{12}$$

where:

$$\tilde{V}_z = \left[\, V_{C12} \ V_{T1} \ \overline{V}_{L2} \ \overline{V}_{L4} \ \overline{V}_{V6} \ \overline{V}_{L8} \ \overline{V}_{L10} \ V_{B1} \ -V_A \,\right] \tag{13}$$

$$\begin{aligned}
\tilde{V}_q = \big[\, & \overline{V}_{L1a} \ \overline{V}_{L1b} \ \overline{V}_{L3a} \ \overline{V}_{L3b} \ \overline{V}_{L5a} \ \overline{V}_{L5b} \ \overline{V}_{L7a} \ \overline{V}_{L7b} \ \overline{V}_{L11,12} \\
& -\overline{V}_{D1} \ -\overline{V}_{D2} \ -\overline{V}_{D3} \ -\overline{V}_{D4} \ -\overline{V}_{D5} \ -\overline{V}_{D6} \ -\overline{V}_{D7} \ -\overline{V}_{D8} \\
& -\overline{V}_{D9} \ -\overline{V}_{OFE} \ -V_{OTH} \ -V_{DCB} \,\big]
\end{aligned} \tag{14}$$

$$\left.\begin{aligned}
\overline{V}_{L8} &= \overline{V}_{L8A} + \overline{V}_{L8B} = (1+\lambda_{8A})\,V_{L8A} + (1+\lambda_{8B})\,V_{L8B} \\
\overline{V}_{L7\gamma} &= \overline{V}_{L7A\gamma} + \overline{V}_{L7B\gamma} = \lambda_{7A}\,V_{L7A\gamma} + \lambda_{7B}\,V_{L7B\gamma} \\
& \quad \gamma = a, b \\
\overline{V}_{L11,12} &= \overline{V}_{L11} + \overline{V}_{L12} = \lambda_{11}\,V_{11} + (1+\lambda_{12})\,V_{L12}
\end{aligned}\right\} \tag{15}$$

$$\overline{V}_{L10} = (1+\lambda_{10})\,V_{L10}$$

V_{DCB} = deposits of other commercial banks with the National Bank of Greece, and all other variables are as in (9) to (11) above, while

$$\left.\begin{aligned}
\tilde{Y}_z &= (i + \hat{m}_z) \\
\hat{m}_z &= \left[\, 0 \ r_T r_{L2} \ r_{L4} \ r_{L6} \ r_{L8} \ r_{L10} \ r_B \ r_A \,\right]
\end{aligned}\right\} \tag{16}$$

where $r_T, r_{L2}, r_{L4}, r_{L6}, r_{L8}, r_B, r_A$ are described by (11) and analogously

$$r_{L10} = R_{10}/(1+\lambda_{10})$$

but r_8 is proxied by

$$r_8 = R_{8A}/(1+\lambda_{8A})$$

Anticipating the possibility of biases arising from any remaining discontinuities, resulting from data imperfections, it seems desirable that the set of arguments employed in explaining the behaviour of $\tilde{V}_z$ be augmented to include appropriate data dummies. The same can be said of seasonal dummies, granted the quarterly and seasonally unadjusted nature of the data. No less importantly one should not preclude the possibility that other influences and conventions[50] bear on the choices of these institutions regarding the quantities of the assets defined here as components of $\tilde{V}_z$. Such considerations suggest a specification of the form[51]

$$\tilde{V}_z = \frac{1}{\alpha} G \tilde{Y}_z - H \tilde{V}_q + JE + C + U \tag{17}$$

where E comprises a vector of data and seasonal dummies and, perhaps, a trend variable, and J is accordingly a matrix of responses of choice set items to such influences; C is a $z \times 1$ vector of constant terms, and U is a $z \times 1$ vector of disturbances. In that eventuality we would have, in addition to the properties of G and H already described

$$i'J = \phi, \ i'C = 0, \ i'U = 0 \tag{18}$$

where ϕ is a row vector of zeros of appropriate order.

Alas, the size of the sample and computer limitations imposed severe constraints on the feasible specification. Such considerations compelled not only that we forgo the dummies and trends, but also that we resort to some prior aggregation regarding the components of V_q. Faced with this problem, the question of course is: what prior aggregation? what criteria are we to adopt in so doing? One possibility considered was to define V_q as comprising only three aggregates, say

$$\tilde{V}_q = [\, \overline{V}_D \ \overline{V}_L \ \overline{V}_O \,] \tag{19}$$

where $\overline{V}_D$, $\overline{V}_L$, $\overline{V}_O$ comprise respectively the sums of adjusted deposits, loans and other assets defined in (14) above. Yet, however appealing, such aggregation is *ad hoc*. And although something more about it will be said below, it cannot *a priori* be said to comprise a more appropriate deviation from (15) than another alternative, namely that of aggregating all components of V_q together. Moving to the latter extreme, the following relationship was therefore defined

$$\tilde{V}_z = \frac{1}{a} G \tilde{Y}_z - Bi' \tilde{V}_q + C + U \tag{20}$$

retaining, it will be noticed, the vector of constant terms as a minimal concession to 'other influences'.

Relationship (20) is in fact what I have elsewhere described as the myopic model of portfolio selection.[52] But in the present context, I repeat that it is adopted in the interests of computational expediency, a course of action, permissible I dare say in an exploratory study, but not one to be recommended if it can be avoided.

5.2 Estimation

Granted (18), the covariance matrix of disturbances $E(uu') = Q$ i
singular since

$$Qi_z = E(uu')i_z = E(uu'i_z) = 0 \qquad (21$$

While this property, which derives from the balance sheet condition
present in our model, implies that the complete, nine equations system
can only be estimated by relying on the generalised inverse[53] of Q, it also
implies that identical estimates can be obtained by deleting one equation
Such deletion resolves the problem of singularity of Q while, granted tha
the density of the resulting vector of disturbances is independent of the
index of the deleted component, the statistical properties of the mode
remain unaltered.

Tables 10.5 and 10.6, the latter emanating from the remarks
regarding current accounts of commercial banks with the Bank o
Greece, present the estimates derived from constrained estimation of the
system defined in (20) above. A comparison between these tables reveals
that the *precise* parameter estimates are susceptible to even relatively
small variation in our 'prior beliefs' regarding the appropriate pattern o
aggregation. Nevertheless, from a traditional viewpoint – looking say a
'*t*' statistics, given in brackets[54] – the statistical performance of the mode
is far from distressing. Similarly, from an economic standpoint, the
estimated coefficients conform to what theory suggests and, indeed
present no less reasonable a pattern than that traced when similar
structures have been estimated for other countries.[55]

Focusing on particular subsets of coefficients, we find that, in both
tables, responses to changes in the sum of the components of V_q conform
broadly to the pattern exhibited by the shares of the various assets
included in V_z (as described in Appendix 10.5). Increases in the sum
available for distribution among V_z lead – bearing in mind that $i'V_q$ is
introduced with a negative sign – to significant increases in demand for
free bonds and loans of various reserve/rebate categories and – as one
would have expected – significant decreases in demand for Bank of
Greece advances. Also, in accordance with prior beliefs, we find that of
the nine *diagonal elements* of the G matrix presented in Table 10.5, *none* is
both negative and significant while several are both positive and
significant. The same positive and significant coefficients appear, it will
be noticed, in Table 10.6. Similarly, the off-diagonal elements of the G
matrix record a great number of significant substitution/complemen-
tarity relationships, and – except for the two equations, $-V_A$ and V_{C12}

TABLE 10.5 Estimates from 'myopic'[a] model: National Bank of Greece, 1969ı to 1977ıv

Dependent variable	Explanatory variable											
	Y_T	Y_B	Y_{L2}	Y_{L4}	Y_{L6}	Y_{L8}	Y_{L10}	Y_A	i	$i'V_q$	C	SE
V_{T1}	3.82 (0.08)	25.21 (2.24)	−162.31 (4.34)	19.31 (0.47)	49.59 (1.57)	265.59 (8.95)	−27.25 (2.10)	−111.53 (4.90)	−62.33 (2.76)	0.01 (0.58)	−7.97 ( )	1.35
V_{B1}	25.21 (2.24)	7.42 (1.72)	15.14 (1.60)	−22.76 (1.91)	21.04 (2.33)	−15.91 (2.03)	−0.26 (0.12)	2.71 (0.38)	−32.58 (4.50)	−0.08 (17.12)	−3.13 ( )	0.46
V_{L2}	−162.31 (4.34)	15.14 (1.60)	755.09 (4.18)	6.76 (0.13)	100.89 (1.57)	−464.42 (4.94)	−231.72 (2.91)	48.67 (2.44)	−68.09 (2.08)	−0.45 (34.15)	−11.53 ( )	1.29
V_{L4}	19.31 (0.47)	−22.76 (1.91)	6.76 (0.13)	−50.48 (0.67)	−2.38 (0.05)	−37.70 (0.92)	−24.70 (1.81)	60.36 (2.72)	51.41 (2.48)	−0.17 (13.64)	9.91 ( )	1.02
V_{L6}	49.29 (1.57)	21.04 (2.33)	100.29 (1.57)	−2.38 (0.05)	−61.52 (1.04)	−134.99 (3.37)	−9.71 (0.55)	−19.39 (0.92)	56.76 (2.82)	−0.14 (11.28)	1.94 ( )	1.35
V_{L8}	265.59 (8.95)	−15.91 (2.03)	−464.42 (4.94)	−37.70 (0.92)	−134.99 (3.37)	164.74 (2.69)	136.12 (3.38)	43.02 (2.31)	43.56 (1.92)	−0.26 (23.02)	9.84 ( )	1.28
V_{L10}	−27.25 (2.10)	−0.26 (0.12)	−231.72 (2.91)	−24.70 (1.81)	9.71 (0.55)	136.12 (3.38)	137.01 (3.19)	0.07 (0.02)	20.58 (1.48)	−0.00 (1.52)	3.56 ( )	0.16
$-V_A$	−111.53 (4.90)	2.71 (0.38)	48.67 (2.44)	60.36 (2.72)	−19.39 (0.92)	43.02 (2.31)	0.07 (0.02)	−3.50 (0.15)	−20.26 (0.94)	0.09 (7.12)	−2.67 ( )	1.64
V_{C12}[b]	−62.33 (2.76)	−32.58 (4.50)	−68.09 (2.08)	51.41 (2.48)	56.76 (2.82)	43.51 (1.92)	20.58 (1.48)	−20.26 (0.94)	10.97 (0.36)	0.01 (0.52)	0.05 ( )	0.91

[a] Homogeneity of response to V_q.
[b] Including current account balances at the Bank of Greece.

TABLE 10.6 Alternative estimates from 'myopic'[a] model: National Bank of Greece, 1969i to 1977iv

Dependent variable	Explanatory variable											
	Y_T	Y_B	Y_{L2}	Y_{L4}	Y_{L6}	Y_{L8}	Y_{L10}	Y_A	i	$i'V_q$	C	SE
V_Π	28.90 (0.58)	22.48 (1.78)	−137.57 (4.85)	−9.97 (0.25)	37.77 (1.15)	246.34 (8.34)	−20.52 (1.60)	−113.07 (1.60)	−4.35 (0.29)	−0.02 (1.31)	−2.67 (1.17)	1.53
V_{B1}	22.48 (1.78)	14.81 (2.90)	25.22 (2.45)	−18.27 (1.48)	2.56 (0.25)	−22.82 (2.84)	0.63 (0.28)	−18.41 (1.75)	−6.15 (1.32)	−0.09 (21.54)	−1.51 (2.43)	0.52
V_{L2}	−187.57 (4.85)	25.22 (2.45)	753.27 (4.18)	50.35 (0.91)	149.04 (2.16)	−473.48 (5.11)	−265.71 (3.41)	20.81 (0.76)	−71.92 (2.46)	−0.45 (38.02)	−14.12 (4.25)	1.29
V_{L4}	−9.97 (0.25)	−18.27 (1.48)	50.35 (0.91)	−22.98 (0.31)	−32.33 (0.70)	−35.30 (0.87)	−17.32 (1.26)	42.45 (0.54)	43.37 (2.37)	−0.16 (14.62)	8.35 (4.16)	1.04
V_{L6}	37.77 (1.15)	2.56 (0.25)	149.04 (2.16)	−32.33 (0.70)	−35.18 (0.54)	−130.29 (3.21)	−0.58 (0.03)	−0.68 (0.03)	9.70 (0.67)	−0.12 (11.09)	1.71 (0.89)	1.36
V_{L8}	246.34 (8.34)	−22.82 (2.84)	−473.48 (5.11)	−35.30 (0.87)	−130.29 (3.21)	200.91 (3.36)	154.07 (3.90)	35.71 (1.41)	24.85 (1.46)	−0.25 (25.92)	7.79 (3.69)	1.25
V_{L10}	−20.52 (1.60)	0.63 (0.28)	−265.71 (3.41)	−17.32 (1.26)	−0.58 (0.03)	154.07 (3.90)	129.11 (3.07)	−1.95 (0.46)	22.26 (1.63)	−0.00 (0.55)	3.57 (2.35)	0.17
$-V_A$ [b]	−113.07 (1.60)	−18.46 (1.75)	20.81 (0.76)	42.45 (0.54)	−0.68 (0.03)	35.71 (1.41)	−1.95 (0.46)	22.76 (0.38)	12.42 (1.16)	0.10 (5.45)	2.00 (0.79)	2.08
V_{C12}	−4.35 (0.29)	−6.15 (1.32)	−71.92 (2.46)	43.37 (2.37)	9.70 (0.67)	24.85 (1.46)	22.26 (1.63)	12.42 (1.16)	−30.19 (3.01)	0.00 (0.86)	−1.70 (1.73)	0.79

[a] Homogeneity of response to Y_i.
[b] Including current account balances at the Bank of Greece.

subject to the alternative aggregation assumptions – the precise pattern of such responses is very robust when comparing the two sets of estimates presented.

No less pertinent than the specific parameter estimates, however, is the *overall* performance of the model described by (20), to other models that may be tendered as possible descriptions of behaviour. One such model is that on which Tables (10.7) and (10.8) are based. As these tables reveal, in addition to the properties pertaining to model (20), it is in this case assumed that the G matrix is such as to suggest the absence of substitution/complementarity relationships between loans of different reserve/rebate ratio categories. Such a constraint reflects the feature, characteristic of monopolistic profit-maximisation models, that the amount of loans of any particular category is independent of the relative yields and other characteristics pertaining to loans of other categories, although it depends on the opportunity cost defined by the security yields or the rate on Central Bank advances. Imposition of this constraint results in reversal of the sign of the coefficient of response to changes in the own rate of return of V_{L8}, an increase in the return to loans of the high rebate category leading (as demand considerations and the over time correspondence between rates charged to borrowers and yields received by the banks from loans of this category suggests) to a decrease in the sum of own funds devoted to such loans. Yet a chi-squared ratio of the log-likelihood values of model (20) to a variant embodying this additional constraint, yielded a value of $\chi^2_{10} = 30.092$ when current accounts with the Bank of Greece are included in V_{C12}, and of $\chi^2_{10} = 40.499$ when current accounts with the Bank of Greece are aggregated with advances, which with 10 degrees of freedom – being the difference in the number of free coefficients estimated in the more and less restrictive models – denotes that the 'no substitution between loans' hypothesis cannot be said to command even a 0.005 probability of occurrence.

Besides shedding some light on the likely performance of a model that abstracts from explicit consideration of decisions pertaining to banks' choices as between loans of different categories, and pointing to the lack of validity of the hypothesis that the 'rate equalisation' scheme ensures the indifference of commercial banks regarding the composition of their loan portfolios, this result does (perhaps?) enhance our confidence in model (20) as a description of the behaviour of the National Bank of Greece during the period under review. Yet we should not forget that model (20) does, itself, rest on at least one highly restrictive assumption, introduced when aggregating over the components of V_q, namely that of homogeneity of response to changes in non-choice set items. Granted

TABLE 10.7 Estimates from 'restricted'[a] model: National Bank of Greece, 1969ı to 1977ıv

Dependent variable	Explanatory variable											
	Y_T	Y_B	Y_{L2}	Y_{L4}	Y_{L6}	Y_{L8}	Y_{L10}	Y_A	i	$i'V_q$	C	SE
V_{T1}	46.95 (0.96)	28.01 (2.47)	-153.81 (4.51)	-13.26 (0.34)	31.75 (1.00)	194.84 (8.16)	-11.47 (1.19)	-84.85 (3.82)	-38.17 (1.69)	0.01 (0.37)	-3.46 (1.34)	1.45
V_{B1}	28.01 (2.47)	8.07 (1.86)	5.87 (0.56)	-20.87 (1.82)	15.52 (1.71)	-13.77 (1.75)	1.98 (0.84)	4.93 (0.68)	-29.75 (4.09)	-0.08 (16.98)	-2.70 (3.80)	0.48
$\bar{V}_{L2}$	-153.81 (4.51)	5.87 (0.56)	103.37 (2.25)	0.00	0.00	0.00	0.00	29.81 (1.33)	14.76 (0.66)	-0.44 (33.84)	-1.71 (0.81)	1.41
$\bar{V}_{L4}$	-13.26 (0.34)	-20.87 (1.82)	0.00	-68.18 (1.42)	0.00	0.00	0.00	47.58 (2.18)	54.73 (2.72)	-0.17 (14.57)	9.32 (4.40)	1.01
$\bar{V}_{L6}$	31.75 (1.00)	15.52 (1.71)	0.00	0.00	-52.43 (1.15)	0.00	0.00	-44.23 (2.22)	49.39 (2.60)	-0.14 (12.13)	-0.13 (0.06)	1.36
$\bar{V}_{L8}$	194.84 (8.16)	-13.77 (1.75)	0.00	0.00	0.00	-175.15 (5.53)	0.00	31.35 (1.78)	-37.27 (2.32)	-0.26 (26.44)	-1.21 (0.80)	1.16
$\bar{V}_{L10}$	-11.47 (1.19)	1.98 (0.84)	0.00	0.00	0.00	0.00	23.70 (2.79)	2.89 (0.67)	-17.11 (4.49)	0.00 (0.44)	-0.72 (4.17)	0.18
$-V_A$	-84.85 (3.82)	4.93 (0.68)	29.81 (1.33)	47.58 (2.18)	-44.23 (2.22)	31.35 (1.78)	2.89 (0.67)	15.64 (0.70)	-3.12 (0.16)	0.09 (7.17)	0.21 (0.10)	1.58
V_{C12}^b	-38.17 (1.69)	-29.75 (4.09)	14.76 (0.66)	54.73 (2.72)	49.39 (2.60)	-37.27 (2.32)	-17.11 (4.49)	-3.12 (0.16)	6.55 (0.23)	-0.01 (0.59)	0.40 (0.08)	

[a] No substitution between loans of different categories.
[b] Including current account balances at the Bank of Greece.

TABLE 10.8 Alternative estimates from 'restricted'[a] model: National Bank of Greece, 1969iv to 1977iv

Dependent variable	Explanatory variable												SE
	Y_T	Y_B	Y_{L2}	Y_{L4}	Y_{L6}	Y_{L8}	Y_{L10}	Y_A	i	$i'V_q$	C		
V_{T1}	61.16 (1.25)	27.36 (2.17)	−182.94 (5.04)	−28.21 (0.76)	21.79 (0.64)	186.57 (8.02)	−7.85 (0.82)	−78.41 (2.65)	0.53 (0.04)	−0.01 (0.76)	0.19 (0.09)		1.63
V_{B1}	27.36 (2.17)	15.78 (3.10)	10.84 (0.96)	−16.35 (1.42)	−2.28 (0.22)	−19.75 (2.49)	2.81 (1.19)	−13.36 (1.27)	−5.06 (1.10)	−0.09 (20.89)	−1.07 (1.77)		0.54
V_{L2}	−182.94 (5.04)	10.84 (0.96)	133.72 (2.83)	0.00	0.00	0.00	0.00	5.76 (0.20)	32.62 (1.89)	−0.45 (39.74)	−1.76 (0.97)		1.36
V_{L4}	−28.21 (0.76)	−16.35 (1.42)	0.00	−35.41 (0.79)	0.00	0.00	0.00	27.72 (1.17)	52.24 (3.13)	−0.16 (16.50)	8.21 (4.60)		1.02
V_{L6}	21.79 (0.64)	−2.28 (0.22)	0.00	0.00	−1.84 (0.44)	0.00	0.00	29.97 (1.20)	12.30 (0.90)	−0.13 (12.07)	−3.46 (1.79)		1.42
V_{L8}	186.57 (8.02)	−19.75 (2.49)	0.00	0.00	0.00	−140.04 (4.55)	0.00	19.50 (0.87)	−46.28 (4.11)	−0.26 (29.47)	−2.65 (2.24)		1.17
V_{L10}	−7.85 (0.82)	2.81 (1.19)	0.00	0.00	0.00	0.00	18.35 (2.18)	1.32 (0.30)	−14.64 (3.90)	−0.00 (0.42)	−0.96 (3.36)		0.18
$-V_A$ [b]	−78.41 (2.65)	−13.36 (1.27)	5.76 (0.20)	27.72 (1.17)	−29.97 (1.20)	19.50 (0.87)	1.33 (0.30)	54.23 (0.96)	13.19 (1.24)	0.11 (6.04)	4.29 (1.85)		2.97
V_{C12}	0.53 (0.76)	−5.06 (1.10)	32.62 (1.89)	52.24 (3.13)	12.30 (0.90)	−46.28 (4.11)	−14.64 (3.90)	13.19 (1.24)	−44.88, (5.06)	0.09 (0.40)	−3.21 (3.24)		

[a] No substitution between loans of different categories.
[b] Including current accounts balances at the Bank of Greece.

this, one more finding should be mentioned, at least for the sake of caution and certainly as a reminder that the above results do not comprise an exhaustive 'explanation' of the behaviour of the institution considered. A comparison of performance of model (20) to that implicit when V_q is defined as in (19) above, does reveal that the hypothesis that no loss in informational content is incurred from relying on the sum of V_q cannot be accepted. A similar verdict, furthermore, is rendered from examination of the symmetry constraint imposed relative to the unconstrained reduced form.

6. CONCLUDING REMARKS

All this still leaves much to be done. At the analytical level there are several assumptions to be relaxed, that is to say less restrictive models of behaviour to be tried.[56] At the empirical level there are comparisons between banks to be made[57] and for different patterns of aggregation to be investigated. Furthermore, there are various questions about data still to be resolved. Yet for a first attempt towards a systematic description of the main elements of control impinging on Greek commercial banks since the mid-1960s and in examining the behaviour of such institutions, a modest claim may be tendered for the content of this chapter. A list of key points to be noted include:

(i) A necessary – though by no means sufficient – condition for acceptance of the structure of rates chosen at any given moment in time by the Greek monetary authorities in their policy design to be efficient, is that they are able to predict demand for the various categories supplied at different rates of interest, that is that they know the demand functions of borrowers for the various categories of credit. While this is a tall order for any monetary authority, the confusion identified in the course of undertaking this study regarding the structure of banking statistics, and revealed also by the amendments to many of the official series that were deemed necessary, possesses a serious challenge to any such claim being made by the Greek monetary authorities at present.

(ii) Even if this condition were satisfied, the complementary aspect of this policy towards suppliers of credit, that is the equalisation of rates received by banks, need not, in general, ensure the indifference of commercial banks for the structure of their loan portfolios, nor their tacit acceptance of whatever composition the Currency

Committee – acting on the presumption that it is endowed with the insight questioned in (i) above – considers fitting.

(iii) If the Currency Committee's presumption of ensuring the particular loan demands it deems consistent with maximisation of social welfare objectives is disregarded, and excess demands are assumed to pertain to various categories of loans *outside* the credit ratio regulations, our empirical findings reveal that – contrary to official beliefs – banks cannot be treated as indifferent of the composition of their loan portfolios.

(iv) Granted (iii), one may not preclude the possibility that deviations of actual loan volumes, from those which the authorities regard as consistent with intertemporal social welfare objectives, are the result of misinterpretation by the authorities of the behavioural functions of these intermediaries and consequent misspecification of the penalties and inducements that are required to secure the 'desired objectives'. Certainly contrary to popular myth, the results suggest that commercial banks in Greece cannot be treated as mindless machines impervious to economic incentives, since their responses cannot be claimed to be independent of the relative yields and other characteristics of the assets that comprise their portfolios.

(v) On a different but related plane, and in view of the tendency of the authorities to regard their activities in the credit sphere as distinct from those pertaining to monetary policy, the links between the two, stressed earlier in this chapter, should be noted.

(vi) Finally, and if only because the particular interpretation often placed on the unwillingness of banks to grant loans of the kinds defined in the context of credit ratios is misdirected, it should be remembered that the rate of return on own funds directed towards loans in the credit ratio categories has been – and is – vastly higher than the authorities have tended to surmise.

APPENDIX 10.1   CASH RATIOS ON LIABILITIES, 1969i TO 1977iva

Quarter		Deposit category					
		Sight deposits – private	*Savings deposits – no notice*	*Savings deposits – at notice*	*Time deposits – private*	*Restricted deposits*	*Deposits in foreign exchange*b
1969	I	0.000	0.000	0.000	0.000	0.000	0.000
	II	0.000	0.000	0.000	0.000	0.000	0.000
	III	0.000	0.000	0.000	0.000	0.000	0.000
	IV	0.030	0.030	0.030	0.000	0.000	0.000
1970	I	0.000	0.000	0.000	0.000	0.000	0.000
	II	0.000	0.000	0.000	0.000	0.000	0.000
	III	0.000	0.000	0.000	0.000	0.000	0.000
	IV	0.000	0.000	0.000	0.000	0.000	0.000
1971	I	0.000	0.000	0.000	0.000	0.000	0.000
	II	0.000	0.000	0.000	0.000	0.000	0.000
	III	0.000	0.000	0.000	0.000	0.000	0.000
	IV	0.030	0.030	0.030	0.000	0.000	0.000
1972	I	0.000	0.000	0.000	0.000	0.000	0.000
	II	0.000	0.000	0.000	0.000	0.000	0.000
	III	0.000	0.000	0.000	0.000	0.000	0.000
	IV	0.430	0.110	0.060	0.030	0.000	0.000
1973	I	0.400	0.080	0.030	0.030	0.400	0.000
	II	0.400	0.080	0.030	0.030	0.400	0.000
	III	0.400	0.080	0.030	0.030	0.400	0.000
	IV	0.400	0.080	0.030	0.030	0.400	0.000
1974	I	0.400	0.060	0.010	0.010	0.400	0.000
	II	0.400	0.060	0.010	0.010	0.400	0.000
	III	0.050	0.005	0.000	0.000	0.050	0.000
	IV	0.050	0.005	0.000	0.000	0.050	0.000
1975	I	0.050	0.005	0.000	0.000	0.050	0.000
	II	0.070	0.070	0.000	0.000	0.070	0.000
	III	0.070	0.070	0.000	0.000	0.070	0.000
	IV	0.070	0.070	0.000	0.000	0.070	0.000
1976	I	0.070	0.070	0.000	0.000	0.070	0.000
	II	0.070	0.070	0.000	0.000	0.070	0.000
	III	0.070	0.070	0.000	0.000	0.070	0.000
	IV	0.105	0.105	0.035	0.000	0.070	0.000
1977	I	0.070	0.070	0.070	0.070	0.070	0.070
	II	0.070	0.070	0.070	0.070	0.070	0.070
	III	0.070	0.070	0.070	0.070	0.070	0.070
	IV	0.070	0.070	0.070	0.070	0.070	0.070

a Including seasonals.
b That are converted into drachmas in the Bank of Greece.

APPENDIX 10.2   SECURITY RATIOS ON LIABILITIES

	Deposit category					
Quarter	Sight deposits – private	Savings deposits – no notice	Savings deposits – at notice	Time deposits – private	Restricted deposits	Deposits in foreign exchange[a]
1969 I	0.280	0.280	0.000	0.000	0.000	0.000
II	0.280	0.280	0.000	0.000	0.000	0.000
III	0.295	0.295	0.000	0.000	0.000	0.000
IV	0.295	0.295	0.000	0.000	0.000	0.000
1970 I	0.315	0.315	0.000	0.000	0.000	0.000
II	0.315	0.315	0.000	0.000	0.000	0.000
III	0.345	0.345	0.000	0.000	0.000	0.000
IV	0.345	0.345	0.000	0.000	0.000	0.000
1971 I	0.345	0.345	0.000	0.000	0.000	0.000
II	0.345	0.345	0.000	0.000	0.000	0.000
III	0.365	0.365	0.040	0.040	0.365	0.000
IV	0.365	0.365	0.040	0.040	0.365	0.000
1972 I	0.365	0.365	0.040	0.040	0.365	0.000
II	0.365	0.365	0.040	0.040	0.365	0.000
III	0.365	0.365	0.040	0.040	0.365	0.000
IV	0.390	0.390	0.040	0.040	0.390	0.000
1973 I	0.390	0.390	0.040	0.040	0.390	0.000
II	0.390	0.390	0.040	0.040	0.390	0.000
III	0.390	0.390	0.040	0.040	0.390	0.000
IV	0.390	0.390	0.040	0.040	0.390	0.000
1974 I	0.390	0.390	0.040	0.040	0.390	0.000
II	0.390	0.390	0.040	0.040	0.390	0.000
III	0.390	0.390	0.040	0.040	0.390	0.000
IV	0.390	0.390	0.040	0.040	0.390	0.000
1975 I	0.390	0.390	0.040	0.040	0.390	0.000
II	0.390	0.390	0.040	0.040	0.390	0.000
III	0.390	0.390	0.040	0.040	0.390	0.000
IV	0.390	0.390	0.040	0.040	0.390	0.000
1976 I	0.390	0.390	0.040	0.040	0.390	0.000
II	0.390	0.390	0.040	0.040	0.390	0.000
III	0.390	0.390	0.040	0.040	0.390	0.000
IV	0.390	0.390	0.040	0.040	0.390	0.000
1977 I	0.300	0.300	0.300	0.300	0.300	0.300
II	0.300	0.300	0.300	0.300	0.300	0.300
III	0.300	0.300	0.300	0.300	0.300	0.300
IV	0.300	0.300	0.300	0.300	0.300	0.300

[a] That are converted into drachmas in the Bank of Greece.

APPENDIX 10.3   TOTAL RESERVE RATIOS ON DEPOSITS, 1969ı TO 1977ıv[a]

Quarter		Deposit category					
		Sight deposits – private	Savings deposits – no notice	Savings deposits – at notice	Time deposits	Restricted deposits	Deposits in foreign exchange[b]
1969	I	0.490	0.490	0.210	0.210	0.210	0.000
	II	0.490	0.490	0.210	0.210	0.210	0.000
	III	0.505	0.505	0.210	0.210	0.210	0.000
	IV	0.505	0.535	0.240	0.210	0.210	0.000
1970	I	0.525	0.525	0.210	0.210	0.210	0.000
	II	0.525	0.525	0.210	0.210	0.210	0.000
	III	0.555	0.555	0.210	0.210	0.210	0.000
	IV	0.555	0.555	0.210	0.210	0.210	0.000
1971	I	0.555	0.555	0.210	0.210	0.210	0.000
	II	0.555	0.555	0.210	0.210	0.210	0.000
	III	0.575	0.575	0.250	0.250	0.575	0.000
	IV	0.605	0.605	0.280	0.250	0.575	0.000
1972	I	0.575	0.575	0.250	0.250	0.575	0.000
	II	0.575	0.575	0.250	0.250	0.575	0.000
	III	0.575	0.575	0.250	0.250	0.575	0.000
	IV	1.030	0.710	0.350	0.280	0.600	0.000
1973	I	1.000	0.680	0.280	0.280	1.000	0.000
	II	1.000	0.680	0.280	0.280	1.000	0.000
	III	1.000	0.680	0.280	0.280	1.000	0.000
	IV	1.000	0.680	0.280	0.280	1.000	0.000
1974	I	1.000	0.660	0.260	0.260	1.000	0.000
	II	1.000	0.660	0.260	0.260	1.000	0.000
	III	0.650	0.605	0.250	0.250	0.650	0.000
	IV	0.650	0.605	0.250	0.250	0.650	0.000
1975	I	0.650	0.605	0.250	0.250	0.650	0.000
	II	0.670	0.670	0.250	0.250	0.670	0.000
	III	0.670	0.670	0.250	0.250	0.670	0.000
	IV	0.670	0.670	0.250	0.250	0.670	0.000
1976	I	0.670	0.670	0.250	0.250	0.670	0.000
	II	0.670	0.670	0.250	0.250	0.670	0.000
	III	0.670	0.670	0.250	0.250	0.670	0.000
	IV	0.705	0.705	0.285	0.250	0.670	0.000
1977	I	0.580	0.580	0.580	0.580	0.580	0.370
	II	0.580	0.580	0.580	0.580	0.580	0.370
	III	0.580	0.580	0.580	0.580	0.580	0.370
	IV	0.580	0.580	0.580	0.580	0.580	0.370

[a] Note that the 6 per cent ratio applies to the increment in deposits relative to December 1965, so that the totals shown do thus deviate from the average reserve ratios corresponding to each category of deposits.
[b] That are converted into drachmas in the Bank of Greece.

APPENDIX 10.4   BANK SHARES IN TOTAL COMMERCIAL
BANKING BUSINESS (PERCENTAGE)

Quarter	National Bank of Greece	Commercial Bank of Greece	Ionian & Popular Bank of Greece	Credit Bank of Greece	Other commercial banks
			Deposits		
1969 IV	55.16	20.02	7.97	2.94	13.91
1975 IV	53.34	17.78	6.76	5.07	17.05
1977 IV	54.74	16.75	6.98	5.47	16.06
			Loans		
1969 IV	61.82	17.49	7.60	3.17	9.92
1975 IV	58.95	17.40	7.13	5.21	11.31
1977 IV	60.40	15.88	6.37	5.52	11.83

APPENDIX 10.5 A COMPARISON OF THE ASSET AND LIABILITY STRUCTURE OF GREEK COMMERCIAL BANKS, DECEMBER 1975[a]

	National Bank	Commercial Bank	Ionian & Popular Bank
Assets	100.00	100.00	100.00
Cash	1.32	1.57	2.18
Non-interest-bearing deposits with B of G – free	0.86	1.00	−1.49
Non-interest-bearing deposits with B of G – compulsory	—	1.36	0.95
Interest-bearing-deposits with B of G – compulsory	2.43	3.20	4.54
Foreign exchange	0.67	3.19	2.62
Treasury bills – free	2.73	0.40	—
Treasury bills – compulsory	15.97	19.56	23.52
Loans 8 % res. rat. category within tert. res. ratios	1.06	0.07	0.01
Loans 8 % res. rat. category outside tert. res. ratios	18.95	23.13	23.46
Loans 25 % res. rat. category within tert. res. ratios	0.16	0.02	0.05
Loans 25 % res. rat. category outside tert. res. ratios	7.32	7.06	7.63
Loans 5 % rebate category within tert. res. ratios	6.45	4.29	3.60
Loans 5 % rebate category outside tert. res. ratios	3.12	3.17	4.68
Loans 23 % rebate category within tert. res. ratios	3.86	3.30	4.10
Loans 23 % rebate category outside tert. res. ratios	14.54	7.03	9.57
Bonds – free	4.00	2.08	2.53
Bonds – compulsory	2.51	5.47	3.09
Bank premises	2.48	14.10	8.96
Other assets	11.57		
Liabilities	100.00	100.00	100.00
Sight deposits – private	6.02	7.05	7.35
Sight deposits – public	2.68	0.99	1.06
Savings deposits – no notice	34.23	38.90	40.13
Savings deposits – at notice	3.94	4.30	6.27
Time deposits – private, more than 3 month	17.40	15.21	15.10
Time deposits – public	0.40	1.17	0.02
Deposits of special credit institutions	1.33	1.64	1.77
Restricted deposits	0.56	0.73	0.81
Deposits in foreign exchange	10.66	5.61	4.90
Various obligations in foreign exchange	—	—	—
Bank of Greece advances	3.20	5.17	5.84
Capital & reserves	5.13		
Other	14.45	19.23	16.75

[a] In percentage of total assets.

APPENDIX 10.6 LOANS AND INVESTMENTS IN THE CATEGORIES DEFINED IN THE 15 PER CENT REGULATION[a]

Quarter	Medium- and long-term loans for fixed investments			Investments and other eligible loans		
	National Bank	Commercial Bank	Ionian & Popular Bank	National Bank	Commercial Bank	Ionian & Popular Bank
1969 I	12.7	3.8	7.5	2.1	10.7	7.2
II	12.2	3.5	7.5	2.2	9.8	7.0
III	12.0	3.6	7.5	3.1	10.6	7.0
IV	11.5	3.4	7.7	N.A.	N.A.	N.A.
1970 I	12.0	3.4	7.7	3.5	10.8	7.2
II	12.0	3.6	7.3	3.3	10.5	7.0
III	11.7	3.7	7.0	4.0	9.4	7.8
IV	11.5	3.9	7.0	4.5	9.8	7.8
1971 I	11.6	3.8	6.6	4.8	9.8	7.7
II	13.9	3.9	6.1	2.4	10.3	8.6
III	14.4	3.8	5.7	2.5	9.2	8.0
IV	14.1	3.8	5.4	2.5	9.1	7.6
1972 I	15.0	4.1	6.4	2.5	8.9	7.1
II	14.8	4.3	5.9	2.9	8.7	7.5
III	15.5	4.7	5.6	2.8	8.5	7.5
IV	15.6	5.7	5.6	2.9	8.3	8.6
1973 I	16.0	6.1	6.4	3.3	7.9	8.9
II	16.5	7.1	7.1	3.6	7.0	6.6
III	16.5	7.3	7.1	3.9	6.6	6.4
IV	15.9	7.6	6.9	4.2	6.8	7.1
1974 I	16.3	8.1	7.4	4.5	6.5	5.9
II	16.2	8.0	7.1	4.6	6.3	5.3
III	17.5	8.3	7.5	5.5	5.8	5.8
IV	15.8	7.8	8.1	4.9	6.1	5.6
1975 I	17.2	7.7	8.1	3.0	6.3	5.5
II	16.7	7.8	7.7	2.8	6.8	4.9
III	16.4	7.0	7.1	3.6	6.6	4.7
IV	15.3	7.7	7.3	4.2	6.5	5.3
1976 I	14.9	7.7	7.6	5.5	6.5	5.0
II	14.8	7.9	7.8	5.1	6.3	5.1
III	16.8	8.2	8.3	4.9	6.1	5.4
IV	16.9	8.4	8.0	4.9	6.0	5.2
1977 I	17.2	8.1	8.2	4.8	5.8	5.1
II	16.8	8.3	8.0	3.9	5.5	4.8
III	16.5	6.4	7.4	3.9	5.0	4.4
IV	16.6	6.4	7.1	4.3	4.9	5.0
Regulation %	15%	15%	15%			

[a] In percentage of eligible liabilities.

APPENDIX 10.7 TREASURY BILLS HELD IN
ACCORDANCE WITH THE ADMINISTRATION OF
THE 15 PER CENT REGULATION [a]

Quarter		National Bank	Commercial Bank	Ionian & Popular Bank
1969	I	0.0	50.4	46.8
	II	0.0	50.2	49.2
	III	9.6	54.5	50.0
	IV	0.0	N.A.	N.A.
1970	I	8.0	58.0	53.6
	II	0.0	60.1	54.0
	III	0.0	67.5	62.3
	IV	0.0	67.5	62.7
1971	I	0.0	69.4	68.3
	II	0.0	61.2	66.3
	III	0.0	65.0	66.3
	IV	0.0	61.3	66.3
1972	I	0.0	60.5	68.3
	II	0.0	57.5	60.3
	III	0.0	56.2	56.1
	IV	0.0	53.9	52.1
1973	I	0.0	45.7	49.8
	II	0.0	54.3	46.4
	III	0.0	46.9	45.9
	IV	0.0	50.6	51.9
1974	I	0.0	44.8	43.1
	II	0.0	38.6	30.4
	III	0.0	31.0	28.1
	IV	0.0	35.1	32.3
1975	I	0.0	37.5	32.3
	II	0.0	31.7	32.9
	III	0.0	29.3	29.9
	IV	0.0	29.3	26.9
1976	I	0.0	29.3	26.4
	II	0.0	28.5	26.2
	III	0.0	28.5	30.1
	IV	0.0	26.7	28.7
1977	I	0.0	26.7	28.6
	II	0.0	25.9	28.6
	III	0.0	26.6	28.5
	IV	0.0	54.1	37.8

[a] In percentage of the 'Investments and other eligible loans' presented in Appendix 10.6.

APPENDIX 10.8   LOANS IN ACCORDANCE WITH
THE 6 PER CENT REGULATION[a]

Quarter	National Bank	Commercial Bank	Ionian & Popular Bank
1969 I	3.7	2.4	3.9
II	3.6	2.4	3.6
III	3.6	2.6	3.4
IV	3.5	2.6	3.4
1970 I	3.8	2.7	3.3
II	3.8	2.8	3.1
III	3.9	2.9	2.8
IV	3.6	3.0	2.6
1971 I	3.5	3.1	2.5
II	3.3	3.2	2.3
III	3.2	3.0	2.1
IV	2.7	2.8	1.9
1972 I	2.5	2.7	1.9
II	2.3	2.7	1.8
III	2.2	2.7	1.7
IV	2.1	2.8	2.0
1973 I	2.2	3.0	2.2
II	2.5	3.5	2.7
III	2.5	3.8	2.8
IV	2.3	3.9	2.9
1974 I	2.2	3.9	3.1
II	2.0	3.5	2.9
III	2.0	3.3	2.9
IV	1.7	2.9	2.6
1975 I	1.8	2.9	2.8
II	1.8	3.0	2.9
III	1.9	3.1	2.8
IV	1.8	3.5	3.2
1976 I	1.9	3.5	3.4
II	2.0	3.5	3.4
III	2.2	3.4	3.3
IV	2.1	3.2	3.2
1977 I	2.2	3.1	3.1
II	2.4	3.3	3.3
III	2.6	3.2	3.2
IV	2.6	3.4	3.4
Regulation %	6%	6%	6%

[a] As a percentage of the since December 1965 increase in eligible
liabilities.

NOTES

1. This study comprises part of a set proposed by me in memorandum submitted to the Governor of the Bank of Greece in January 1977. Some of the analysis presented here was undertaken during short visits to the Bank of Greece in 1977 and 1978. The bulk of the study was, however, pursued in Oxford and hence the usual disclaimer that the Bank of Greece carries no responsibility for the views expressed here applies with particular force. I am most grateful to Professor Xenophon Zolotas, Governor of the Bank of Greece, for inviting me to the Bank and to Dimitros Halikias, Chief Economic Adviser of the Bank, for his refreshing interest in my work on Greece. A special debt of gratitude is due to Mrs Barbara Rhodis for her help with collection of much of the data here employed. I also thank Mrs E. Ringas and Mrs K. Marketou for typing drafts of this paper. Finally, I wish to *stress* that this paper was written before my appointment to the Government's Committee on Interest Rates and does not, therefore, derive from views put forward in the Committee or recommendations to be made to the Minister of Coordination by the Committee.

2. In the context of this paper, the term 'Monetary Authorities' is to be understood as including the Bank of Greece and the 'Currency Committee', that is to say, the body formally responsible for monetary and credit policy in Greece. This is appropriate as the Bank of Greece has in fact played a dominant role on all such policy decisions, in addition to being the body responsible for policy implementation. Detailed descriptions of this and other such features of Greek reality can be found in D. J. Halikias (1978), for example pp. 3–4 and 28–31, and X. Zolotas (1965), for example pp. 62–63.

3. Bank of Greece memorandum, 22 May 1976. A similar statement had been made less than a month before by Governor X. Zolotas. Addressing the 'Shareholders', the Governor noted that 'For the near future the authorities are contemplating a reform of the present system of credit controls and regulations' (see X. Zolotas (1976) pp. 9–10). This in turn was but a mere repetition of the position expressed in *the previous year*, cf. X. Zolotas (1975) pp. 15–16. Since the time of writing – winter 1978 – a Committee has been set up to advise the Minister of Coordination on the reforms deemed desirable in the light of the defects of the existing system and of entry into the EEC. The Committee is expected to tender its final report before spring 1980. See also A. S. Courakis (1980a).

4. See A. S. Courakis (1980a).

5. See J. Pesmatzoglou (1956), X. Zolotas (1963, 1965, 1967, 1976), D. J. Halikias (1978) and, for example, Bank of Greece Report for the Year 1977, p. 41.

6. See, for example, D. J. Halikias (1978) p. 59 and Bank of Greece Report for the Year 1977, pp. 42–4.

7. For there are obviously other groupings one may adopt.

8. Besides having periodically included so-called 'seasonal' components of specified duration. It should be noted that changes in required ratios are introduced subject to adaptation periods designed to allow banks to adjust their portfolios. With effect from beginning 1977, for example, the authorities, having changed reserve ratios, instructed the commercial banks

to '. . . make an additional withholding of 15 per cent of the increase in current deposits until the balance of commercial bank deposits at the end of 1976 meets the newly established reserve requirements and the appropriate portion invested in Treasury Bills and government bonds' (Bank of Greece Report for the Year 1976) p. 44.

9. See Appendix 10.1.
10. See Appendix 10.2.
11. See, for example, Tables 10.1, 10.2 and 10.3.
12. That is, the four banks listed in Appendix 10.4.
13. Appendices 10.6 to 10.8 provide some indication of the extent to which commercial banks have, over the period under review, met the desired loan volumes envisaged by these regulations.
14. It should be noted that the complexity of the system almost inevitably results in confusion as to the precise content of the regulatory framework. Thus although *the letter* of the 15 per cent regulation makes no reference to rebates for credit given *in excess* of the amount corresponding to 15 per cent of the eligible bank liabilities, the records kept by the Bank of Greece/Currency Committee pertaining to the monthly observance of this regulation, exhibit 100 per cent rebates (to, for example, the National Bank of Greece) against such excess, as listed in the accounts pertaining to the 'Calculation of the 15 per cent Compulsory Deposits of Commercial Banks for Medium/Long-Term Loans in Accordance with NE 1509/14.9.68' (see Appendix 10.6). So far as I could establish from the parties responsible for such statistics, these are just notional items, rather than *de facto* rebates made as a result of interpretation of the NE 1509/1/4.9.68 regulation of a kind other than its precise text allows.
15. See Table 10.3, first row.
16. C. A. E. Goodhart (1975) p. 149.
17. J. Tobin (1963). I wish to stress that this is due to the deposit interest rate ceilings and not as Tobin intimates due to both (or either) 'special reserve requirements and interest rate ceilings to which banks are subject'. J. Tobin (1963) p. 418.
18. Put differently, suppose that, starting from a particular volume of deposits, the government runs a deficit of GD during some interval of time. Suppose that of this the first kGD (where k is the fraction denoting the compulsory cash ratio) is financed through creation of monetary liabilities of the government/central bank. Suppose also that the incremental cash to deposits ratio of the public is zero. The deposit of kGD by the recipients of the government's excess spending generates a compulsory excess demand for public sector debt of $gkGD$, where g is the bank's security ratio, thus reducing the multiple expansion of deposits (and consequently of the money supply) which a deficit of GD will otherwise have implied for any particular level of security rates: see also A. S. Courakis (1980a). Other things equal, deposits will eventually increase by $(1/(k + g))GD$ if we assume that banks can meet their required 15 and 6 per cent ratios through the granting of appropriate loans.
19. The total absence of transactions in such securities between the banks and the public, that is.
20. See Appendices 10.5 to 10.7.

21. This policy of 'equalisation of interest rates' received by banks has applied since September 1966; see D. J. Halikias (1978) p. 52. In earlier years, considerable differentials existed. But today also, the reader may note, that 'equalisation' is not exact, differences of more than half a percentage point being recorded from time to time; see, for example, Table 10.3, second row.

22. See A. S. Courakis (1980, a and b).

23. See also A. S. Courakis (1974, 1975b, 1976).

24. For a very clear exposition see M. Monti. (1971 and 1972); see also M. A. Klein (1971), although his definition of the problem in terms of portfolio shares raises awkward questions to say the least.

25. Within the context of such models, one may in turn distinguish between models in the Edgeworth (1888) tradition, emphasising precautionary aspects resulting from stochastic quantities, for example R. C. Porter (1961), and models in the Hicksian (1935)–Tobin (1958)–Markowitz (1952) tradition, stressing stochastic prices (yields).

26. See also A. S. Courakis (1980a).

27. The model here presented is that found in J. M. Parkin (1970) and A. S. Courakis (1974). It is a limiting case of the more general models presented in A. S. Courakis (1975b and 1976).

28. It should be noted that insofar as the rates set by the Bank of Greece are maxima rather than fixed rates, this involves a simplification, but one which by all accounts is in general justifiable to adopt. See also below, and A. S. Courakis (1980a).

29. See J. M. Parkin (1970), A. S. Courakis (1974, 1975b and 1976) and C. D. Hart and D. M. Jaffee (1974). Yet the restrictiveness of this assumption should not be disregarded, see E. Baltensperger (1973).

30. From a longer run standpoint, of course, this assumption cannot be sustained on the grounds of price taking alone.

31. As I have argued elsewhere, one may of course choose to distinguish between different categories of securities included in the securities ratio, see A. S. Courakis (1975b). No such attempt is undertaken in this preliminary study, however.

32. For loans outside the credit ratios categories, $r_i = R_i/(1 + \lambda_i)$, where R_i denotes the rate charged to the borrower and λ_i the corresponding reserve or rebate ratio.

   For loans inside the credit ratios categories, $r_i = (R_i - C)/\lambda_i$ where C is the interest paid on the corresponding compulsory reserves (that is, 5 per cent in December 1975), if $\lambda_i > 0$, where $r_i > 100$ per cent if $\lambda_i < 0$. The rationale for this calculation is as follows. Consider a bank receiving a deposit of (100/0.21) drachma. Immediately, 100 dr. have to be placed with the Bank of Greece at 5 per cent in accordance with the 15 and 6 per cent credit ratios. Suppose now that the bank finds a customer willing to borrow at the going rate 100 dr. for expenditures classifying for the 15 and 6 per cent regulations. Then if the loan falls in the 8 per cent reserve ratio category, *a net outlay* of 8 dr. by the commercial bank will secure for it a yearly income (12.5 − 5.0) dr. Thus the rate of return per drachma on own funds is (12.5 − 5.0)/8 = 93.970 per cent.

   Note that these calculations do not take into account the option that commercial banks can secure to hold part of their compulsory reserves in the

form of Treasury bills. But even if banks are able to so choose and even if the rate on 12 month bills is taken as the proxy for C, it is still the case that the rates on own funds for loans within the credit ratios are considerably higher than those for loans not qualifying for this privilege. For December 1975 they are respectively equal to 34.375, 19.000, more than 100 per cent and more than 100 per cent.
33. D. J. Halikias (1978) p. 185.
34. Ibid.
35. Ibid., emphasis added.
36. Assuming, of course, always that this is not due to unwillingness on their part to supply such loans in accordance with default considerations or other characteristics of their loan portfolios.
37. See in this context also, note 14 above.
38. In this context, see T. J. Valentine (1973).
39. For previous models of this kind that embody distributed lags, see W. R. White (1975). See also A. S. Courakis (1975b).
40. See also below.
41. See J. M. Parkin (1970) and A. S. Courakis (1974).
42. Followed, for example, in J. M. Parkin (1970) and A. S. Courakis (1974).
43. See A. S. Courakis (1975b).
44. See Appendix 10.3.
45. See, for example, Bank of Greece Report for the Year 1975, p. 51.
46. A more thorough discussion of such issues is presented in A. S. Courakis (1975b).
47. See Appendix 10.4.
48. See, however, also A. S. Courakis (1980a).
49. The end product in the case of some series bore no resemblance, either in absolute size or over time variation, to the original.
50. See, for example, A. S. Courakis (1974 and 1975b).
51. See, for example, J. M. Parkin (1970) and A. S. Courakis (1974 and 1975b).
52. A. S. Courakis (1974).
53. See, for example, A. Barten (1969) and J. Theil (1971).
54. We may also – in passing only, of course, granted the simultaneous nature of the model – note that the ratios of the 'variance explained' to the 'total variance' also point to a very high proportion of the total variance in each dependent variable being explained.
55. See, for example, J. M. Parkin (1970) and A. S. Courakis (1974, 1975b, 1976) and also W. R. White (1975).
56. Models that incorporate both demand and supply characteristics are an obvious avenue for further research; see A. S. Courakis (1980a).
57. See also Appendices 10.4 to 10.8.

REFERENCES

Baltensperger, E. (1973) 'Optimal Bank Portfolios: The Liability Side', *Jahrbücher für Nationalökonomie und Statistik*.
Barten, A. (1969) 'Maximum Likelihood Estimation of a Complete System of

Demand Equations', *European Economic Review*, no. 1.

Courakis, A. S. (1974) 'Clearing Bank Asset Choice Behaviour: A Mean Variance Treatment', *Oxford Bulletin of Economics and Statistics* (August).

Courakis, A. S. (1975a) 'Testing Theories of Discount House Portfolio Selection', *Review of Economic Studies* (October).

Courakis, A. S. (1975b) 'In Search of an Explanation of Clearing Bank Portfolio Selection' (Paper presented to the Money Study Group–Oxford Conference in Honour of G. L. S. Shackle in September).

Courakis, A. S. (1976) 'Bank Behaviour: Theories and Evidence' (Oxford: Brasenose College, mimeograph).

Courakis, A. S. (1980a) 'Bank Behaviour and the Structure of Controls', *The Greek Economic Review* (forthcoming).

Courakis, A. S. (1980b) 'Banking Policy in Greece: Retrospect and Prospect', *The Banker*.

Edgeworth, F. (1888) 'The Mathematical Theory of Banking', *Journal of the Royal Statistical Society*, Part I.

Goodhart, C. A. E. (1975) *Money, Information and Uncertainty* (London: Macmillan).

Halikias, D. J. (1978) *Money and Credit in a Developing Economy: The Greek Case* (New York University Press).

Hart, C. D. and D. M. Jaffee (1974) 'On the Application of Portfolio Theory to Depository Financial Intermediaries', *Review of Economic Studies* (January).

Hicks, J. R. (1935) 'A Suggestion for Simplifying the Theory of Money', *Economica* (February).

Klein, M. A. (1971) 'A Theory of the Banking Firms', *Journal of Money, Credit and Banking* (May).

Markowitz, H. M. (1952) 'Portfolio Selection', *Journal of Finance* (March).

Monti, M. (1971) 'A Theoretical Model of Bank Behaviour and its Implications for monetary Policy', *L'Industria*, no. 2.

Monti, M. (1972) 'Deposit, Credit and Interest Rate Determination under Alternative Bank Objective Functions' in G. P. Szego and K. Shell (eds), *Mathematical Methods in Investment and Finance* (Amsterdam: North Holland).

Parkin, J. M. (1970) 'The Portfolio Behaviour of Commercial Banks', in K. Hilton and D. F. Heathfield (eds), *The Econometric Study of the United Kingdom* (London: Macmillan).

Pesmatzoglou, J. (1956) *The Relation between Monetary and Fiscal Policy* (Athens: Bank of Greece).

Porter, R. C. (1961) 'A Model of Bank Portfolio Selection', in *Yale Economic Essays*, in D. Hester and J. Tobin (eds), *Financial Markets and Economic Activity*, Cowles Foundation Monograph 21 (New York: John Wiley).

Theil, J. (1971) *Principles of Econometrics* (Amsterdam: North Holland).

Tobin, J. (1958) 'Liquidity Preference as a Behaviour Towards Risk' *Review of Economic Studies* (February).

Tobin, J. (1963) 'Commercial Banks as Creators of Money', in D. Carson (ed.), *Banking and Monetary Studies*, (Homewood, Ill.: R. D. Irwin Inc.).

Valentine, T. J. (1973) 'The Demand for Very Liquid Assets in Australia', *Australian Economic Papers* (December).

White, W. R. (1975) 'Some Econometric Models of Deposit Bank Portfolio

Behaviour in the United Kingdom 1963–70', in G. A. Reuton (ed.), *Modelling the Economy* (London: Heinemann Educational Books).

Zolotas, X. (1963) *The Role of Banks in a Developing Country* (Athens: Bank of Greece).

Zolotas, X. (1965) *Monetary Equilibrium and Economic Development* (Princeton University Press).

Zolotas, X. (1967) 'Monetary Planning in Economic Development', *The Banker* (July). Reprinted in X. Zolotas (1977) *International Monetary Issues and Development Policies* (Athens: Bank of Greece).

Zolotas, X. (1975) 'Developments and Prospects of the Greek Economy: An Address', *Bank of Greece Papers and Lectures*, no. 30.

Zolotas, X. (1976) 'Problems and Prospects of the Greek Economy', in Bank of Greece, *Summary of the Statement of Governor Xenophon Zolotas at the Annual Meeting of Shareholders*, 29 April (Athens).

Comment on Courakis

GÉRARD VILA

First, I must thank the Centre for Economic Studies of the Catholic University of Leuven for providing me with this opportunity to lower my level of ignorance about Greek monetary policy and institutional features.

Second, we must all thank Courakis for having established that, contrary to what is often said, the business of central bankers is not beyond the reach of analytical investigation. We are all familiar with attitudes which imply that only long years spent in the higher ranks of a central bank or ministry of finance can qualify one to speak intelligently about matters relating to the setting up of interest rates and the drafting of bank regulations.

The chapter of Courakis, however, vividly depicts a group of regulators so wrapped up in the intricacies of their regulations that they can no longer think coherently or even count.

The Bank of Greece is certainly not unique in this respect. Courakis shows us the way to bring analytical economics to bear upon matters erroneously considered too complex for non-bureaucrats to understand.

At this point, however, I would like to make a few technical remarks about the specific methodology Courakis has been using.

Courakis resorts to a mean–variance portfolio analysis, using a negative exponential utility function of the Freund–Parkin type.[1] Central to this approach is the assumption that every asset and liability is characterised by statistical returns which are normally distributed.

This follows from the approach by which the portfolio allocation of commercial banks is derived from their utility maximising response to the quantity and rate constraint imposed by the regulators upon those assets that they use as exogenous instruments.

In turn, the derivation assumes that the matrices G, H and B in equation (7) are of sufficient rank, a condition which is met only if stochastic returns on all assets are normally distributed or, more generally, if the covariances among those returns are small enough. This assumption has been questioned by M. S. Feldstein and S. Fischer.[2]

Indeed, when one realises that during most periods a single principal components analysis of various yields reveals that the first and second component account for almost all of the variance in a universe encompassing all the market, we must remain sceptical about this approach.

If, however, we abandon the assumption that matrices G, H and B are of sufficient rank, it becomes impossible to derive econometric conclusions of any practical relevance.

We are left with a valuable analytical representation of the type of feedback that must be triggered by regulations and of which regulators are not even aware, but we fall short of being able to provide a robust and convincing alternative to the pointless and routine proliferation of regulations proceeding from shortsighted bureaucratic logic.

In turn, this limitation of Courakis's technique, which applies also to the whole mean–variance approach to the analysis of banking regulations, leads me to make a few more general comments beyond the scope of Courakis's chapter but with a bearing on the general theme of this colloquium.

Many participants made clear that, in their view, regulations in general were at best inept and, at worst, harmful. Indeed, if the idea that financial markets are essentially composed of a population of assets and liabilities yielding stochastic returns normally distributed, the Le Chatelier principle applies in full: fewer constraints of any kind will always produce a better outcome. This representation may not, however, be the most useful way to think about financial markets.

If, indeed, financial markets are primarily a complex cybernetic process, as contended, for example, by A. Brender,[3] defined by a historically determined set of usages, habit and regulations, it does not follow at all that doing away with all frictions and inhibitions is always better.

The record of experience in the United States during the past fifteen years suggests strongly that the opposite may be true. In that country, largely under the influence of theoreticians arguing forcefully the case for the removal of all 'purposeless regulations', many traditional constraints on banks and financial intermediaries have, one after the other, been removed. Savings and loans institutions, which used to be prohibited from offering cheque books and which suffered from Regulation Q when rates moved upward, now offer deposits with the same chequing privileges as banks and issue money market certificates when interest rates rise.

As a result of this and many other 'improvements', the money multiplier appears no longer to be stable, and monetary policy no longer to have any teeth. Similar observations may be made of other countries in addition to the United States.[4]

Furthermore, it appears that the combination of the certainty always to find a lender of last resort and the relaxation of preventive regulations has also resulted in bank balance sheets that would be considered to reveal nearbankruptcy under any honest accounting system.

In other words, if the alternative to a proliferation of unenlightened bureaucratic regulations is to be a trend towards a financial system without constraints and safeguards, are we not heading towards hyperinflation and financial crashes?

In this respect, attempts to define principles of rational regulation would appear an urgent supplement to the general attack on any kind of 'rigidity' encountered in the financial markets in the name of the 'mean–variance portfolio approach'. In spite of many generations of routine bureaucracy, some of the features of the financial markets which have evolved from everyday experience during a long period of time may not all be so foolish.

NOTES

1. R. Freund (1956) 'The Introduction of Risk into a Programming Model', *Econometrica*, pp. 253–63; J. M. Parkin (1970) 'Discount House Portfolio and Debt Selection', *Review of Economic Studies* (October) pp. 469–97.
2. M. S. Feldstein (1969) 'Mean–Variance Analysis in the Theory of Liquidity Preference and Portfolio Selection', *Review of Economic Studies* (January) pp. 5–12; S. Fischer (1969) *Essays on Assets and Contingent Commodities* (Cambridge, Mass.: Ph D Dissertation, Department of Economics, Massachussetts Institute of Technology).
3. A. Brender (1977) *Une Analyse Cybernétique de l'Intermédiation Financière* (Paris: Ph D Dissertation, University of Paris).
4. M. Fratianni and M. Nabli (1979) 'Money Stock Control in the EEC Countries', *Weltwirtschaftliches Archiv*, no. 3, pp. 401–23.

11. Competition and Regulation in Financial Markets: Concluding Observations

ALMARIN PHILLIPS

1. AN OVERVIEW

These are troubled but fascinating times for economists and policy-makers concerned with the structure of financial markets, financial regulations and financial market performance. Both the trouble and the fascination come from much the same source. The central paradigms used to study and explain the largely separate macroanalytics and the microanalytics of money and banking, central banking and regulatory aspects of financial markets are no longer usefully applicable to today's problems. Market segmentation has broken down. Issues in aggregative economics – the supply and demand for money, interest rates, relations between money, interest rates and income and employment – are so intimately affected by regulatory structures and the competitive behaviour of financial institutions that the latter cannot be ignored in macroanalysis. Regulatory and competitive issues which in the past could be viewed in terms of microeconomic efficiency and equity standards are now seen to have significant aggregative impacts. The trouble and the fascination, mixed liberally with considerable frustration, come from the absence of alternative paradigms that successfully blend the macro- and microeconomics of financial markets. We are groping about without a reliable theoretical guidance system.

The chapters in this volume reflect this problem. While they do address regulatory and competitive phenomena that have important microeconomic implications, the stress in most of the chapters is on the macroeconomic effects. More specifically, most of the chapters are not cast in the structure–conduct–performance mould that characterises industrial economics. Problems relating to mergers, holding companies, chartering, branching and consequent competitive results for particular markets are not highlighted. Instead, a host of regulatory and competitive issues are viewed in terms of their effects on monetary policy, and the functioning of financial markets generally. The banking *system*, not specific banking markets, is the general focus.

There is, too, an air of potential crisis in several of the chapters. They deal with the possibility of market failure not in the terms of allocative inefficiencies but rather in terms of systematic breakdowns. There appears to be some feeling that the hosts of structural and prudential regulations imposed on financial systems – each one of which may have ostensible beneficial effects – have created system characteristics pointing to the grave possibility of being dysfunctional. But again, there is no micro-based macrotheory to explain this.

2. SOME SPECIFIC COMMENTS

The first three chapters of this volume illustrate the points above. Franklin Edwards espouses the abolition of a vast majority of structural regulations and of those prudential regulations that, on examination, are found to be aimed primarily at limiting competition rather than the promotion of safety and soundness for the system. At the same time, Edwards proposes the imposition of mandatory reserve requirements for all financial institutions that offer demand deposits or other deposits that can be used for third-party payments. More will be said of this below, but it can be noted at this point that Edwards's main concern is with the effects of the present structural regulations on the payments system. The regulations invite institutions other than commercial banks to engage in commercial bank loan and deposit markets, with extremely complicating consequences for the central bank.

The chapter by Jack R. S. Revell is both a historic review and a prophetic look at things to come. Many of my learned colleagues, I suspect, would argue that Revell's view is nothing more than another Doomsday forecast, lacking in rigorous analysis and founded on nothing save fear. Those who greet the paper with such thoughts should be forced to reread it. Economists too frequently seek special cases – that is, use unrealistic simplifying assumptions – in order to obtain theoretical tractability. They cater to their own bounded rationality and consider only those problems for which analytic clarity is possible.[1] Revell admittedly addresses problems so complex that analytic clarity is impossible. But that in no way makes the problems less severe. He holds, as do some few others, that financial systems are likely to suffer severe crises in the relatively near future because of the accumulated impacts of regulations over the past decades.

Robert Taggart's chapter is a good illustration of one reason why Revell may be correct. Deposit financial institutions in the United States have been subject to the infamous 'Regulation Q' since 1933. The regulation, as amended by law and changed by regulatory discretion, imposes ceilings on the interest that can be paid on savings and time deposits. The objective of the regulations, along with that prohibiting any interest payments on demand deposits, was to limit competition among the affected institutions.

As Taggart points out, economic and technological conditions have changed drastically since the regulations were imposed. The most suggestive parts of the Taggart chapter deal with the adaptive responses of the regulators to the changed conditions and to the concomitant changes in the behaviour of both regulated and unregulated institutions. In truth, Regulation Q has been changed piecemeal as particular events gave rise to particular adverse consequences of the regulation. There has been virtual unanimity among economists for over two decades that Regulation Q does more harm than good. Yet continuity of short-run modifications rather than outright elimination of the regulation is all that has been politically feasible. Is it not possible that a series of short-run 'solutions' serve only to exacerbate the long-run problems?

Another series of chapters in the book concerns financial structures and performance. The one by Albert Verheirstraeten and Jozef Pacolet sets forth an enormous compilation of concentration data for the banks of Belgium and provides some interesting estimates of scale economies. Based on the latter, it is concluded that there are no scale efficiency justifications for the levels of concentration that exist. A larger number of smaller institutions could exist without losses due to cost increases.

There are some problems here that suggest caution before the policy conclusion is reached that Belgium banking markets require de-concentrating efforts. There is first the question of relevant product and geographic markets. It is probably true that small commercial and industrial concerns, along with most households, have access to only one or a few local banking sources. It is conceivable that if what are now branches of major national banks became independent local banks, the degree of competition for such customers might increase. But it is also conceivable that these local customers now benefit from the degree of competition among the major banks in other, larger markets. It is also conceivable that, were the smaller, local institutions substituted for the present branches, the array of services would diminish and that price competition would be lessened. If the United States experience has any validity, the suppression of competition that occurs among small unit banks because of the protective regulations needed to keep them in existence and because of their own collusive propensities is likely to outweigh any gains from deconcentration.

With respect to large commercial and industrial customers, the concentration data probably exaggerate market reality. The relatively small loans and deposits held by branches of major foreign banks in Belgium belies their potential competitive effect. Were one to ask the managers of Belgium banks where their competition comes from, it is a safe guess that the foreign banks would not be far down their list. Non-bank financial institutions would probably be indicated as a growing source of competition as well, with the disparity in regulations as one reason why that source of rivalry is growing. In any case, concentration data for Belgium alone are perhaps necessary but surely insufficient for the determination of competitive policy. Regulations and private modes of conduct are probably much more important than structure in determining banking performances.

Given their results, it is unlikely that the scale economy studies of Verheirstraeten and Pacolet suffer much from the problem, but it should be noted that the method used does tend to produce some bias. In short, an association between bank size and costs, shown by simple regression, does not address the question of whether costs are low (high) because a bank is large (small), or whether a bank is large (small) or growing (declining) because its costs are low (high). More sophisticated techniques must be used.

Lieven Gheysens shows that the Belgian banks have radically varying levels of performance and risk. These are reflected in market evaluations of the banks. Over time, these differences surely affect bank sizes both because of their effect on internal growth and because of merger opportunities and merger consequences. Gheysens' data, if surveyed by bank managers and by bank shareholders, would raise serious questions about different qualities of management in the several banks. The modern banking world, I suspect, will not allow such ostensible differences in efficiency to remain for long.

The last part of the book is devoted to an analysis of government intervention in the financial sector in different European countries. Reconsidering the foregoing chapters in that context, one gets a clearer view of the dysfunctional aspects of the present regimes of regulation, competition and monetary control. Brian Griffiths and Roy A. Batchelor give an excellent illustration of how the private behaviour of banks and discount houses in England reflect anticipations of and adaptive responses to regulations. The results of regulation are not those intended by the regulators, because structure and conduct adapt in ways unanticipated by the regulators. Roberto Wessels' paper shows the not surprising result that control of a price (interest rate) at below market equilibrating levels, without limits on the quantity demanded (and supplied), leads to disastrous monetary control consequences.

The other chapters are in a similar vein. Central banks and the banking intermediaries are subjected to many sorts of abortive regulations. Mario Monti and Angelo Porta analyse the effects on the Italian banking system, while Florin Aftalion describes the extensive use of bank credit schemes for numerous sectors of the French economy. Finally, Anthony S. Courakis, with analytic ingenuity, traces the results of central bank and regulatory credit schemes in Greece. In all cases, the conclusion is that the central bank, as the controller of the money supply, loses direction and influence when it assumes or is burdened with administrative functions aimed at attaining distributional and political goals. In some of the cases – particularly in Courakis' work – the adaptive responses of financial institutions and their customers are shown to be rational responses to what turn out to be irrational policies.

3. SOME PESSIMISTIC CONCLUSIONS

This conference may be unique among those given in recent years. There has been no argument about the proper definition of money, no argument about whether M1, M2, M3 – or M22.7 – is correct. All of the participants who approached the matter, although with varying emphasis, agree that it is not really the definition of money that matters. However money is defined, market facts in the several countries surveyed show that monetary controls are at best ineffective and, at worst, dysfunctional.

Inspection of the market facts shows that regulatory influences are the primary reason for the breakdown in monetary control. In some countries, regulations have encouraged or forced the central bank and traditional bank lenders to expand their liabilities. In other countries, regulations have destroyed the historic market segmentation among various classes of financial institutions. That breakdown, over time, has resulted in the development of new types of institutional liabilities which have moneylike characteristics from the point of view of those holding the liabilities as assets. In all countries, private borrowers and lenders have adapted responsively and seemingly rationally to regulations with the end result that controls at the aggregate level are lost.

This is nowhere more obvious than in the United States. Segmentation between the thrift institutions and the commercial banks in the market for savings and time deposits vanished two decades ago. Segmentation between the same institutions for third-party payments began to disappear a decade ago. On the lending side, the markets of the thrifts and the commercial banks are still largely separate.

Regulations aimed at controlling the disintermediation between the thrifts and commercial banks, as discussed by Taggart, had the unintended effect of causing disintermediation between the two classes of deposit institutions, on the one hand, and the rest of the money market on the other. The Eurodollar market, the commercial paper market and, more recently, money market funds developed. Investment bankers, who by law cannot engage in commercial banking, found means to attract funds that alternatively would have been in bank deposits and to use those funds to make loans that alternatively would have been bank loans. For their part, commercial banks, acting through their trust departments, began in fact to distribute securities (fund shares), even though by law they are prohibited from doing so.[2]

At first, the central bank saw these developments only hazily. It appeared that the velocity of M1 was rising. In the inflationary environment, the answer given by the old macroeconomics was to control the growth in the money supply and/or to raise interest rates, although it was seldom obvious whether it was a money target or an interest rate target that was being pursued. The old microeconomics suggested that 'competitive equality' necessitated the imposition of uniform reserve requirements on all institutions with liabilities that can be used for third-party payments. The central bank went to great lengths to demonstrate – unconvincingly – that effective monetary policy depended on such uniform, mandatory reserves.

Curious market responses occurred. First, the demand for and supply of money became highly interdependent. Using the simple Keynesian version for illustration only, the central bank's actions caused the liquidity preference schedule to shift back and forth. When it was reported that the money supply rose over a *past* week, the market anticipated *future* tightening, and liquidity preference rose. Interest rates increased and, at least with interest rate targets, the need to contract the money supply in the subsequent period was obviated. Added to this reason not to contract was the precarious position of many of the thrift institutions and some commercial banks, with returns on assets less than the marginal cost of buying funds.

Second, with each wrenching upward of interest rates, the incentives for old institutions to thwart rate ceiling regulations and for new institutions to enter the markets are increased. Something like a black market appeared, but in this case the new liabilities create a new supply of things that are close substitutes for the old liabilities that – due to regulation – cannot grow as fast as market rates would dictate. In the end, both the old kind of money and the new kind of money increased.

This process has been and will continue to be abetted by new technologies that fall within the rubric of electronic funds transfer. As this technology develops, the ability of any holder of marketable assets to exchange them for other marketable assets will increase. Many private and public debt instruments are already easily used as 'money', and there is growing use of equity assets for the same purpose. This is what is wrong with Edwards' proposal for mandatory reserves. Unless such reserves bear a rate of interest that is sufficient to make holders wish to hold them, the required reserves have taxlike effects. Such a new regulation would only serve to encourage other institutions which are exempt from that tax to issue liabilities for the same purpose. The technology of electronic funds transfer makes this possible.

All of this raises the spectre discussed by Jack R. S. Revell. The system is not working to achieve desired ends under the present regulatory regime. Old regulations are patched up and new ones are added, with the effect of inducing new means of avoidance. The means of avoidance involve the creation of uninsured liabilities that are used as money. At this writing, money market funds are growing at a rate of over $1 billion per week in the United States while at the same time the central bank is releasing statistics to show that M1 and M2 are growing at slower and more satisfactory rates.

One would hope that enough understanding of the intermeshing of micro- and macrophenomena that leads to these results would quickly solve the problem. But it will not. The level of theoretical sophistication required to produce a disaggregated macroanalytic dynamic model with anticipatory and adaptively responsive elements in it is, unfortunately, unlikely to emerge. Even were it to appear, it would probably be neglected by policy-makers and theorists alike since it would be at variance with the accepted paradigms. After the crisis it might gain credence as an explanation of events past.

NOTES

1. See H. A. Simon (1979).
2. For details, see A. Phillips (1978).

REFERENCES

Phillips, A. (1978) 'The Metamorphosis of Markets: Commercial and Investment Banking', *Journal of Corporate Law and Securities Regulation* (November) pp. 227–43.
Simon, H. A. (1979) 'Rational Behavior in Business Organizations', *American Economic Review* (September) pp. 393–473.

Index